FASHION IN FOO

1600–2009

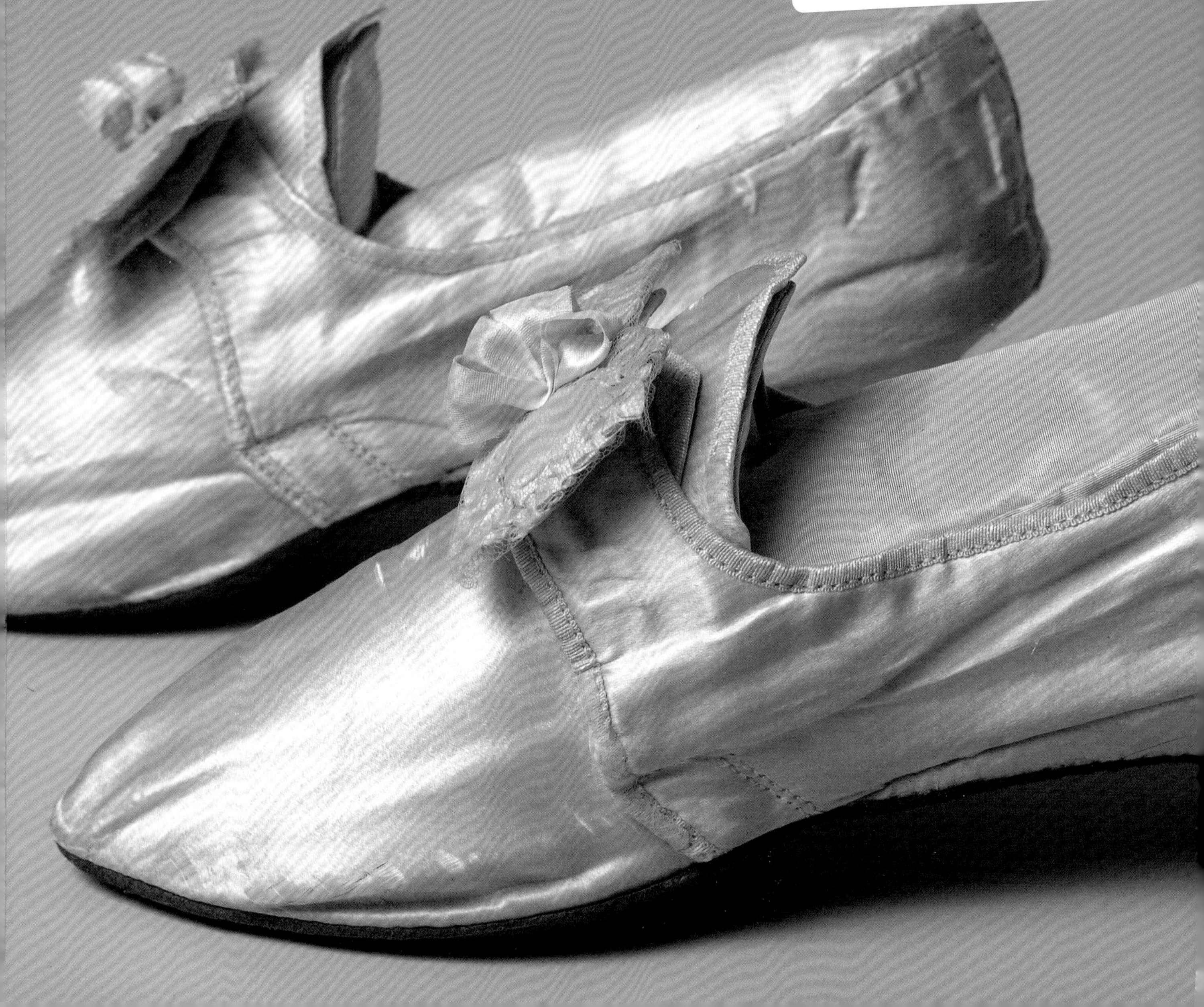

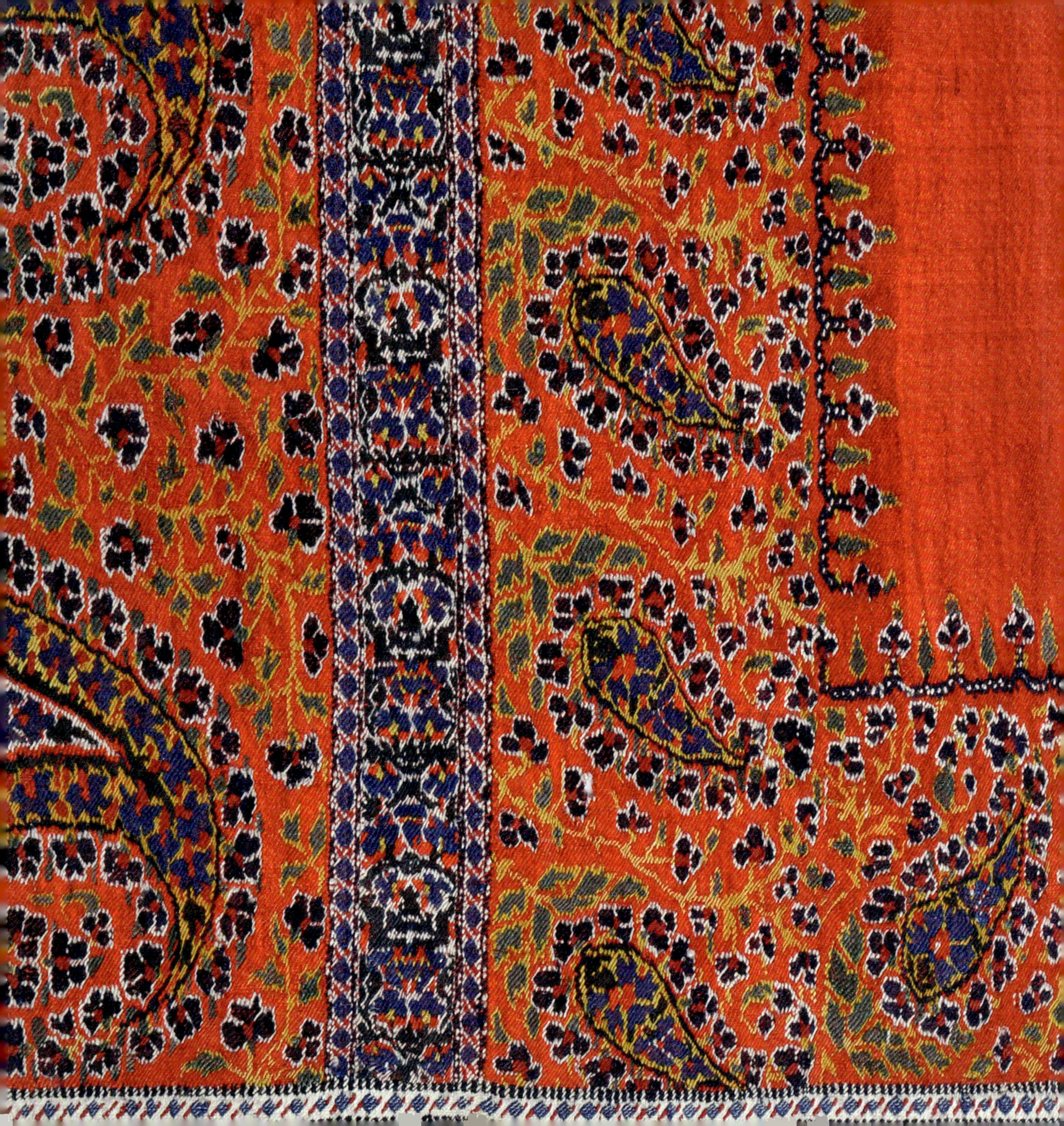

FASHION IN FOCUS
1600–2009

Treasures from the Olive Matthews Collection

GRACE EVANS

Photography by John Chase

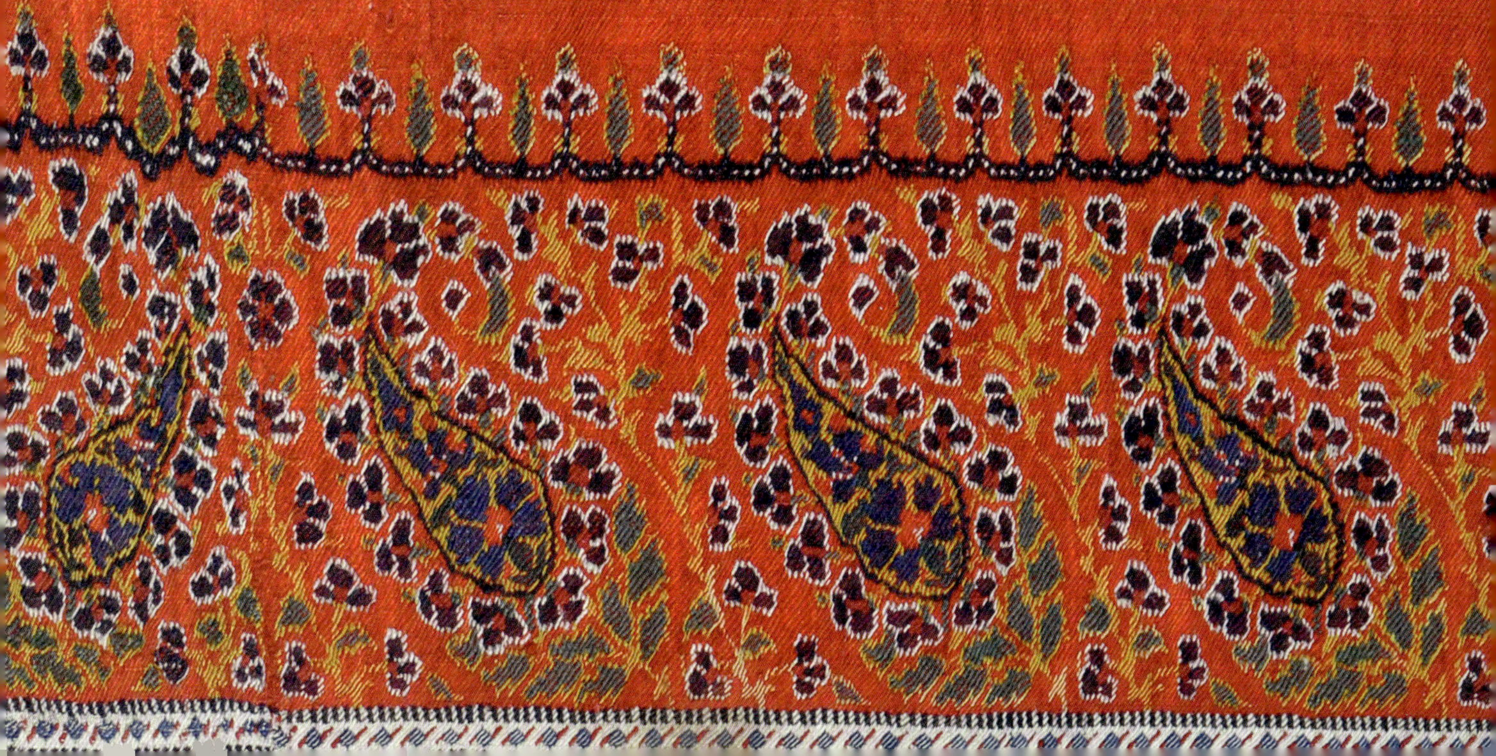

Published by Chertsey Museum
33 Windsor Street
Chertsey
Surrey KT16 8AT
www.chertseymuseum.org.uk

A catalogue record for this book is available from the British Library

ISBN 978-0-9568135-0-3

Design: Anne Wilson
annewilson@thornpress.co.uk

Photography: John Chase
www.johnchasephotography.com

Printed and bound in the UK by Butler Tanner and Dennis Limited, Frome and London

GREAT BRITISH BOOKS PUBLISHED & PRINTED IN THE UK

FRONT COVER Detail showing the bodice back of a silk brocade wedding dress, 1780.
BACK COVER Detail showing silk and metal work embroidery from a stomacher, 1725–1735.
PAGE 1 Pair of cream silk satin shoes with wedged heels. Part of a wedding ensemble, 1780.
PAGES 2–3 Detail of a red wool 'Kashmir' shawl, 1820–1830.
RIGHT Detail showing the back of a woman's cap of white linen embroidered in black work, 1700–1720.

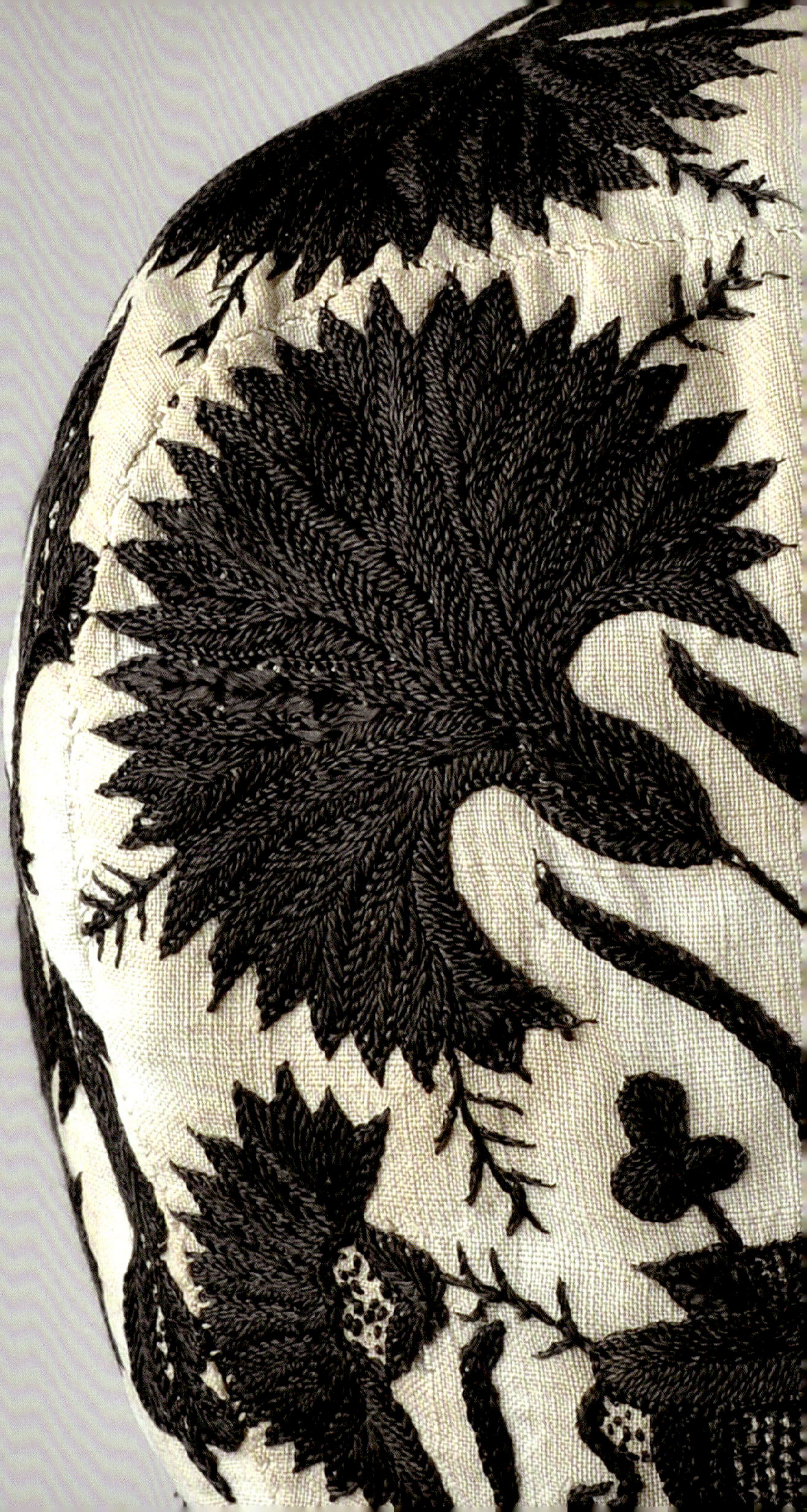

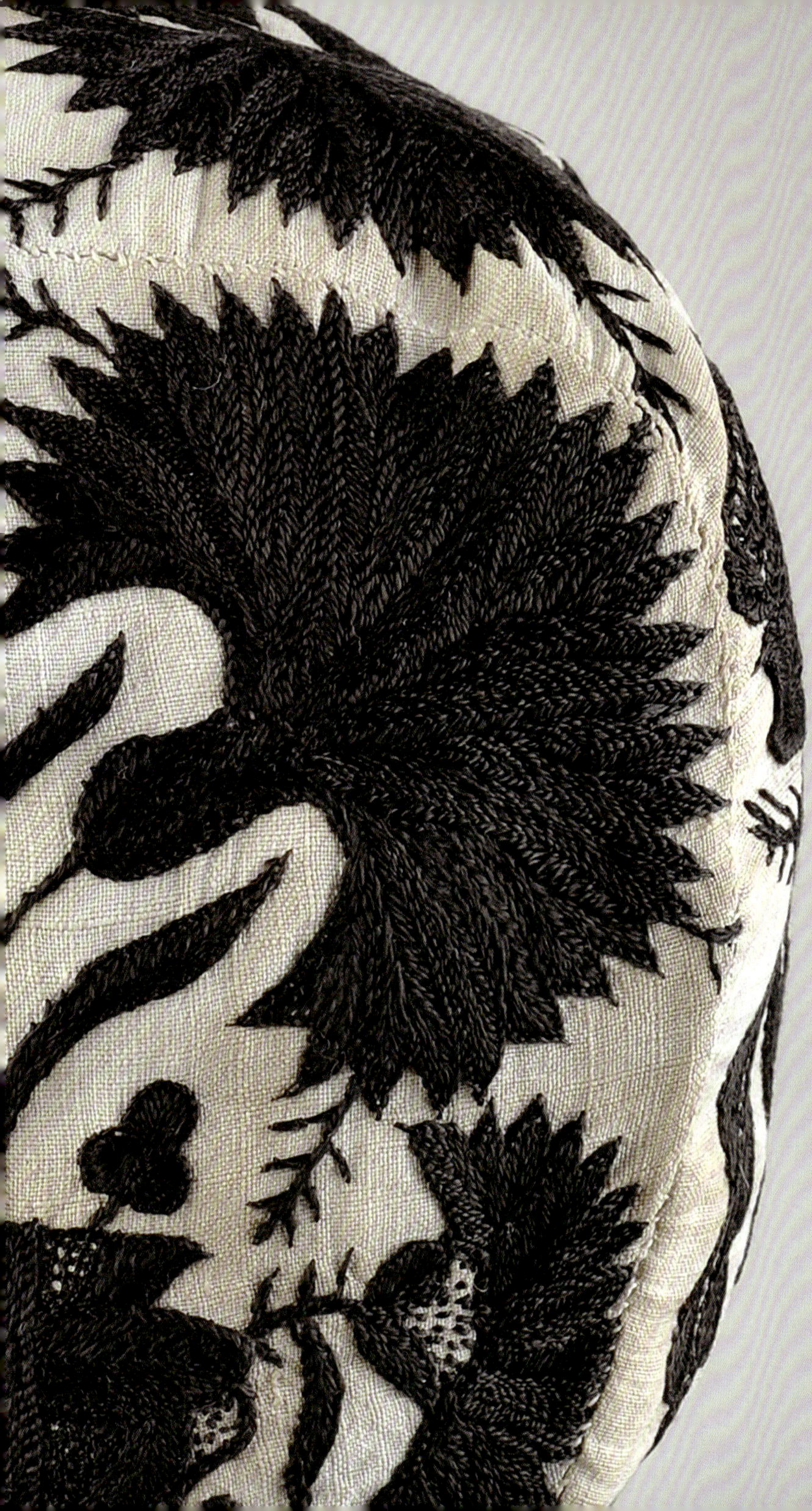

Contents

FOREWORD

In 1976 a sixteen page booklet was published by Runnymede District Council. *Costume in Chertsey Museum 1700–1800* is a modest catalogue, illustrated with black and white photography which discusses the eighteenth century material in; 'The collection of costume (that) covers the period 1700–1960 with one important 17th century item, an embroidered nightcap dating from 1600–1610'. Christina Rowley, the author, was then the Assistant Curator whose main responsibility was to care for the Olive Matthews Collection and the smaller group of dress and textiles within the wider Chertsey Museum collections. The fact that this catalogue was written and published during the lifetime of Olive Matthews is significant; it was tangible proof that the collection that this shy but knowledgeable woman had assembled over many years could compete with other, longer established and larger collections. It is appropriate that the last ten years of her long life which included the founding of the Olive Matthews Collection trust in 1969, the opening of a museum displaying her material in 1972, and the catalogue of 1976, offered public recognition for her life's work as collector and benefactor.

Personal collections are idiosyncratic; they reflect the discernment and preoccupations of the individual who assembles them but can be infuriatingly unbalanced. This is particularly obvious in 'closed collections' because the finite and un-endowed legacy of a specific time and set of circumstances will invariably be incomplete. Fortunately Olive Matthews was a generous and farsighted woman and her bequests to the trust offered opportunities for the collection to evolve and, as this book demonstrates, the collection has expanded considerably since her death in 1979. However, its exceptional quality has never been in doubt and successive curators have attempted to emulate Olive Matthews' instinct for and knowledge of what is outstanding and thus a candidate for inclusion.

The test of a major collection is whether it can continue to delight its many audiences from occasional visitors to informed researchers and also to offer new challenges to those who curate it. The Olive Matthews Collection entered the public domain at much the same time as the teaching of dress history; the training of costume curators and the growth in museum provision transformed this area of the arts and heritage from the mid-1960s onwards. In 1972, when the first displays of dress and textiles were presented in Chertsey Museum, the idea that fashion would emerge as a major draw for museum visitors was unproven. It is now indisputably a significant element within the increased visitor figures at Chertsey and in other museums which regularly programme exhibitions and activities with fashion themes. In partnership with Runnymede Borough Council the Olive Matthews Collection trustees ensure that the collection is added to, conserved and displayed within a variety of contexts – an annual exhibition, an accessories gallery and in other displays which benefit from dress and textile exhibits. The trustees support and promote the collection within Runnymede and in the wider world of fashion collections, displays and publications. This is made easier because Chertsey Museum is acknowledged as a regional centre of excellence due to its joint funding, its first-rate staff, informed volunteers, active Friends' organisation and innovative approach to museum services.

There have been fewer trustees than curators of costume; I have the unique distinction of having been the first person to curate the Olive Matthews Collection, the first professional museum trustee and, since 2003, chairman of the trust. In the period since the mid-1980s when I became a trustee I have known all of the costume curators who have worked at Chertsey Museum; they invariably recall the collection and museum with genuine affection. Grace Evans, the Keeper of Costume and author of this book, has made important acquisitions, researched and installed exhibitions and played a major role in the planning of new galleries in the period of museum expansion over the last ten years. She has also lectured and written about the collection and has a flair for presenting information to a range of audiences. This book with its fine photography by John Chase offers the first rounded view of the Olive Matthews Collection's many strengths and would, I feel sure, have delighted the woman whose collection Grace curates and writes about so elegantly.

Valerie Cumming
Chairman, The Olive Matthews Collection

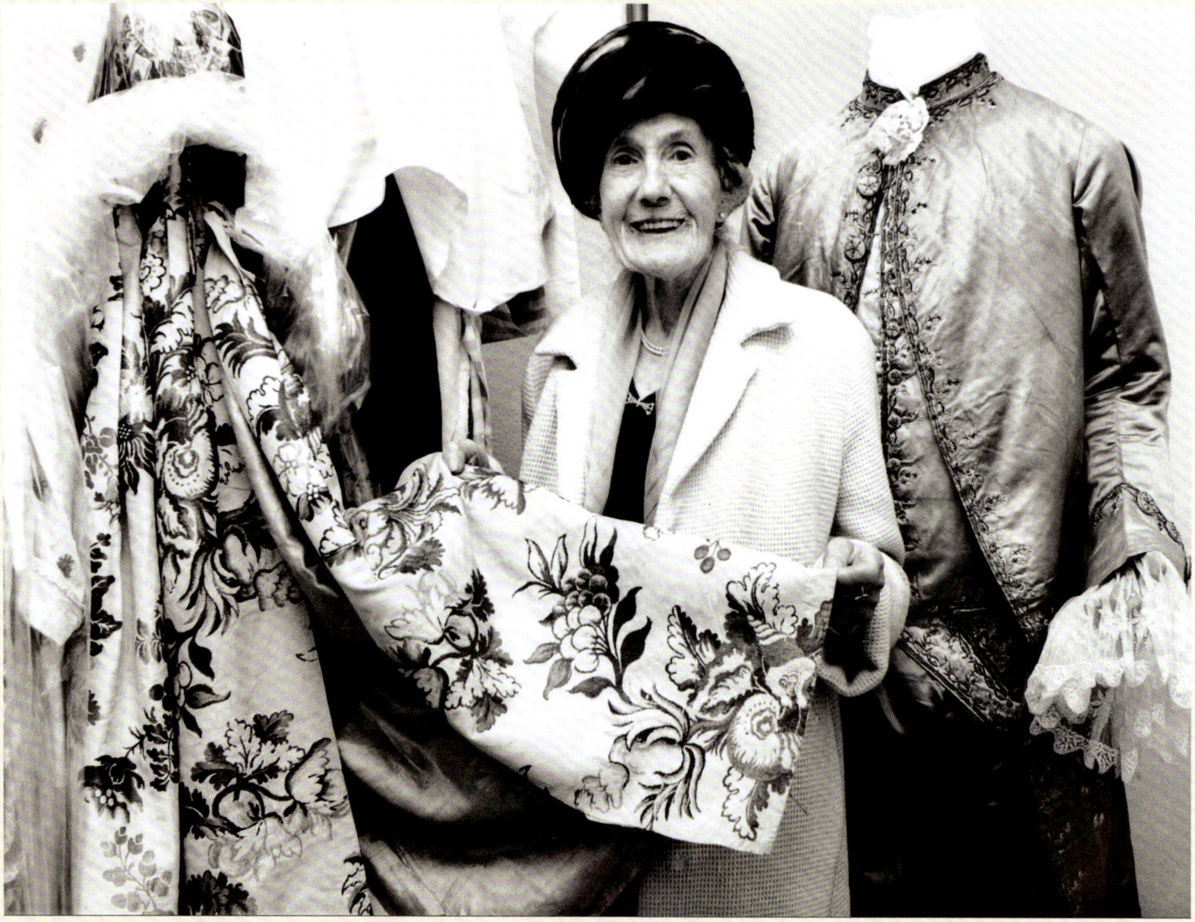

ABOVE Miss Matthews with favourite pieces from her collection, including a silk brocade gown of the 1730s, April 1972.
OPPOSITE Chertsey Museum, The Cedars, 33 Windsor Street, Chertsey.

INTRODUCTION

Olive Matthews and her Collection

The Olive Matthews Collection is a nationally significant group of items which today consists of over 4,000 articles of men's, women's and children's fashionable dress and accessories, as well as groups of textiles, fashion plates, needlework tools, furniture, silver, ceramics and fine art.

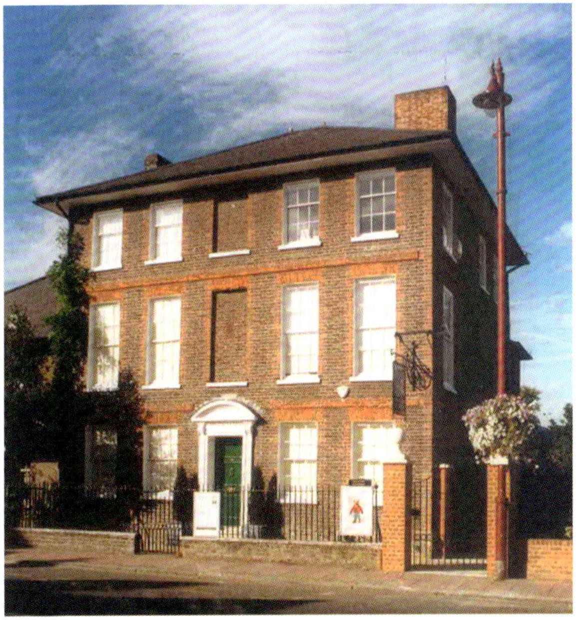

The dress items date from 1600 to the present day, and around 3,000 were collected by Miss Olive Mary Matthews over a period of about forty years. The collection contains a considerable number of exceptional pieces, many of which are in remarkably pristine condition. They incorporate qualities that Miss Matthews particularly admired, such as intricate surface decoration and superior workmanship, but also serve as excellent examples of key fashionable trends. The collection is now owned by the Olive Matthews Collection Trust and is housed at Chertsey Museum in Surrey.

The museum, which also contains important artefacts relating to the local area, is run by Runnymede Borough Council in partnership with the Olive Matthews Collection Trust.

Olive Matthews was born in 1887. She came from a comfortable middle class background, and her family lived in Camden Town in London. Her father was a successful saddler and harness maker whose business had a lucrative contract with the railways. Sadly her mother died when she was just two years old, and as a result she was brought up by her father and aunts. Olive was educated at home by a governess and, in line with the practices of the Victorian middle classes, self-improving hobbies were encouraged. Collecting was a Victorian passion, and vast groups of items relating to a wide array of themes were amassed, stored and catalogued. Some of the best now form the bedrock of museum collections throughout the country. In Olive's case her father is said to have encouraged her to collect by giving her a small allowance of between 2s 6d and 5s a week. Miss Matthews never wrote extensively about her collection, but some information about its creation has been gathered from a variety of sources. These range from conversations she had with museum staff and Matthews Collection trustees later in life, letters she wrote to the museum curator and small amounts of printed ephemera relating to the acquisition of certain pieces. Alongside the objects themselves and the circumstances of her life, it is possible to build up a picture of how and why the collection was formed.

It seems that Olive began collecting from around twelve years of age. Initially she collected historic furniture, but her father is said to have disapproved due to the lack of storage space available in the family home. It is at this point that Miss Matthews began her collection of antique dress and accessories. These items were much more easily stored within her bedroom, and they embodied all the features that she felt to be valuable and important. In common with many other collectors of her era, Miss Matthews was passionate about material culture from a golden age of hand craftsmanship that was felt to be 'lost' by her generation. In this sense, her attitudes were very much in line with those of the British Arts and Crafts movement of the late nineteenth century. Mechanisation and mass production had heralded the end of skilled workmanship on any real scale, and she sought to preserve and treasure examples that still survived. Olive was therefore keen to collect items which dated up to the early nineteenth century. The majority of the pieces she acquired date from the 1740s to around the 1840s, but there are some notable earlier examples, and a few later ones. In a letter to Bob Trett, the Curator at the time the collection entered Chertsey Museum, she stated: 'I am interested in costumes up to about early Victoria...styles I have known and worn I don't care about. They are not Antiques to me'[1]. This is one of the only written pieces of information that Miss Matthews supplied about her motivation for collecting, but it is very telling, and makes absolute sense when taken in conjunction with the objects she held dear. They hailed from an era just beyond living memory, and this allowed Olive to romanticise about them, their origins and context.

Miss Matthews' own personal situation may also have had a bearing on her reasons for collecting and her choice of objects. She was an only child, and lost her mother at an

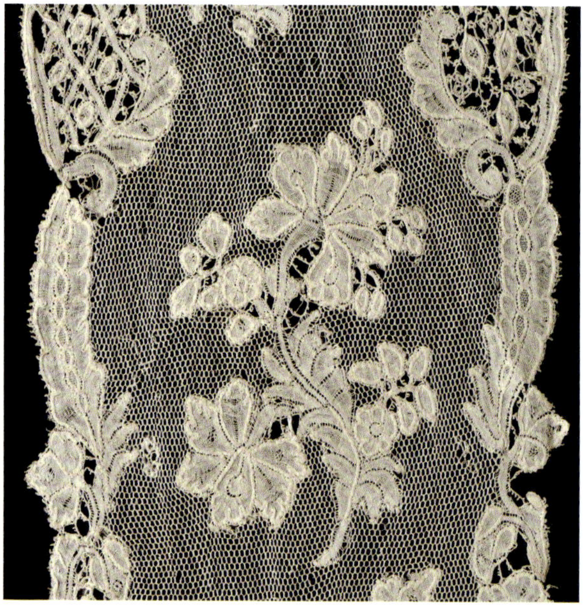

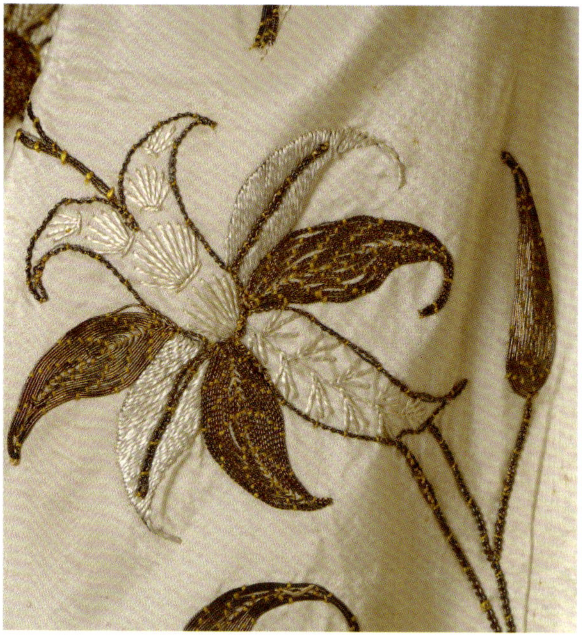

early age. Her father never re-married and he, her aunts and cousins were her closest family members. Olive never married and spent her middle age caring for her father and maiden aunt until their deaths. Miss Matthews was a very private person and did not talk openly about her own life, but some hints to acquaintances and members of museum staff indicate that her father may have been quite authoritarian, in the traditional mode of fathers of the period.[2] At some points in her life she seems to have been nervous about angering him, and this, as well as her rather isolated situation, may have led her to retreat into collecting. It had the advantage of providing her with a private realm over which she had control, and by her own admission she collected sets of items that might go together, such as a dress, a stomacher and a pair of shoes. She spoke about her collector's fantasies, in which she saw groups of people wearing the clothes.

Olive was blessed with 'a good eye' but she also read diligently around her subject throughout her life, later communicating regularly with curators from the Victoria and Albert Museum. As a result she had an excellent working knowledge of the history of dress and decorative arts, though she would perhaps have been too modest to describe herself as an expert. As a result of this research and natural aptitude, the majority of the pieces she found were genuine, high quality, well preserved examples of their type. As already discussed, she preferred items that were handmade, but in addition she was particularly keen on pieces that were, even for their time, examples of exceptional skill in terms of their intricate methods of creation or decoration. This is evident from the presence of over 900 pieces of lace ranging from the seventeenth through to the nineteenth century, and large numbers of beadwork bags from the early to mid nineteenth century. High quality silk and metalwork embroidery also attracted her, and the collection contains some particularly fine examples.

The means by which Miss Matthews collected her pieces varied during the course of her lifetime. Though she later purchased from dealers and bid for items at auction, as a child she was a regular visitor to the Caledonian Road Market in Camden Town.

OPPOSITE ABOVE Flower detail from a Brussels lace lappet, mid 1740s.
OPPOSITE BELOW Detail from a hand embroidered apron, showing couched gilt metal thread and silk, 1740–1750.
BELOW Auction catalogue for antiques sold by department store Debenham and Freebody, 1920s to '30s.

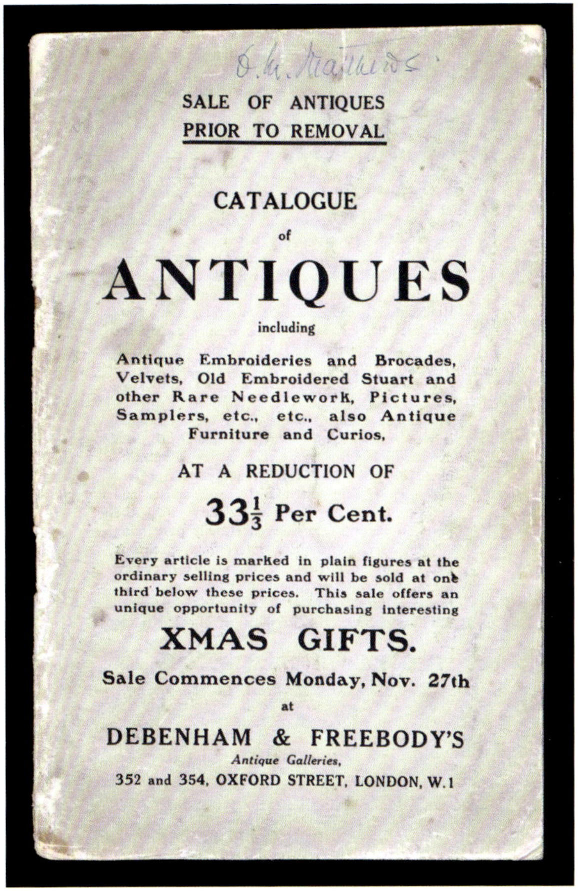
SALE OF ANTIQUES
PRIOR TO REMOVAL

CATALOGUE
of
ANTIQUES
including
Antique Embroideries and Brocades, Velvets, Old Embroidered Stuart and other Rare Needlework, Pictures, Samplers, etc., etc., also Antique Furniture and Curios,

AT A REDUCTION OF
$33\frac{1}{3}$ Per Cent.

Every article is marked in plain figures at the ordinary selling prices and will be sold at one third below these prices. This sale offers an unique opportunity of purchasing interesting
XMAS GIFTS.
Sale Commences Monday, Nov. 27th
at
DEBENHAM & FREEBODY'S
Antique Galleries,
352 and 354, OXFORD STREET, LONDON, W.1

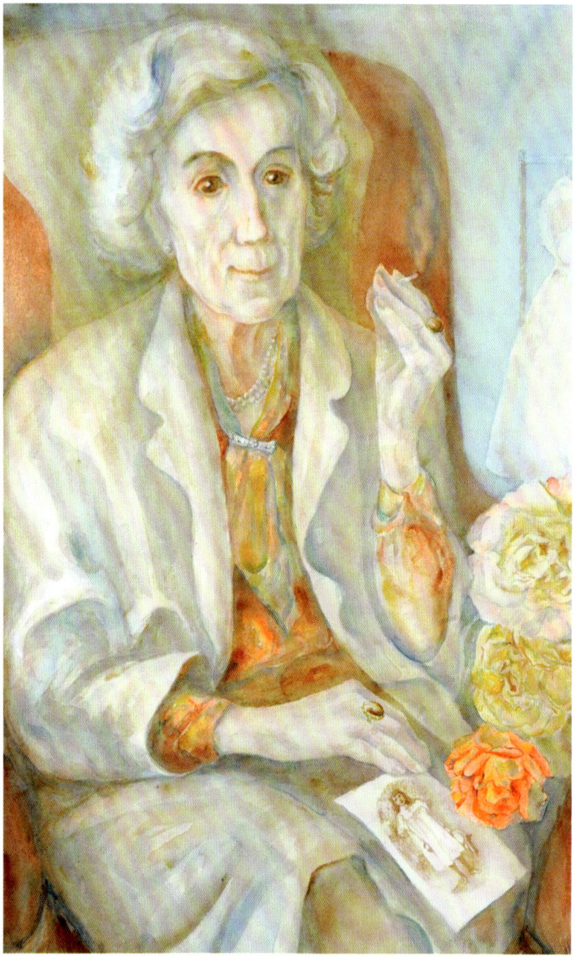

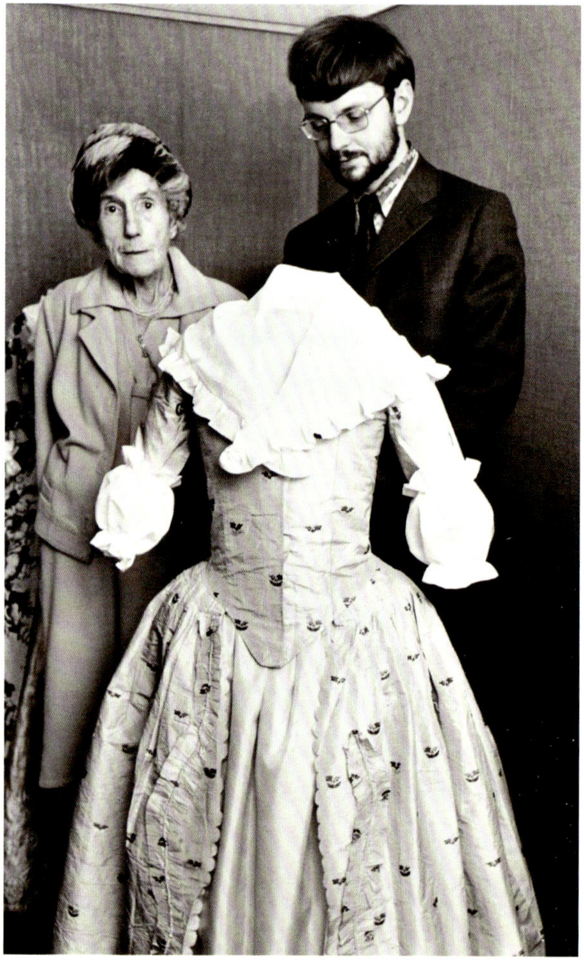

ABOVE Watercolour portrait of Olive Matthews by Chertsey artist Margaret Robinson. It was painted in 1973. The painting incorporates a number of aspects of Miss Matthews' life and items relating to her background and personality. Behind her hangs a piece from her dress collection. In her hand she holds a photograph of herself as a young girl. Miss Matthews was quite a heavy smoker and she is shown holding a cigarette in her hand.

ABOVE Olive Matthews with Curator of Chertsey Museum, Bob Trett at the time when Chertsey Museum was opened in 1972.They are standing amongst her garments which are mounted ready for display, and in the foreground is a late 1770s silk brocade gown.

OPPOSITE Women's shoe shown with a clog. Shoe 1735–1745, clog 1720–1740.

The stalls contained many examples of antique clothing and textiles, and the young Olive prided herself in finding bargains. She later said that she never paid more than £5 for a piece, and the thrill of finding a treasure as a result of her knowledge, keen eyes and persistence was another impetus for her collecting. She was, for example, discreetly proud when relating how she purchased a pair of silk brocade shoes dating to around 1735–1745 for half a crown from a stallholder, only to find a pair of brocade clogs which fitted them perfectly the next time she visited the market.

Miss Matthews' family were said to have been particularly careful with money, and this must have rubbed off on Olive.[3] In fact she was making extremely shrewd purchases with her limited funds. Antique costume was not valued at the time when she was gathering her items. It was seen by most as fancy dress or a source of authentic theatrical costume. As such, Olive and a handful of her contemporaries were able to pick up many rare and important pieces, such as her early seventeenth century nightcap or her pair of early eighteenth century stomachers, for what was effectively pocket money. It was not until the second half of the twentieth century that historic dress would be taken seriously as an important subject for study and museum display. At this point collectors such as the Cunningtons, Doris Langley Moore and indeed Olive Matthews began to be acknowledged by the establishment – their collections making their way into museums to be preserved in perpetuity.

Olive Matthews' collection came to be part of Chertsey Museum through a variety of opportune circumstances and the actions of a number of far sighted individuals. She and her family had moved to nearby Virginia Water at the outbreak of the Second World War and Olive remained there, outliving her father and aunt. Her collection had come with her and was tucked away in boxes stacked in cupboards around the house and in her garage. During the 1960s Miss Matthews became friends with local antique dealer and fellow collector Sydney Oliver who quickly realised the significance of her collection. Now nearing the end of her life, and perhaps encouraged by Mr Oliver, Miss Matthews began to seek a suitable home for it. She approached the Victoria and Albert Museum, but they wished to select individual items rather than taking it in totality. This disappointed Olive and led her to look elsewhere. Mr Oliver and other members of the local community including Bernard Pardoe, a local historian, stepped in to offer her a credible alternative which would allow the collection to remain together. They were involved with the newly opened Chertsey Museum, which was run by Chertsey Urban District Council and housed a variety of antiquities and important local artefacts in rather cramped conditions. In 1969 the Olive Matthews Collection Trust was formed and a mutually beneficial arrangement with the council was mooted. This enabled the collection to be kept in its entirety whilst also forming an intrinsic part of a new and more dynamic Chertsey Museum. The Trust purchased The Cedars, a late Regency house on Windsor Street in Chertsey, and the new museum was opened there in 1972. Miss Matthews was at last able to see her pieces displayed in a public museum, with a gallery devoted to her costumes. Sadly she passed away just a few years later in 1979. She was 92 years old.

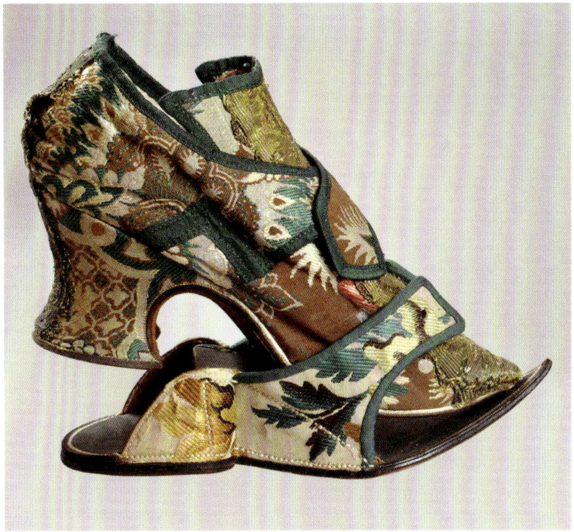

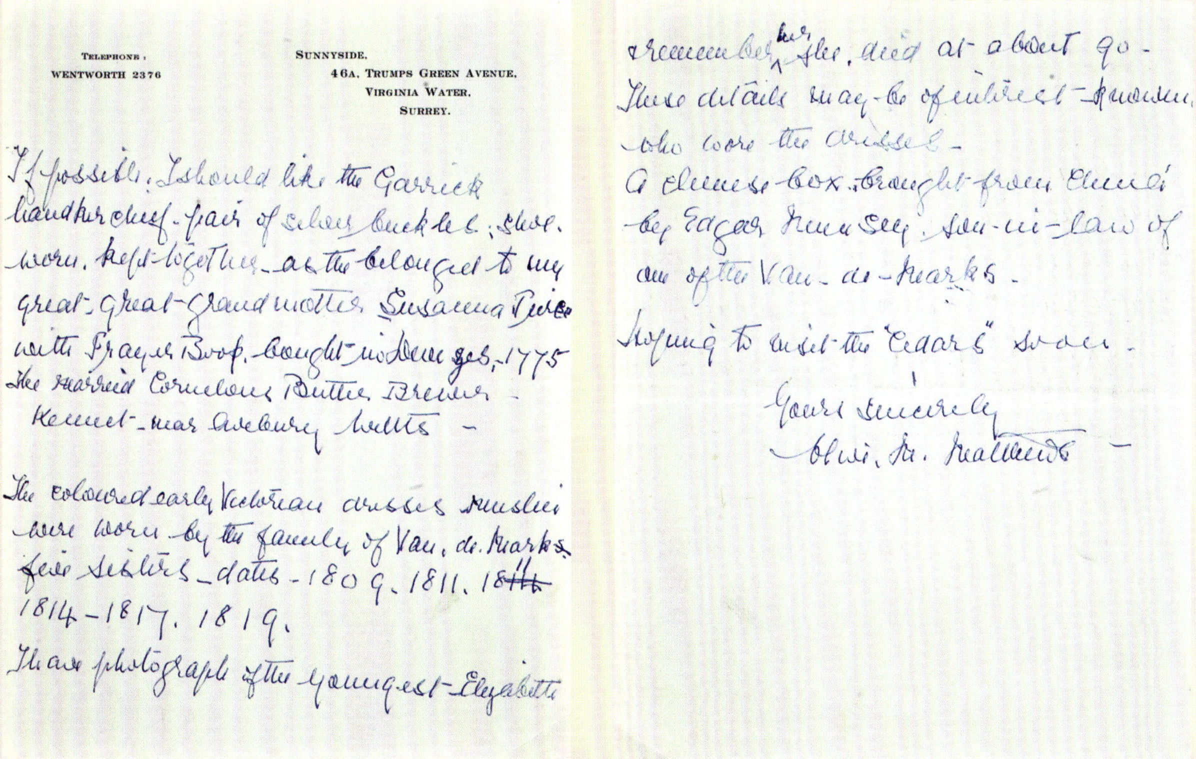

TELEPHONE: WENTWORTH 2376

SUNNYSIDE,
46A, TRUMPS GREEN AVENUE,
VIRGINIA WATER,
SURREY.

If possible, I should like the Garrick handkerchief - pair of silver buckles; shoe worn, kept together - as they belonged to my great-great-grandmother Susanna Pearce with Prayer Book, bought in Devizes, 1775. She married Cornelius Butler, Brewer - Kennet - near Avebury hills -

The coloured early Victorian dresses muslin were worn by the family of Van de Marks five sisters - dates - 1809. 1811. ~~18~~ 1814 - 1817. 1819.

I have photograph of the youngest - Elizabeth

remember her, she died at about 90 - These details may be of interest - knowing who wore the dresses -

A dress-box, bought from Devizes by Edgar Munsey, son-in-law of one of the Van de Marks.

Hoping to visit the "Cedars" soon.

Yours sincerely
Olive M. Matthews -

ABOVE A letter written around 1973 by Miss Matthews to the Curator of Chertsey Museum. In it she lists a group of family items that she wished to be kept together. She also refers to other pieces which now form part of the Olive Matthews collection.

OPPOSITE The items, as mentioned in the letter above, which Olive Matthews wished to be kept together. They belonged to her great, great grandmother Susanna Pearce. They are a linen handkerchief printed with images of David Garrick, the great eighteenth century theatrical actor-manager, alongside other actors and embroidered with 'Susanna Pearce, July the 9 1774'; a pair of silver shoe buckles dated 1770–1784; a shoe of black and buff coloured silk, dated c.1775 and a Book of Common Prayer published by T. Wright and W. Gill, Oxford 1772 which is embossed on the cover with 'Susanna Pearce Monckton, 1775'.

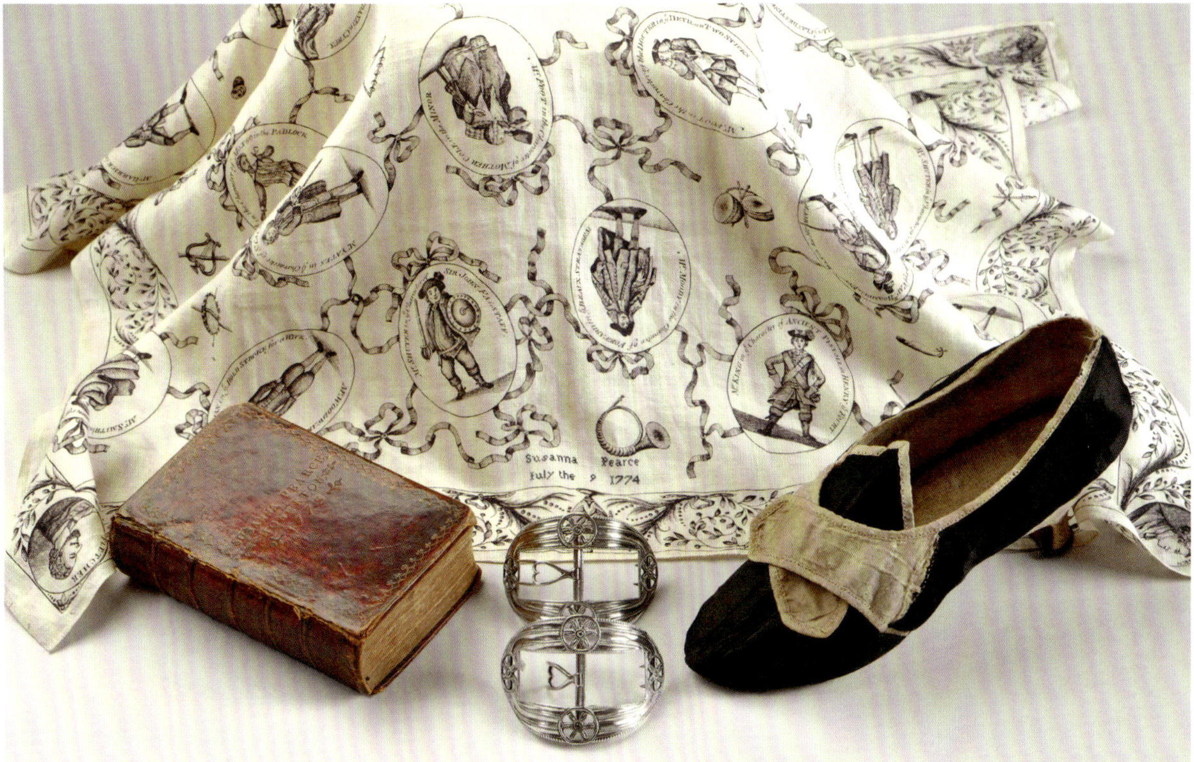

The Collection archive contains a number of pieces of correspondence between the Curator and Miss Matthews during the early days of Chertsey Museum. The most revealing relate to Olive's obvious interest in the new displays and her ongoing attachment to her collection after it had entered the public domain. She offers suggestions of suitable display methods, and in one letter she makes a point of requesting that a selection of items should be kept together as a group. They date from the 1770s and belonged to her great, great grandmother Susanna Pearce. They are a printed handkerchief featuring David Garrick, a pair of silver shoe buckles, a shoe and a prayer book. Miss Matthews inherited these items when she was a child, and it is fascinating to speculate as to whether they may have triggered her interest in historic dress and accessories, particularly since they date from the late eighteenth century – the era of dress history about which she was especially enthusiastic.

No longer a private passion kept hidden away for only a select few to enjoy, the collection has taken on a new life since entering Chertsey Museum. It is now available for all to discover, and successive curators have added pieces to the collection, filling gaps and incorporating garments from later periods in order to make it relevant to modern audiences. There are now two galleries in the museum which are dedicated to the fashion collection. One features annually changing themed exhibitions which show and interpret a wide variety of pieces. The other gallery houses a large number

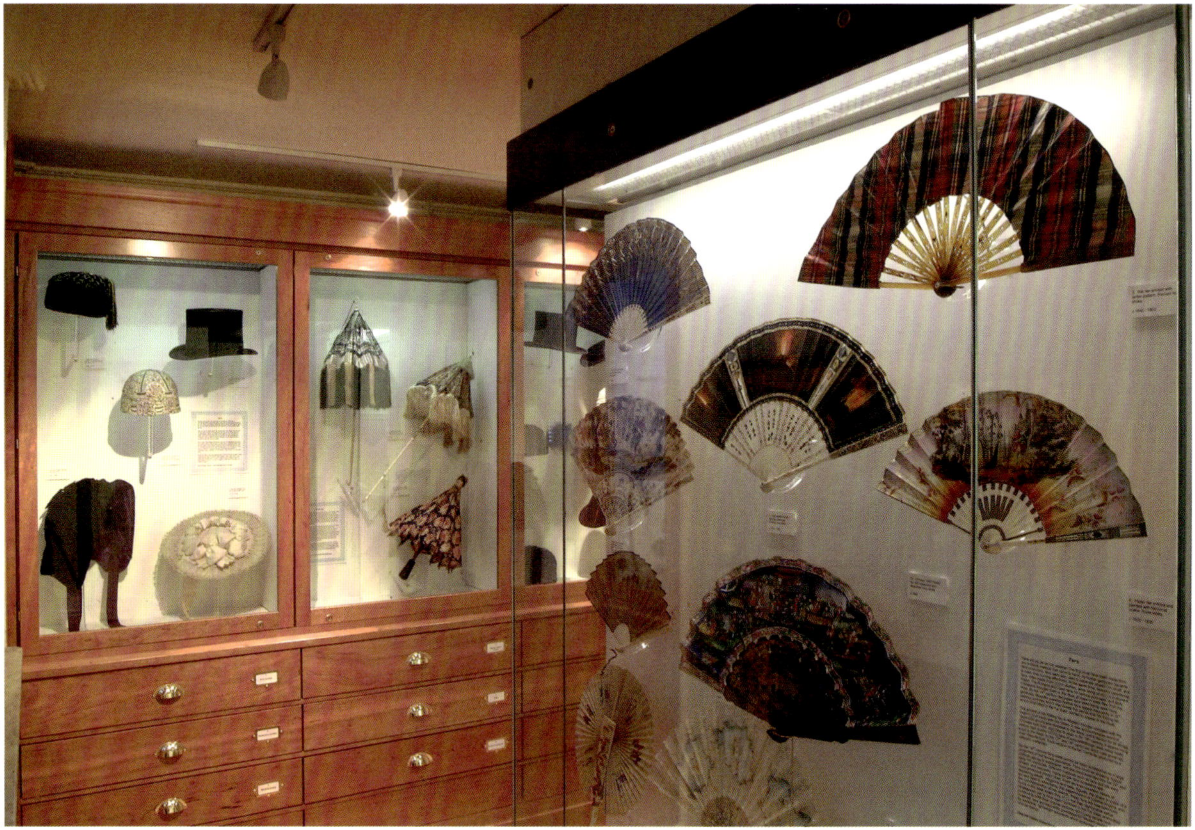

ABOVE The Olive Matthews Fashion Accessories Gallery at Chertsey Museum. It features pieces from the seventeenth to the twentieth century and includes many of the exquisite smaller objects that Miss Matthews collected with such enthusiasm. OPPOSITE Opening case from the 2010–2011 exhibition of wedding dresses entitled 'Brides Revisited'. Photograph by Grace Evans.

of fashion accessories – an area of collecting which was of particular interest to Miss Matthews. The collection has a reputation internationally for its important and exceptionally well-preserved pieces, and researchers regularly consult items for in-depth study. The museum also runs a lively events programme, offering fashion-related workshops, talks and re-enactment days to packed audiences.

The following chapters take the reader on a chronological tour through some of the most fascinating and important pieces contained within the Olive Matthews Collection. Though space constraints have meant difficult choices in terms of what to include, the garments have been carefully

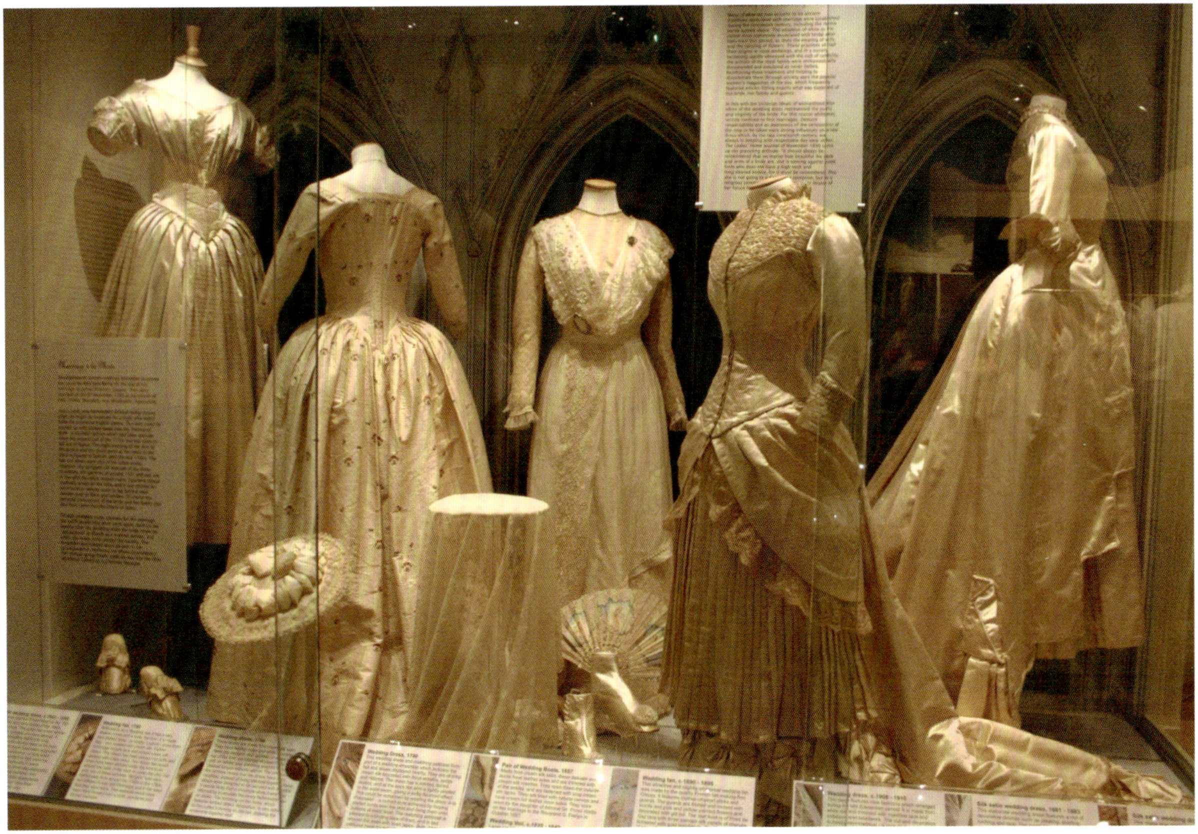

selected to give an overview of the quality and historical value of the treasures contained within the collection's holdings. Above all they reveal the preferences and enthusiasms of Olive Matthews herself. Their intricate and sometimes awe-inspiring workmanship has been expertly captured in sumptuous images by the photographer John Chase, while the text seeks to explain their significance, both in terms of fashion history and as part of the Olive Matthews Collection.

[1] Excerpt from a letter from Olive Matthews to Mr Bob Trett dated 22nd April 1974.

[2] Cumming, Valerie, *Understanding Fashion History*, (Batsford, London 2004), p.64.

[3] Letter from Bernard Pardoe, Olive Matthews Collection trustee, dated 30th September 1996.

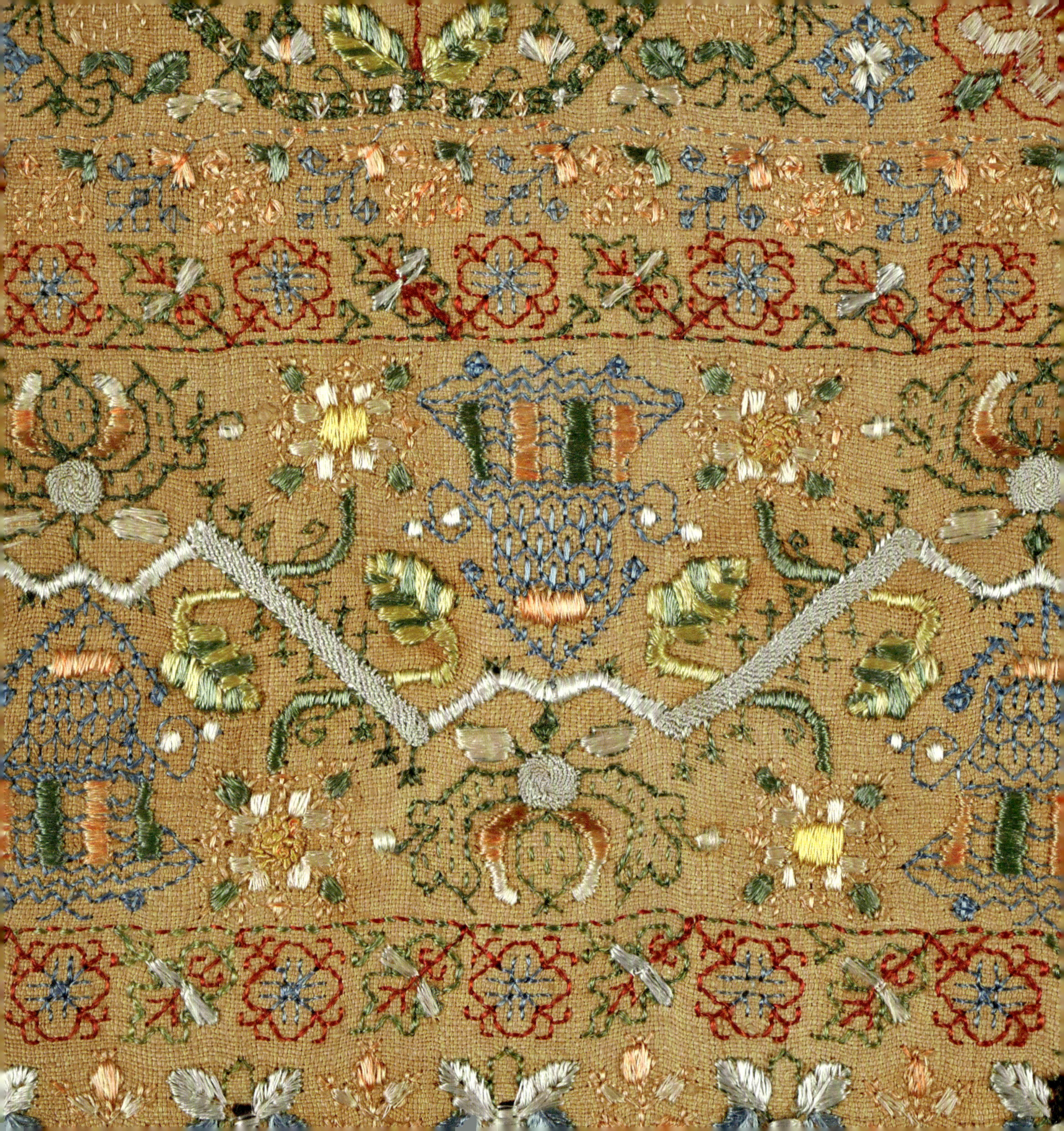

THE SEVENTEENTH CENTURY

*'The Needle's Excellency'**

Despite having an immense enthusiasm for the dress and accessories of the eighteenth and early nineteenth centuries, Olive Matthews could not resist including a few key pieces from the seventeenth century in her collection. These consist of accessories, lace and samplers rather than full garments, and it is no surprise that we do not find seventeenth century items in any great abundance since so few of them survive.

Given the opportunity Miss Matthews would no doubt have jumped at the chance to collect more and larger pieces from the 1600s. We know that the items that she did own she loved, particularly the embroidered nightcap she cleverly spotted as the early and important piece it was. These items epitomise her love of fine, beautifully hand-crafted work, but their great age must have been an equally important factor. These objects, perhaps more than any others in Miss Matthews' collection, embody the enormous appeal of survivals from a distant and largely intangible past; qualities which fired her imagination and motivated her collecting.

* The title of an embroiderer's pattern book published by James Boler in 1631.

LEFT Detail of a sampler, 1650–1690 (see pages 26–27).

Nightcap, 1600–1620

Man's nightcap of fine linen embroidered with silks, silver gilt thread and silver gilt spangles. It is made from one piece of fabric, but the crown has been shaped into six segments, producing a neat fit around the head (neater than would have been the case with more common four segment examples). Each section is picked out with embroidered pillars which frame snakes coiling around swords. Flowers and insects surround and emanate from the snakes. The same pattern is echoed on the turned back brim. Originally the cap would have been lined with coarser linen, but only fragments of this remain. The embroidery stitches consist of stem, chain, buttonhole, plaited braid and rope stitch.

The embroidered motifs are imbued with meaning. They may have been chosen specifically for their relevance to the owner of the cap, and would have been derived from sources which were readily available. The pillars represent fortitude and constancy, the snakes wisdom, and the swords justice and military honour. Flowers were often taken to mean hope and joy. The use of emblems in art and textiles was very common at this time, and books such as Claude Paradin's *Devises Heroiques* (1557) and Thomas Trevelyon's *Miscellany* (1608) are known to have influenced the designs of many sixteenth and seventeenth century embroideries. The floral elements could have been derived from books on herbs and plants, some of which were aimed specifically at the embroiderer, such as Jacques Le Moyne de Morgue's *La Clef des Champs* (1586). This period saw a flowering of domestic embroidery in England. Wealthy women employed pattern drawers to sketch out designs freehand or prick the outlines and dust them with charcoal to make them easy to follow. Amateur pieces could rival those of the professionals and items such as this nightcap may well have been executed at home and given as gifts.

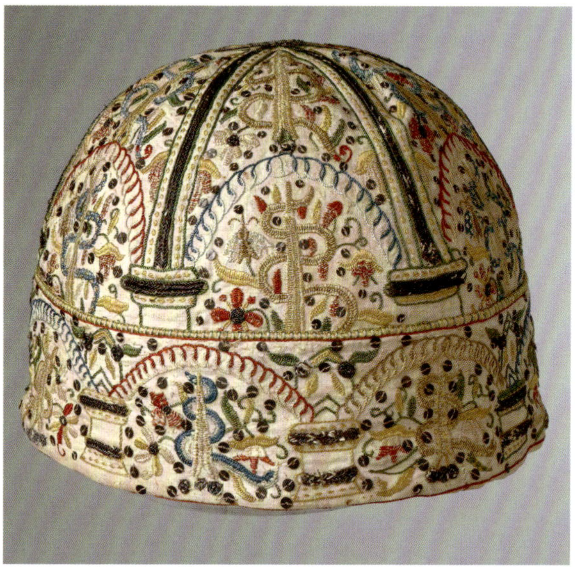

The cap would have been worn by a wealthy man when at home in informal circumstances, though not in bed as the name might suggest. They were worn throughout the seventeenth and eighteenth centuries and later provided comfortable relief from hot, itchy wigs. Olive Matthews purchased this example for £2.00 at the Old Caledonian Road Market, Camden Town during the first half of the twentieth century. It had been crudely lined with pink silk and a tassel tacked to the crown, suggesting it had been used for fancy dress, or as a smoking cap in the Victorian era. She recognised it as a much earlier piece, and was delighted to add it to her collection. It was the earliest and one of the most important articles she owned.

OBJECT NUMBER – MT.0183

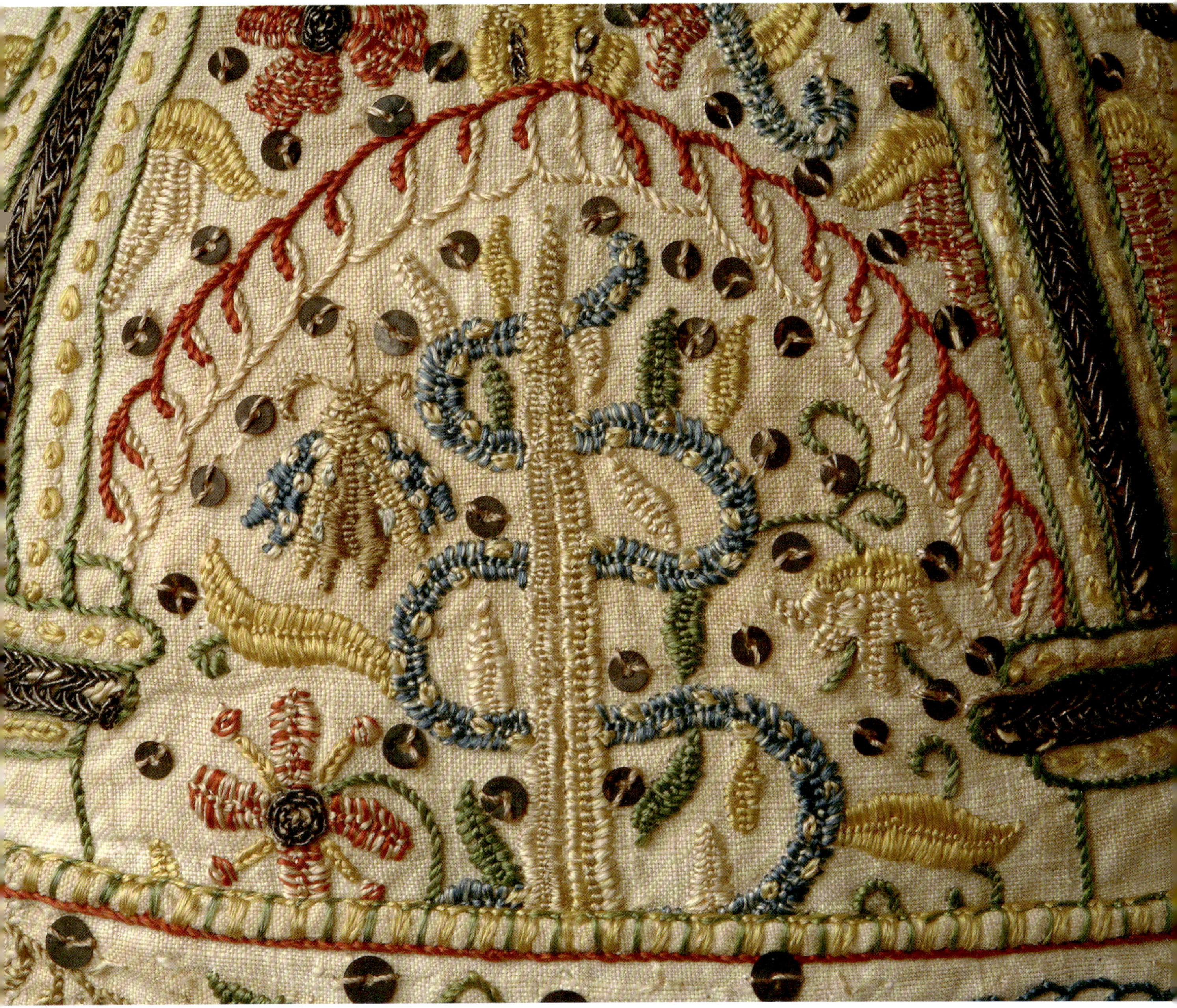

Drawstring bag, 1640–1670

Drawstring bag made from linen canvas; it is embroidered in silk thread with three rows of stylised flowers in rococo stitch and a background of silver metal thread worked in plaited gobelin stitch. The upper edge is bound in cream silk and holes for the drawstring cords are worked in buttonhole stitch with red and green silk thread. The cord itself is of plaited silk, finished with tassels. Three further tassels at the base of the purse are suspended on bound rings and it is lined with cream silk.

The embroidery style represents an intermediate period in pattern development. The design of larger stylised flowers dates the bag to the middle of the seventeenth century. Earlier designs often feature scrolling, naturalistic flowers, and those found towards the end of the century tend to be worked in abstract diaper patterns. Embroidery such as this could be carried out by women at home, who worked from published pattern books such as *The Needle's Excellency* published by James Boler in 1631. However, there was also a considerable trade in professionally made luxury goods, many of which were produced in France.

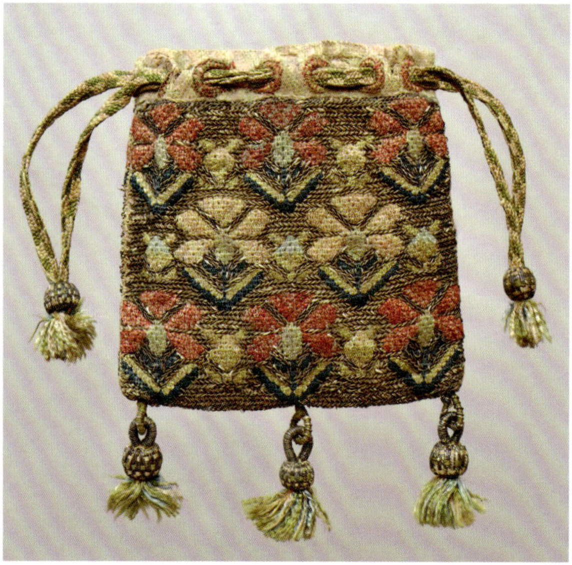

Although their original purpose is not fully known, such bags are often referred to as 'swete bags'. In the seventeenth century the term 'swete' could be used to describe sweet-smelling things, and these small decorative bags were filled with sachets of perfumed powder or herbs. They were carried on the person, filling the air around the wearer with pleasant scent. They were even thought to have disinfectant properties. Richly embroidered bags could also be used as containers for presents of coin between wealthy givers, or given as gifts in themselves. The lists of New Year's gifts received by Elizabeth I contain many references to embroidered bags and sweet bags. When money was given strict rules were adhered to and noblemen gave set sums according to rank. The value of the purse was also regularly referred to in these instructions, and the use of beautiful purses may have detracted from the perceived vulgarity of giving money to the monarch. Other examples of bags similar to this one are found with matching pincushions attached, suggesting a further use as containers for needlework tools such as small needles, thread and miniature scissors. The owner of this bag would certainly have been wealthy as only the higher levels of society could have afforded such richly embroidered accessories.

OBJECT NUMBER – MT.0074

Drawstring bag, 1680–1700

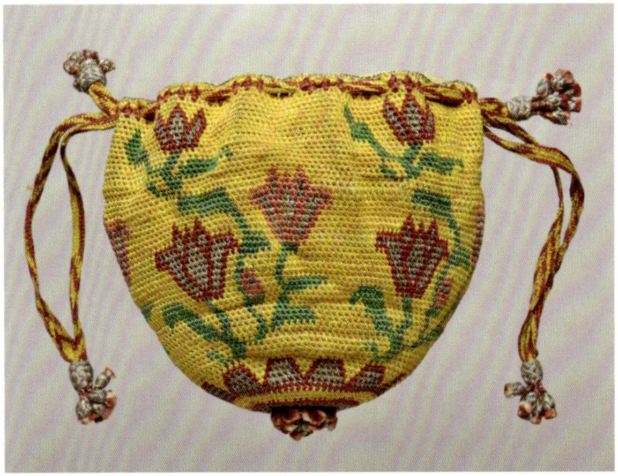

A basin-shaped drawstring bag made from silk and silver metal thread. It has a design of tulips in red, green, pink and silver on a bright yellow ground. A drawstring pulls the bag closed, and this is finished with plaited silver and red silk floss tassels. A generous bunch of tassels has been added to the base. The bag is made from detached buttonhole stitch (a technique also employed for needlepoint lace) and would have been worked over a wooden mould. Moulds had rounded ends and were pierced with holes at the top. Bands of threads were wound around and secured by stitches through the holes. These threads then formed the anchor for the buttonhole stitches which covered the mould. Once the purse was finished off at the base, the threads holding it would be cut and the purse released. The tassels would then be stitched in place and the drawstring threaded through.

Tulip designs are seen in many pieces of fine and decorative art during the seventeenth century. Many are contemporary with the phenomenon of 'Tulip Mania' which occurred from the early 1600s until 1637, when the value of Dutch-cultivated tulip bulbs reached extraordinarily high levels – some more than ten times the annual income of a skilled craftsman – before crashing spectacularly. The value of tulips made them into a high-status decorative motif which found its way onto pottery, paintings and accessories. The date of this bag is too late for the tulip design to have coincided with 'Tulip Mania'. However, since tulips had been established as a Dutch flower, it is possible that their use here may link to the 'Glorious Revolution' of 1688, when the Dutch William of Orange became King William III of England.

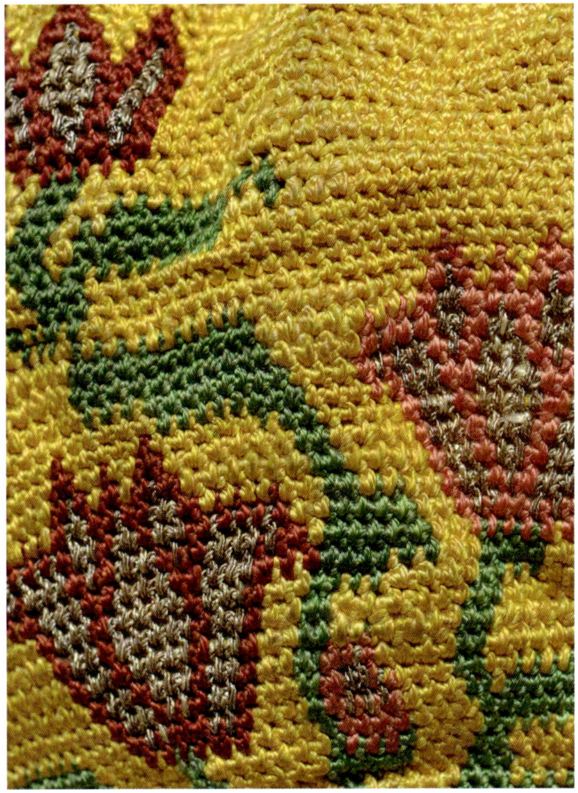

OBJECT NUMBER – MT.0075

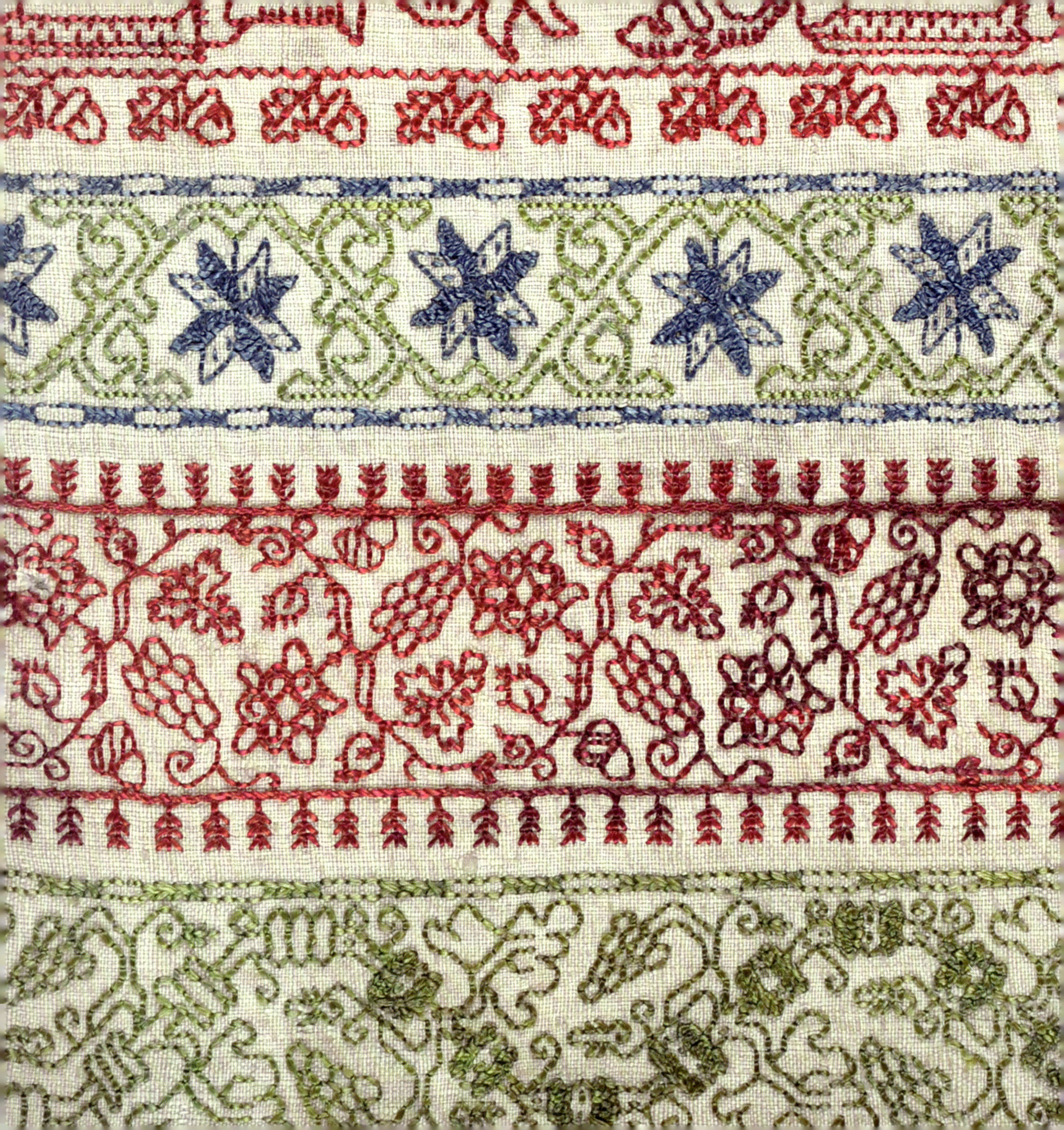

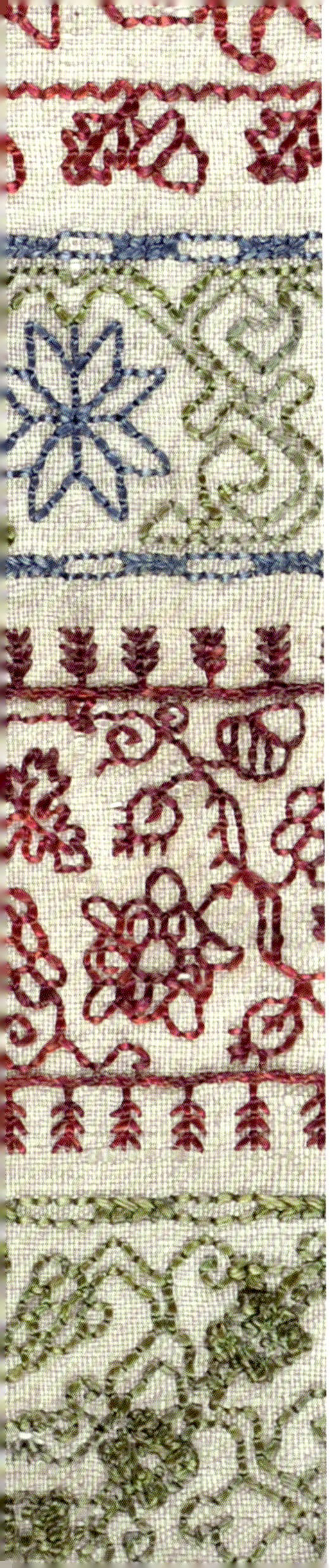

Band sampler, 1660–1700

Long, narrow linen sampler featuring bands of embroidered repeat patterns in coloured silks. A separate section has much narrower bands with smaller patterns. The stitches are extremely regular and display a high level of competence and skill. They include double-running stitch, cross stitch, Algerian eye and stem stitch. The designs range in style from scrolling Italianate motifs to angular patterns featuring birds, fruit and flowers. All would have been derived from published pattern books. Samplers were usually worked on a complete narrow loom width of linen. This is one of the longest of its kind at 91.5cm (36").

The name 'Sampler' is derived from the Old French word 'essamplaire' which related to any work copied or imitated. Band samplers such as these were reference works for patterns or stitches which were copied from other pieces or pattern books and then used elsewhere. This piece has been worked from both ends, and was rolled up and kept in a workbox ready to be consulted when needed. The designs would have been embroidered on collars, cuffs, pillowcases and coverlets, and could be scaled up or down according to the size of the object to be decorated. By this date they were also increasingly used in the education of young girls.

The patterns present in this piece are found in a number of band samplers from the second half of the seventeenth century. They had established decorative value, but many were also symbolic, with origins in religious and heraldic imagery. For example the strawberry, usually shown flowering and fruiting simultaneously, is commonly found in paintings of the Virgin and Child. The fruiting vine is also strongly associated with earlier church embroidery, and though this ceased to be produced in England after the Reformation of the mid sixteenth century, religious symbols lived on in secular pieces. Pea pods are also present in another pattern. These are thought to have heraldic origins, possibly deriving from the broom pod used in the arms of the Plantagenets.

OBJECT NUMBER – M.2008.34

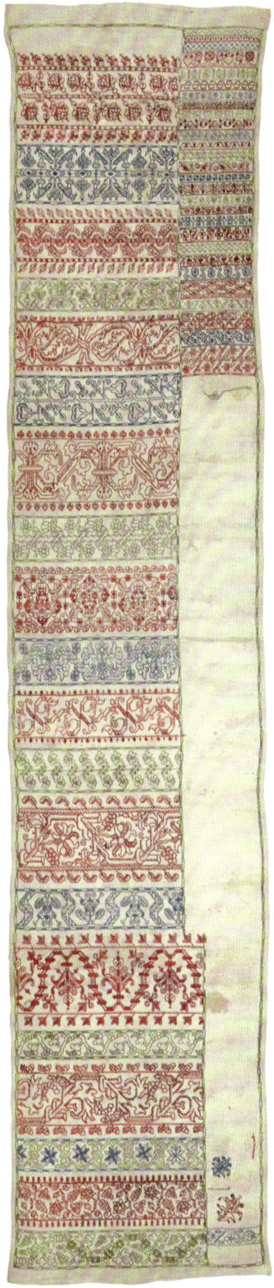

Sampler, 1650–1690

A linen band sampler showing skill in a wide variety of techniques, it features intricate designs incorporating roses, honeysuckle, carnations and pomegranates in silks and metal thread. A number of the patterns are familiar from other surviving samplers of the second half of the seventeenth century, suggesting widespread use of pattern books such as *A Schole-House for the Needle* by Richard Shorleyker (1624). The large central honeysuckle and chains motif with coiling snakes is particularly common. The inclusion of a female figure surrounded by a floral bower and crowned with flowers is also found in other samplers of the seventeenth century. In this case she is composed of detached buttonhole stitch and adorned with couched metal thread and seed pearls. She is flanked by fruit trees, birds, moths and a caterpillar. A pair of rabbits sit at her feet. She wears clothing contemporary with the sampler's date, but the roots of the motif can be traced back to medieval images of the *Enclosed Garden of the Holy Virgin*. By this period, the meaning may not have been widely known, but rather included as a traditional subject alongside many others inherited from earlier religious embroideries. The stitches used include double-running stitch, satin stitch, detached buttonhole, cross stitch and couching, and the embroiderer has added the alphabet and her name: 'Mary Tovey'. The bottom of the sampler has a raw, unfinished edge, suggesting that it may have been cut, possibly to fit into a frame during the nineteenth century. It is very likely that the sampler also included a date which has now been lost.

Samplers such as this were usually undertaken by girls from well off families who were aged around 8 or 9. They were a first step towards becoming a skilled embroiderer, establishing the techniques needed for the embellishment of household linen, clothing and furnishings. Mary may have progressed to the embroidered decoration of cushions, caskets and mirror surrounds, but a sampler's completion represented a milestone in a child's early education.

OBJECT NUMBER – MT.1318

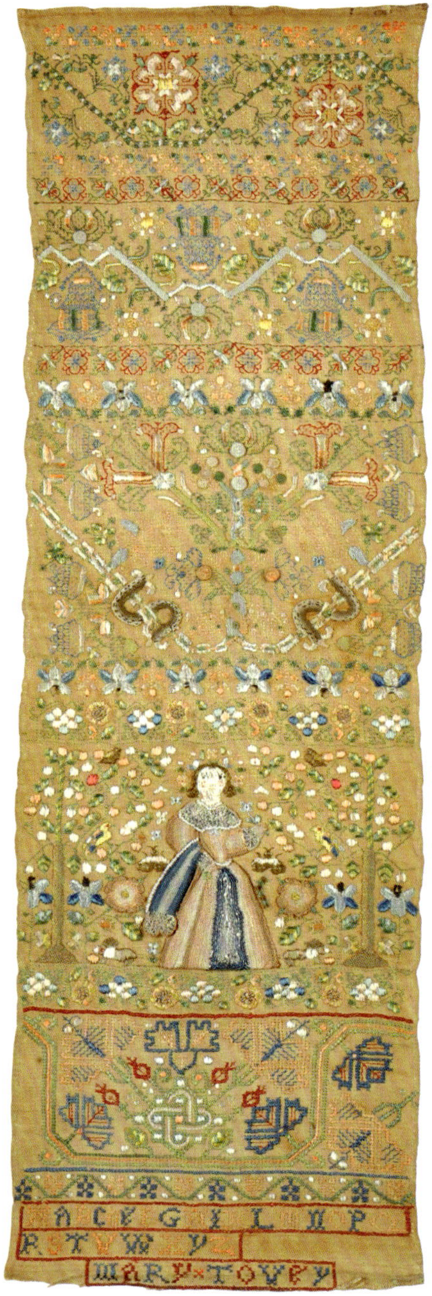

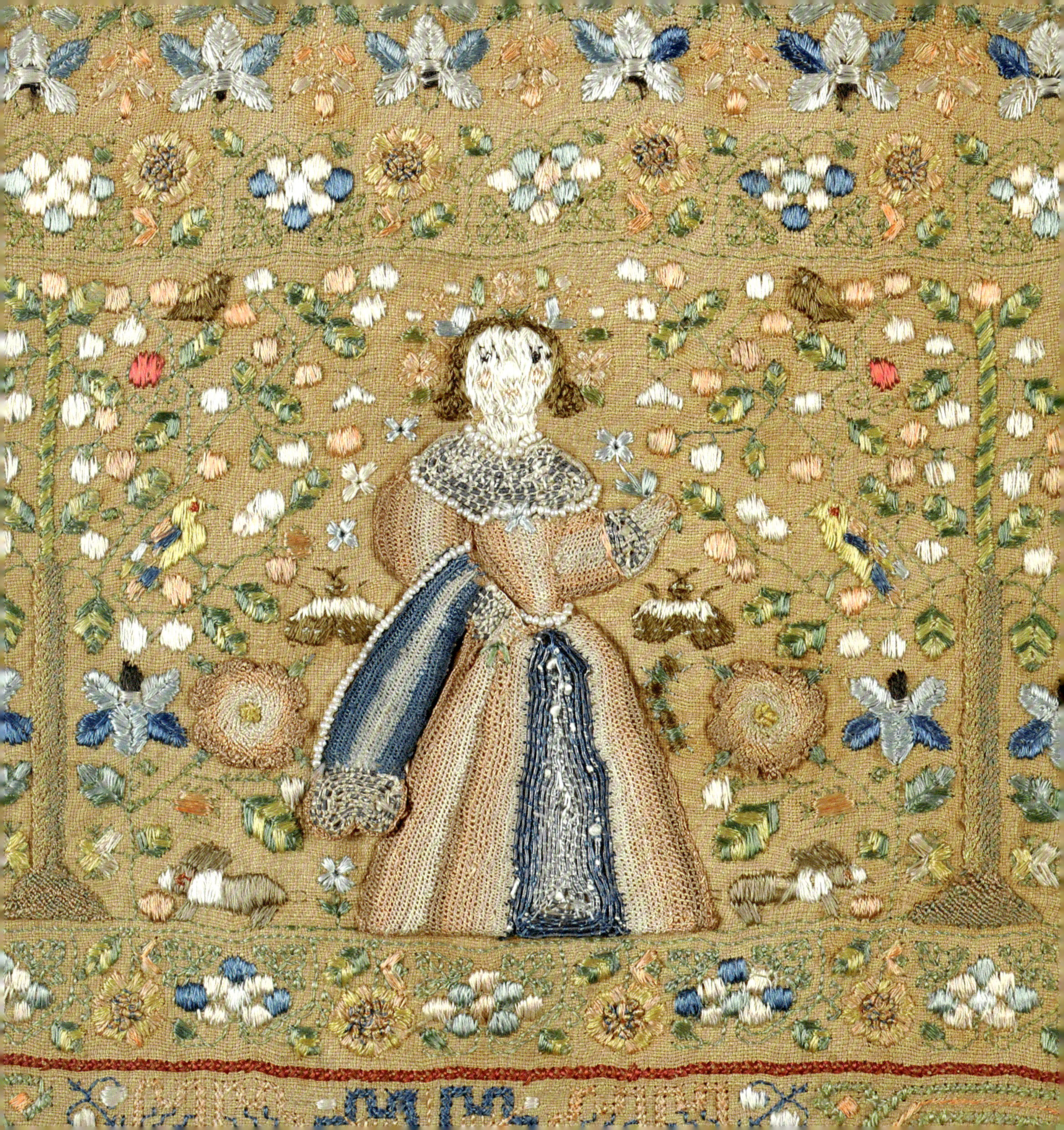

Lace

Olive Matthews was a keen lace collector. Her extensive collection of over 900 pieces dates from the seventeenth to the nineteenth century, and includes a few key examples from the early era of lace production. Her enthusiasm for lace was in line with contemporary tastes. During the nineteenth century there was a widespread revival of interest in historic lace, much of which was altered and incorporated into fashionable garments. This group includes some of the best of the seventeenth century pieces in the collection, and spans a few of the different types of lace produced at this time. The lace collection epitomises Miss Matthews' preference for all things that were skilfully hand made. It satisfied her love of beautiful and painstakingly intricate things.

The lace collection incorporates needle, bobbin and machine made lace. Needle lace is constructed using a needle and thread and is based on embroidery. Detached buttonhole stitches are worked to create the pattern. Bobbin lace is produced using a weaving or plaiting technique in which threads are wound onto small bobbins, secured at the ends to a lace pillow and the lace is worked over a pricked pattern with the threads held in place by pins. Linen tended to be used for all lace (except silk and metal laces) until the 1830s when cotton thread was produced that was strong enough for making hand made lace. The items discussed here are made from linen.

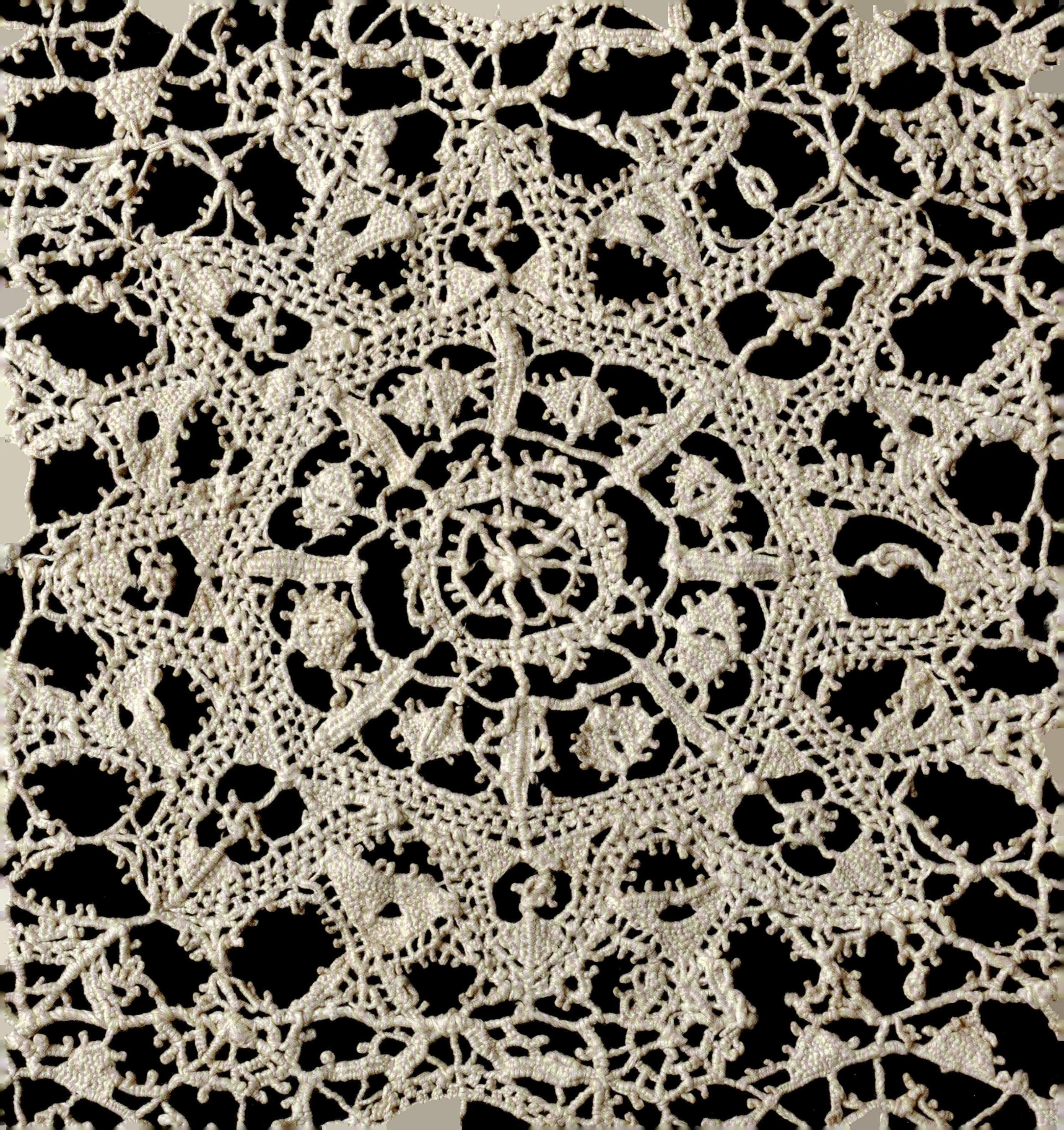

Geometric needle lace, 1600–1625

This early form of Italian geometric needle lace has its origins in cutwork – where embroidery was stitched onto a woven linen ground from which areas were cut away. A development from this technique was a kind of embroidered insertion, sometimes called *reticella*. It required the extensive removal of threads from the linen cloth to create a bare framework over which the design was worked. This type of early lace is identified by its geometric patterns, which were a necessary element of the insertion technique and limited the variety of patterns that could be produced to about 50 or so. Despite having no evidence of a woven ground, this example retains the characteristic rigid geometric patterns embellished with a variety of decorative fillings. It shows needle lace on the brink of change as it was shortly to break free of all ties to its cutwork origins. The development, during the first quarter of the seventeenth century of freely formed needle lace (termed *Punto in Aria* meaning 'stitches in air'), meant that lace became a textile in its own right. Patterns were freed from their rigid framework and became much more varied and imaginative.

OBJECT NUMBER – MT.0616

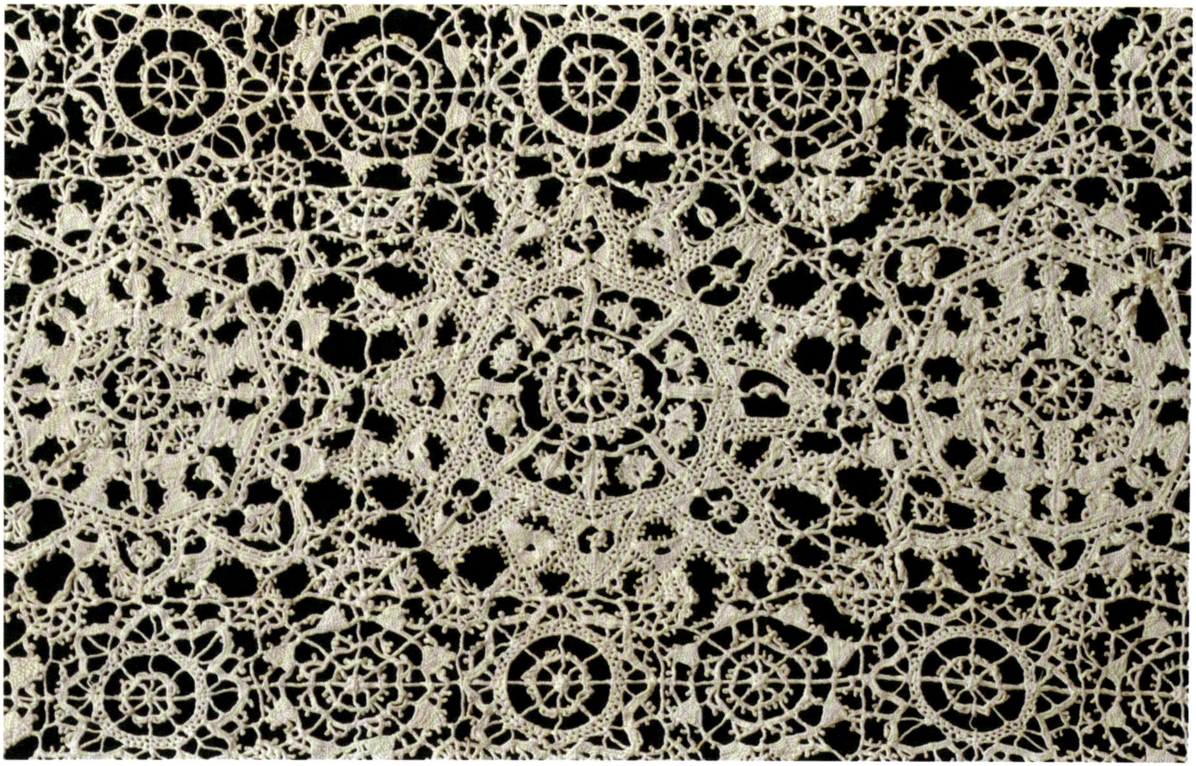

Bobbin lace, Flemish, 1630s

This bobbin lace was probably produced to decorate a wide collar and consists of deep scallops with a repeated pattern of urns and foliage. Flemish bobbin lace, with its fine, delicate texture and appearance was particularly popular for edging the soft draping collars which had come to replace ruffs in men's and women's fashion. Flanders was the centre of the bobbin lace making industry during the seventeenth century, and produced the most fashionable lace until around the 1660s. Though more famous for its needle lace, Italy also produced bobbin lace at this time; however its heavier texture was more suited to furnishings and the trimming of liturgical vestments.

OBJECT NUMBER – MT.0508

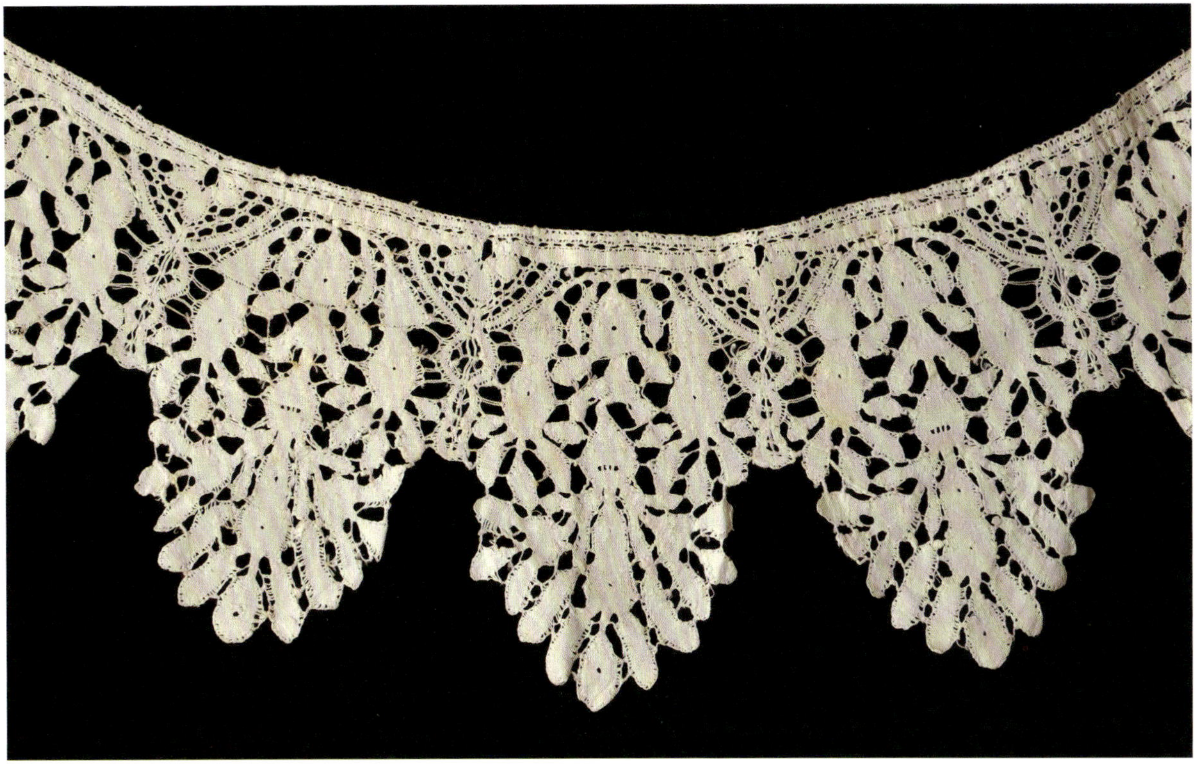

Italian needle lace, 1660–1680

This piece of Venetian needle lace has an added bobbin lace footing and a picot heading. Another name for this type of lace is *Gros point* which relates to the large, bold design. This type of *Gros point* was also known as *Rose point*. Its scrolling flower pattern is baroque in style, and the wool-padded cordonnet gives this needle lace a wonderfully three-dimensional character. The flowers have fillings of *Hollie point*, produced by leaving small holes in a variety of different patterns along rows of buttonhole stitch. Despite the popularity of Flemish bobbin lace during the majority of the seventeenth century, the French court of Louis XIV (1643–1715) popularised Venetian needle lace during the 1660s, and it soon took over as the dominant fashion. By this date needle laces were produced by drawing the pattern on a strip of parchment. Outline threads were tacked to this and the space between them was stitched to follow the design. When this was completed, linking brides were added to hold everything in place and these were often embellished with picots. Finally, the tacking stitches were cut to free the lace and the parchment re-used. Various versions of Venetian needle lace were produced, ranging from this large-scale type to the incredibly delicate *Point de Neige* (see band collar overleaf).

This lace has a dealer's label associated with it. Olive Matthews carefully kept the labels for the lace she

purchased, and they record the type of lace and the sum she paid for it. They may have been a useful cataloguing device. As the lace market expanded during the nineteenth century, lace dealers prospered from the sale of contemporary and historic laces. We do not know which dealer Olive Matthews patronised, but it may have been A. Blackborne and Co., which was founded in 1850. This London lace dealer boasted many fashionable and aristocratic clients who purchased modified historic pieces to wear, but they also sold to museums and collectors like Miss Matthews.

OBJECT NUMBER – MT.0174

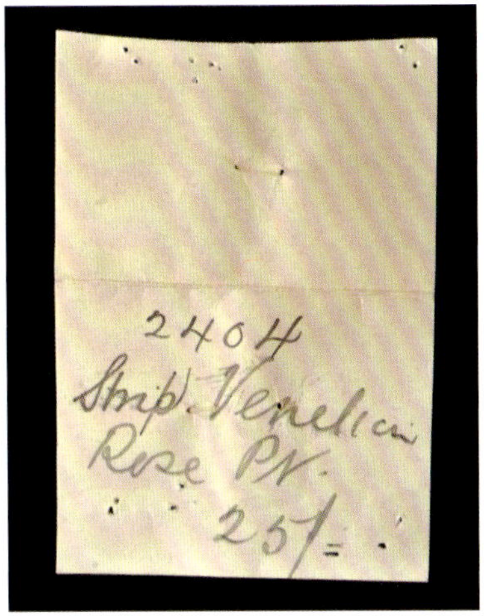

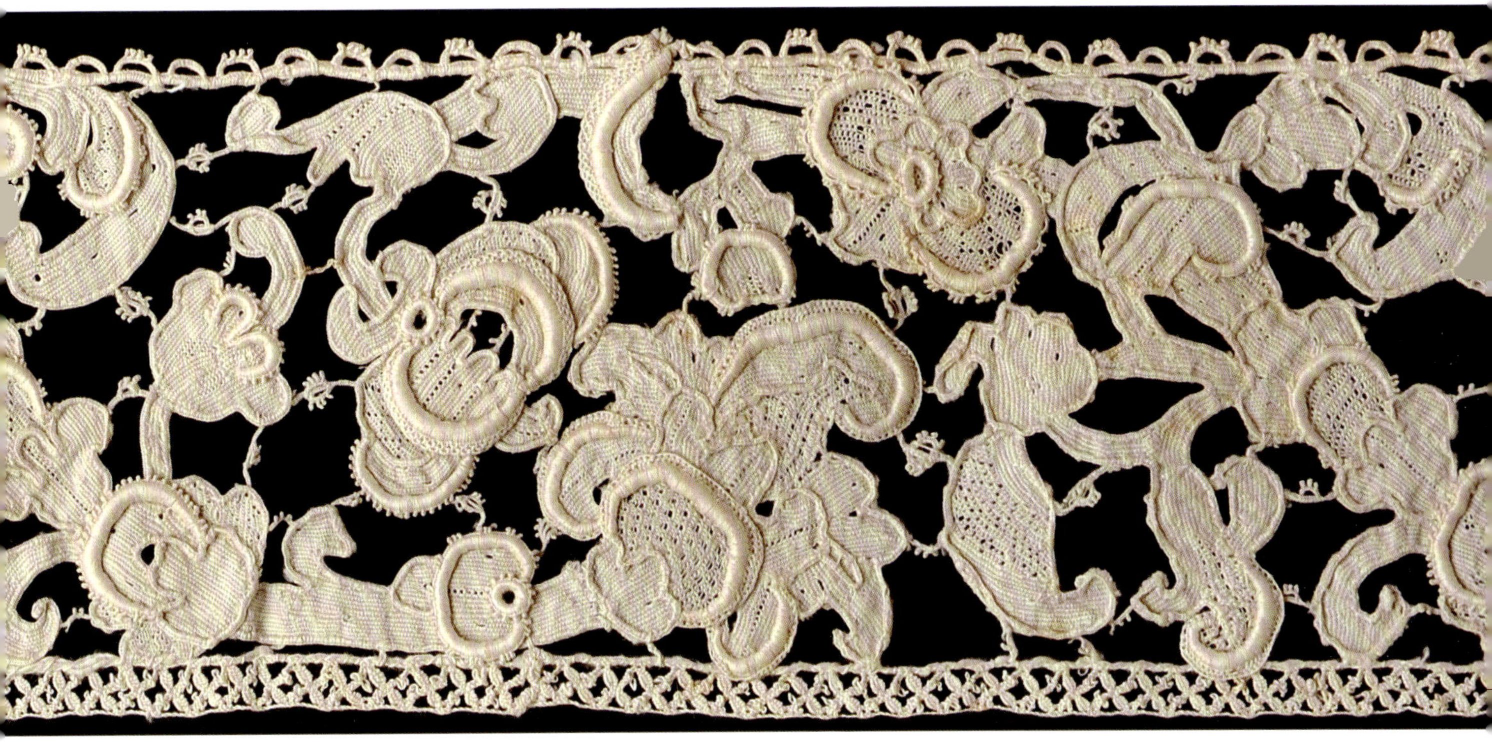

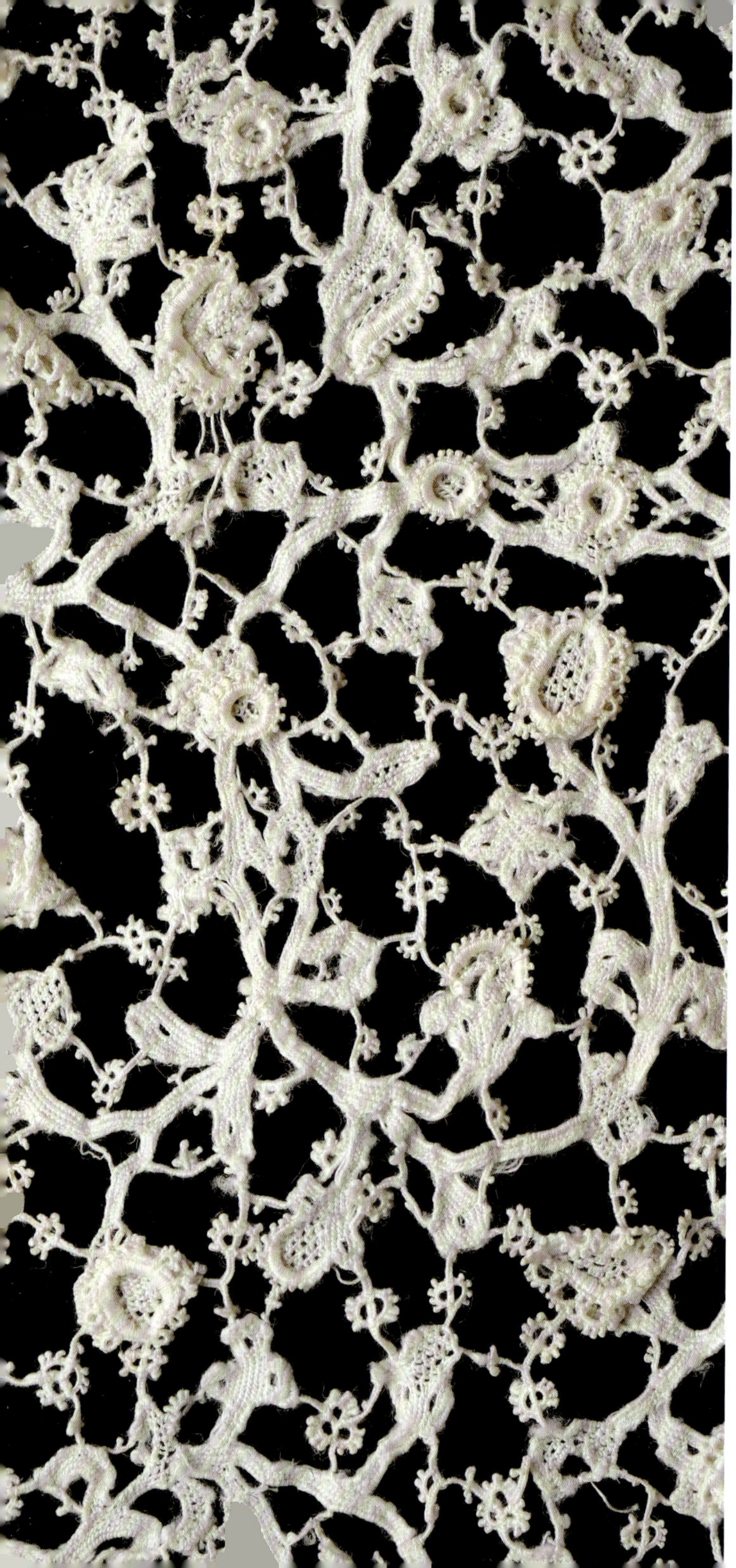

Man's bib-fronted band collar, Italian needle lace, 1690s

The collar is made from the very finest Venetian needle lace, sometimes known as *Point de Neige*. It features tiny layered floral patterns, said to resemble snow crystals. The flowers are joined by brides picotées or decorated linking threads, and some areas have *Hollie point* fillings. The lace is mounted on a linen band with linen tapes at either end. There have been some nineteenth century modifications, probably carried out by a lace dealer. These include tiny alterations and some mending. The collar is also missing its lace 'header' – a strip of plainer lace to provide a firm anchor for the linen band. The band would have been removed and replaced when it became too dirty or worn.

During the late seventeenth century wide linen collars edged with lace were replaced by band collars such as this one. Lace was moved to the highly visible throat area as a result of changes in men's hair fashions. The increasingly large wigs worn by men would have hidden expensive trimmings around the shoulders. These new collar styles ensured that costly lace could be seen, and were often worn over dark colours to make them stand out. In bib-fronted bands the lace design was created in mirror image, and here scrolling floral motifs wind delicately upwards, setting off the face. Though here it features as part of a man's fashion accessory, this very fine type of needle lace was often used in women's headdresses.

The lace industry was worth a great deal of money as lace was an expensive luxury item. Attempts were made to protect the native English lace makers, and in 1662 legislation banned the importation and selling of foreign lace. However, the royal family were exempt from this law, and it was generally flouted by wealthy people of fashion who favoured the more showy Continental laces. The lace trade continued to flourish, particularly in London, much of it fed by lucrative smuggling rings. Not surprisingly, the theft of lace was also a common occurrence.

OBJECT NUMBER – MT.0637

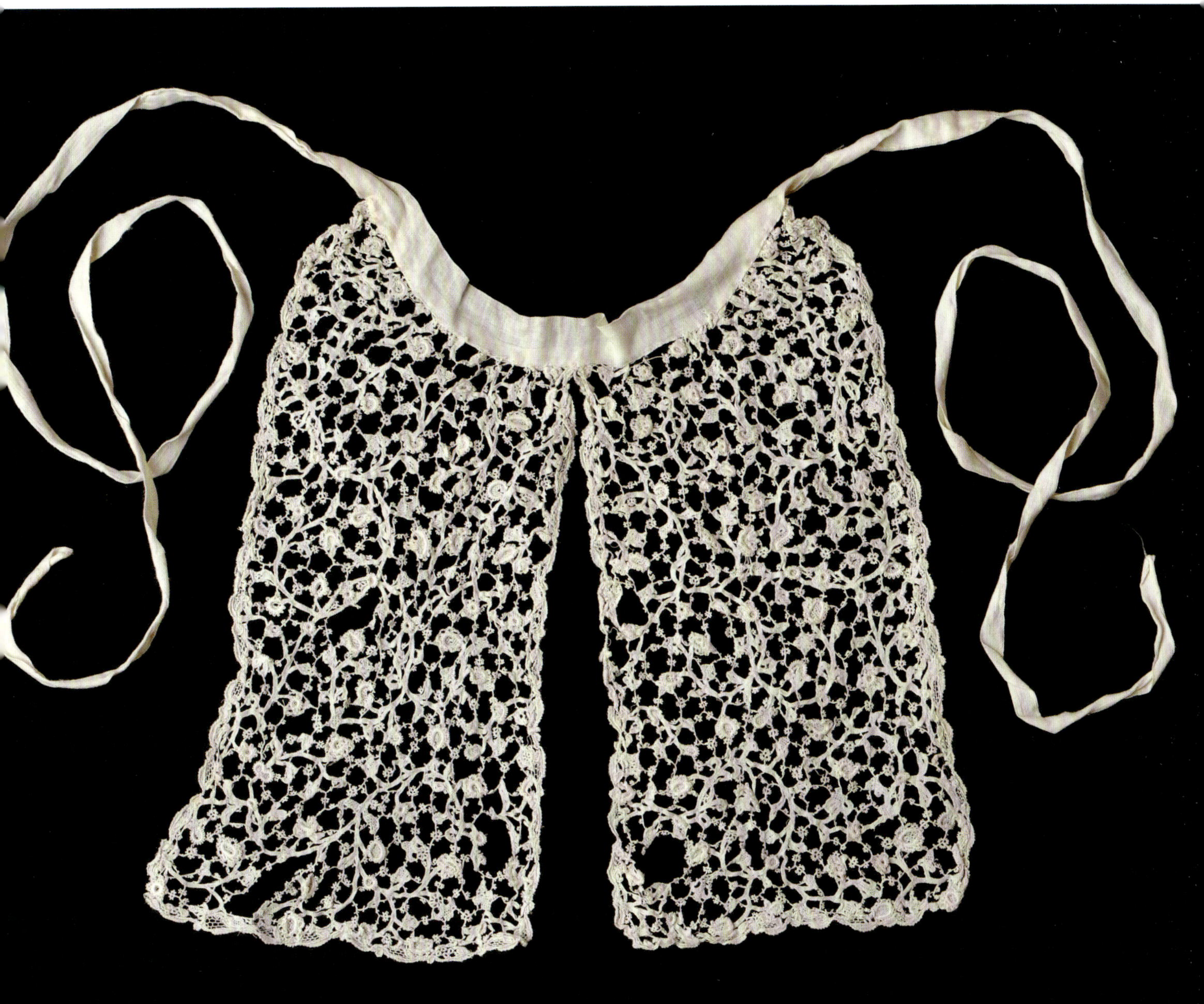

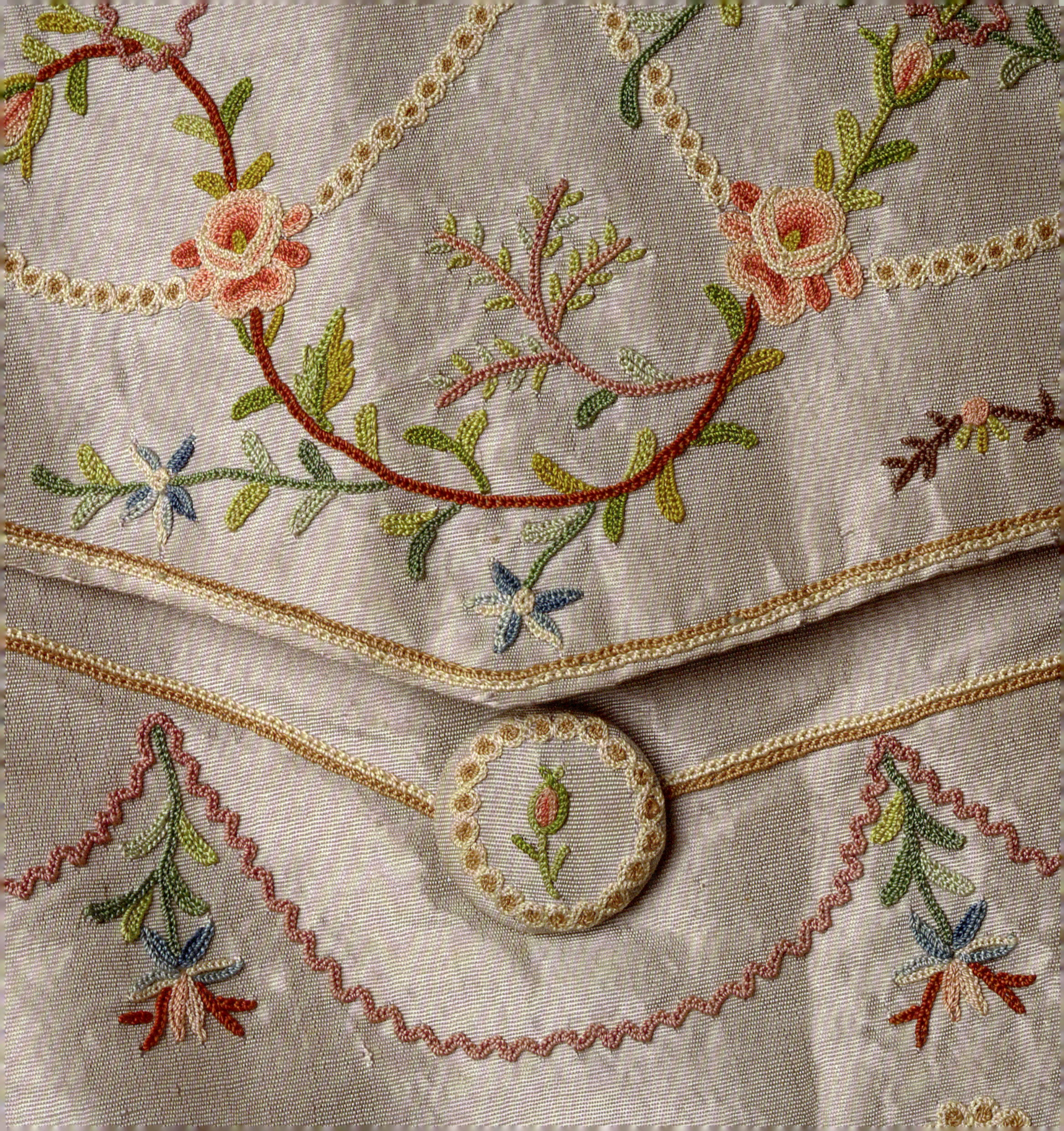

THE EIGHTEENTH CENTURY

*'Lightness, freshness, elegance and decency …'**

The Olive Matthews Collection is known for the quality of its eighteenth century holdings. The fashionable dress of the 1700s had a distinctive elegance and exuberance all its own which held a particular fascination for Olive Matthews. The collection contains an abundance of important and beautifully preserved pieces from this era, rivalling the quality of items held by much larger institutions. In contrast to the seventeenth century group, there are a number of full garments as well as accessories, and the collection spans the entire century, with both male and female clothing represented. These high quality high fashion items have survived in remarkably good condition, and once again Miss Matthews' love of intricately hand worked decoration and craftsmanship is much in evidence.

* Mercier, Louis-Sebastian, *Tableau de Paris* discussing the fashions of the 1780s, quoted in Waugh, Norah, *The Cut of Women's Clothes, 1600–1930*, (Faber & Faber, London, 1968), p.122.

LEFT Detail from a man's suit, 1780–1788 (see pages 70–71).

Cap with black work embroidery, 1700–1720

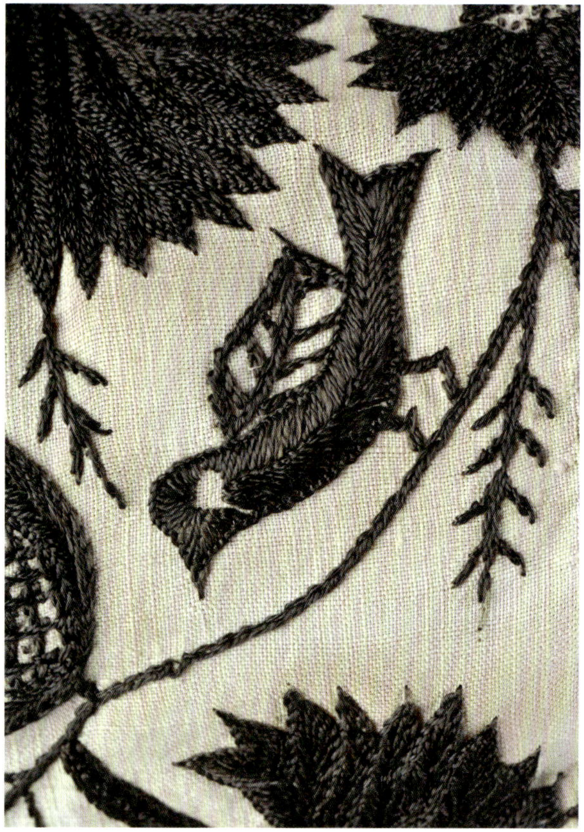

Woman's white linen cap made from two shaped panels. A double draw cord of linen allows for the fit to be altered at the back of the neck. A strip of flat woven braid with a repeat flower design is stitched to the front edges and gathered at the temples. Two linen tapes should tie under the chin, but only one of these survives.

The cap is decorated with black work embroidery in silk thread. The bold, symmetrical design features vases of carnation flowers with birds perched on the stems. The high quality embroidered fabric used for this cap has been recycled from another garment. It is likely to be Spanish in origin, and probably originally part of a woman's smock, though the cap itself may be Dutch. Black work embroidery became fashionable during the sixteenth century. It was usually worked on linen, and often covered the fabric in scrolling designs. It tended to be used to decorate collars, cuffs and smocks. The re-using of good quality fabrics was common in this period and earlier. These textiles were very expensive to buy, and it made sense to remake garments in new styles, or even to cut them up to make entirely new items as has been done here.

OBJECT NUMBER – MT.0073

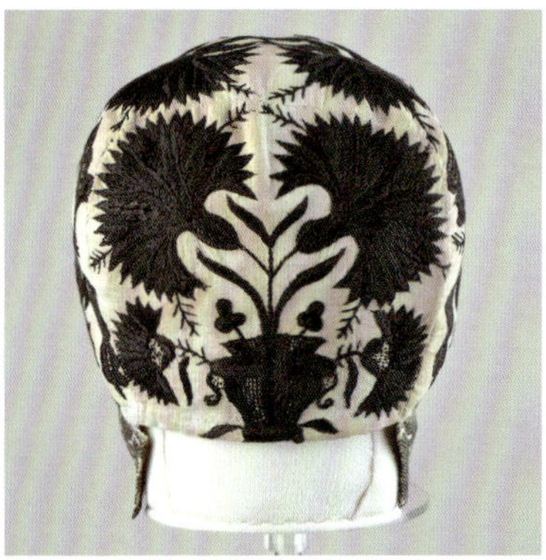

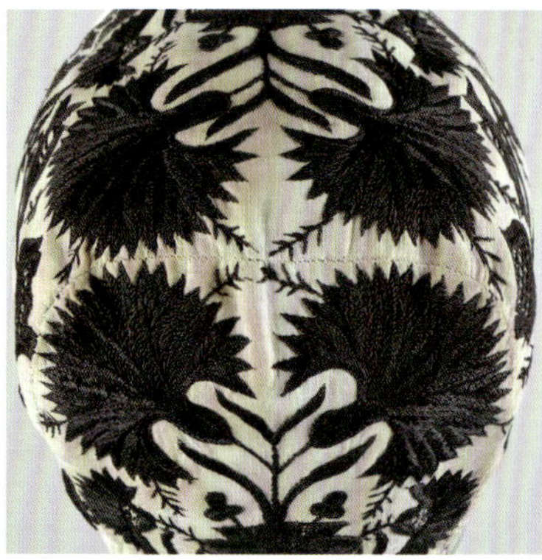

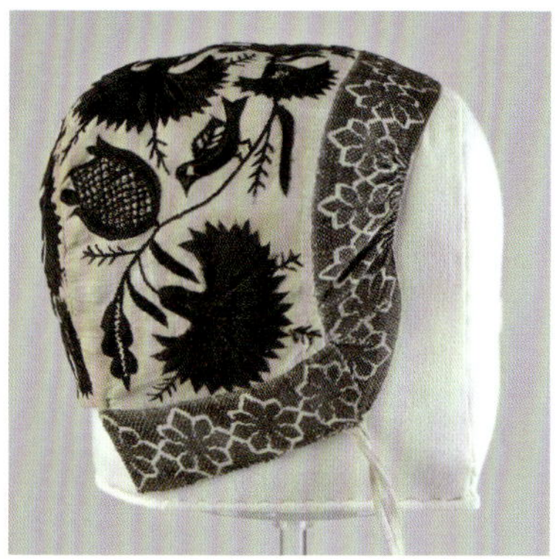

Gloves, 1700–1715

One-piece gauntlet gloves made from cream kid leather, and embroidered with silver thread in a design of pomegranates, flowers and spots. A narrow fringe of silver thread has been stitched to the edges of the gauntlets, and they are part lined with blue silk taffeta to cover the back of the embroidery stitches. An opening has been made at the outside edge of the gauntlet so that the wearer's cuffs would not be crushed. They could have been worn by either sex, and are transitional in style, having links with the lavishly embroidered long gauntlet gloves of the seventeenth century and the short, plain leather gloves with vented sides adopted for day to day wear during the early eighteenth century.

Gauntlet gloves were first fashionable from the sixteenth century through to the 1740s, although plain versions continued to be worn for riding after that date. The style originated from armour, where the gauntlet sections provided flexible protection for the wrist. Practical gauntlet gloves were also used for hawking, but the expanse of leather provided ample space for the addition of decoration. Fashionable versions soon evolved, becoming status symbols and featuring in much of the portraiture of the period. The earlier examples were highly decorated with coloured and metalwork embroidery on long gauntlet sections which were either added or all one piece with the glove. Glove fashions gradually become less elaborate and more practical, and by the time this pair was produced in the early eighteenth century, we see only a remnant of the lavish seventeenth century style in the short gauntlets and relatively muted metalwork embroidery.

OBJECT NUMBER – MT.3166

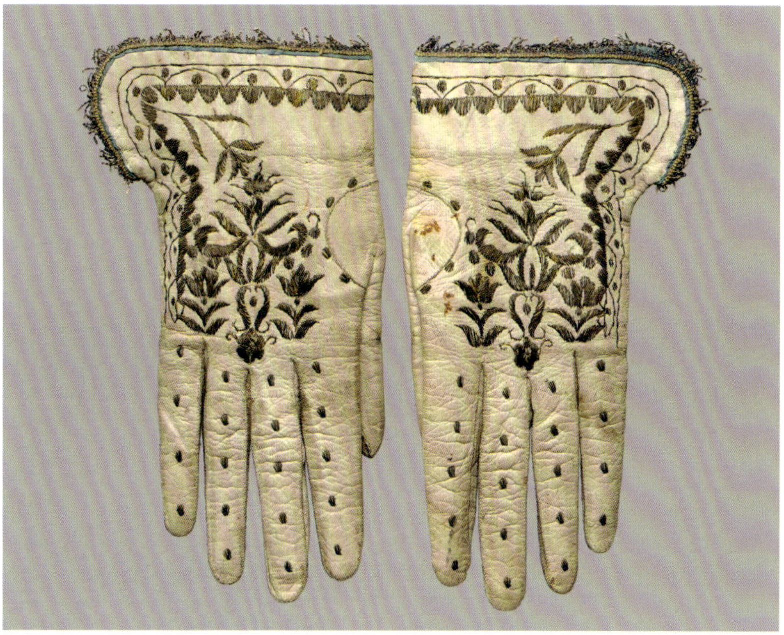

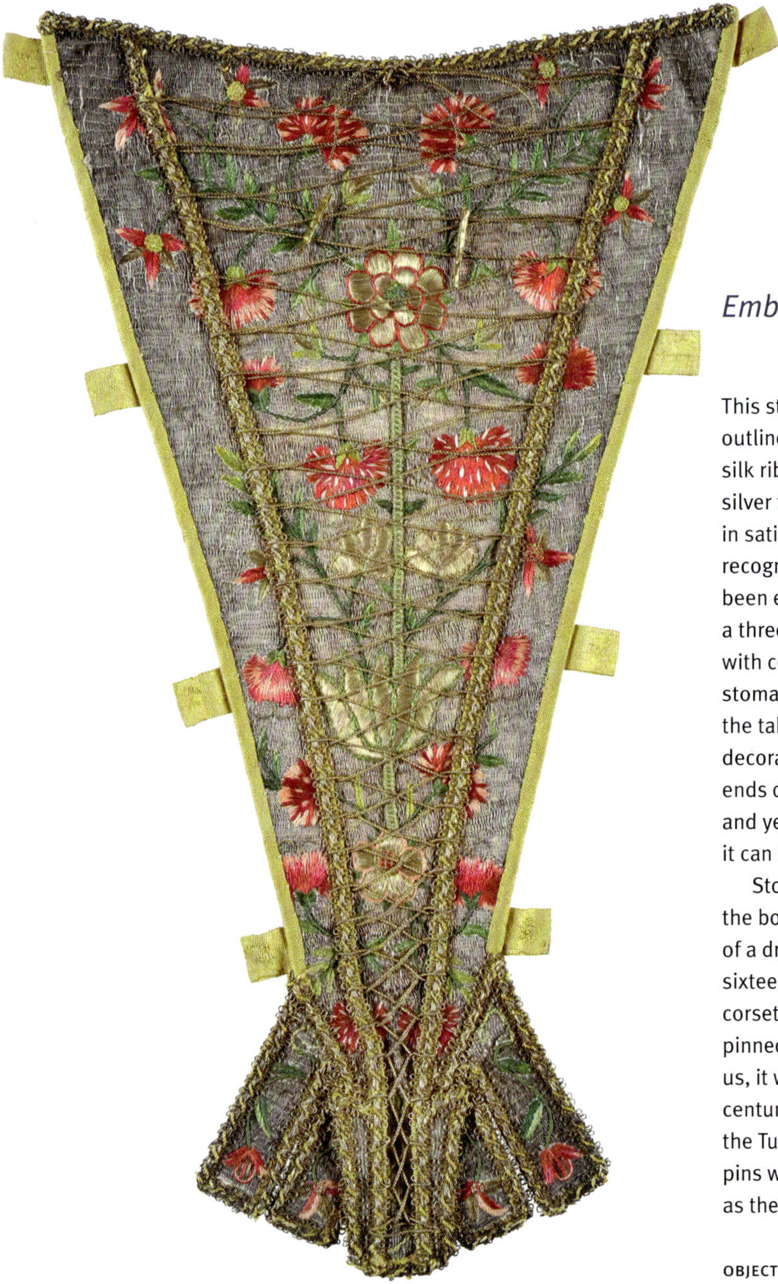

Embroidered stomacher, 1725–1735

This stomacher is made from linen, covered with silk and outlined with gilt metal braid. It is embellished with yellow silk ribbon and gilt cord and embroidered all over with silver thread. A naturalistic flower pattern has been worked in satin stitch with silk and gold thread. The flowers are recognisable as carnations, roses and tulips. Some have been embroidered in raised work or stump work, giving a three dimensional effect which is achieved by padding with cotton wool. The criss-cross lacing is a continuation of stomacher fashions from the late seventeenth century, as are the tabs at the bottom. The lacing was by this time largely decorative, though it did provide a neat way to secure the ends of a kerchief. The stomacher is lined with cream silk, and yellow silk ribbon loops are stitched to the sides so that it can be laced, stitched or pinned in place.

Stomachers were decorative panels worn at the front of the bodice to fill in the central gap between the two sides of a dress. They were part of women's clothing from the sixteenth to the eighteenth century, and were fixed to the corset by means of pins or stitches. Though the idea of being pinned or sewn into clothing on a daily basis seems odd to us, it was quite normal at the time, and had been for many centuries. When excavations were carried out at the site of the Tudor Globe Theatre in London, large numbers of brass pins were found. These had dropped from people's clothing as they watched the performances.

OBJECT NUMBER – MT.1319

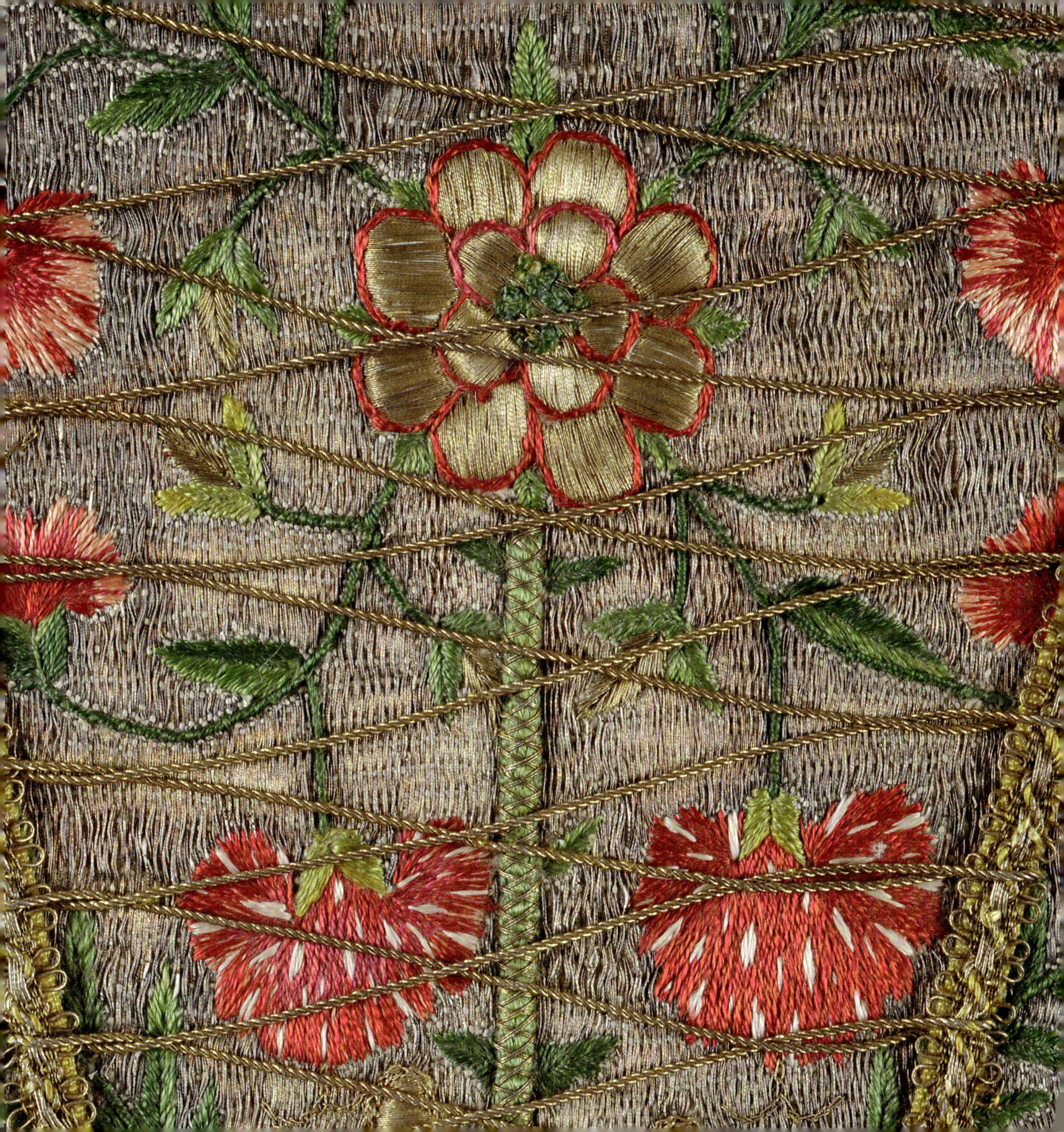

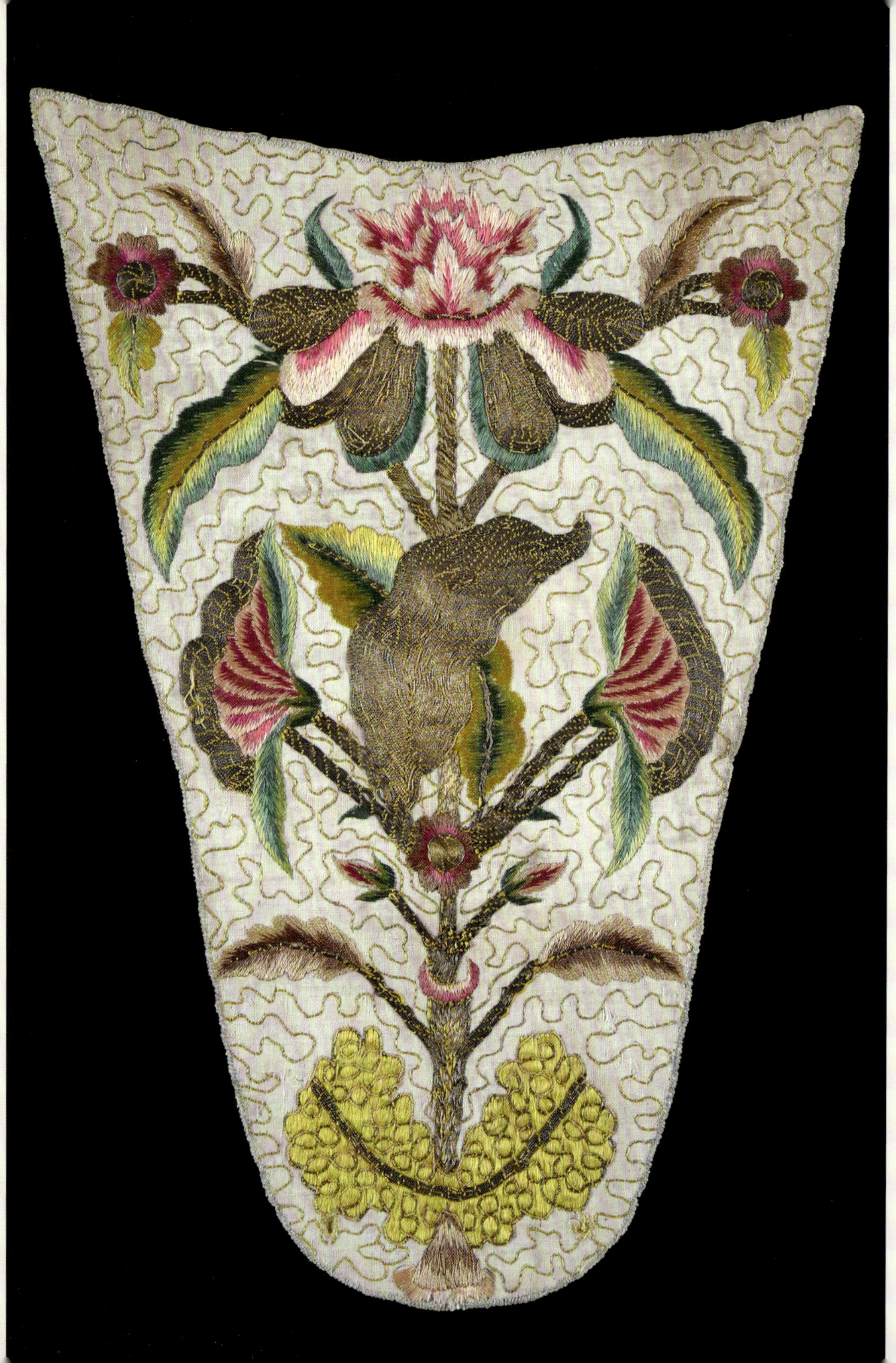

Embroidered stomacher, 1725–1735

This stomacher is made from linen and hand embroidered. The background has been worked with a meander pattern in couched yellow silk thread. The central floral motif has been richly embroidered in pink, green and yellow silks and silver metal thread couched with yellow silk. The edge has been neatened with pale green buttonhole stitch.

Although stomachers were an important element of fashionable dress until the mid eighteenth century, by the 1770s they were reserved for use in formal dress only. Often stiffened with layers of fabric or buckram, stomachers were designed to emphasise the flatness of the front of the body – a shape created by tightly laced whalebone stays. The central prominence of the stomacher made it a favoured place for decoration. This example is beautifully embroidered with a bold, stylised design, but other methods of embellishment were also used. For formal occasions sets of three graduated stomacher brooches could be pinned in place, and during the 1750s at the height of the Rococo era, rows of bows or *échelles* were added for maximum texture and opulence.

OBJECT NUMBER – MT.1314

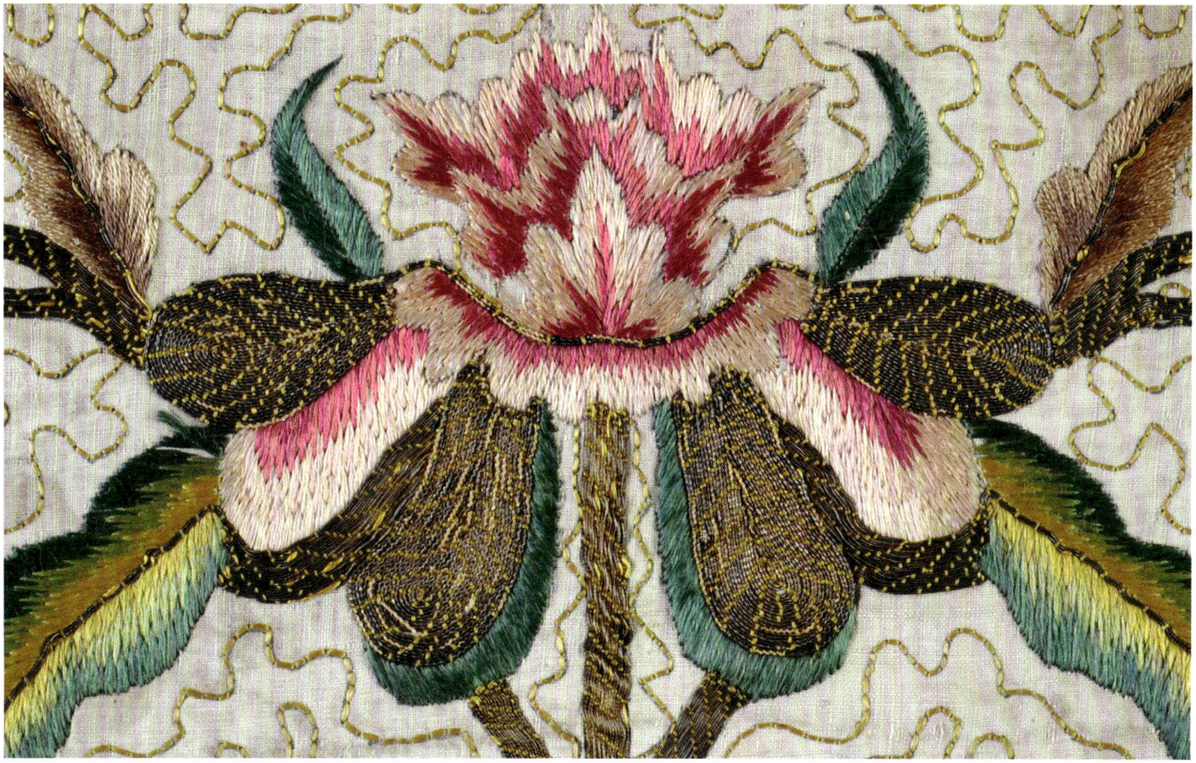

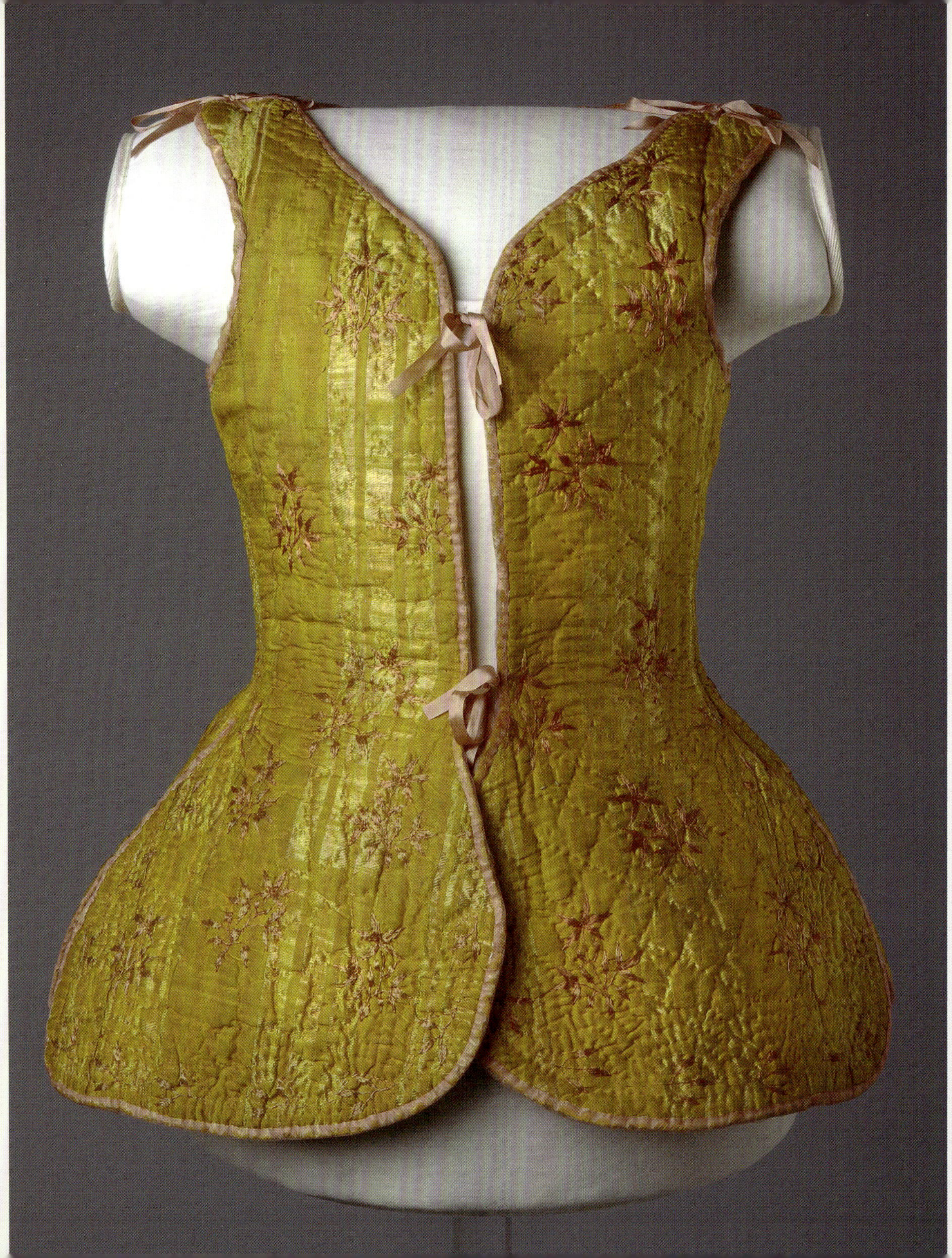

Woman's quilted waistcoat, 1730–1735

Made from bright yellow silk satin with damask stripes, the edges are bound with pink silk ribbon. Pink silk thread has been used for the quilting. The interlining is likely to be wool. It has been embroidered with bunches of flowers in pink silks, and is tied at the shoulders and centre front with pink silk ribbons (these are modern replacements). The waistcoat has a brown block printed linen lining. Investigations during conservation work have revealed that this is a replacement. The original lining is still present beneath, and is of linen block printed with stylised maroon rosebuds in a diamond trellis pattern. This is of particular interest since the original lining was carefully chosen to complement the embroidery on the quilted section of the waistcoat, making it a much more coherent garment.

This type of waistcoat tended to be worn for comfort and warmth. It replaced the corset and was for informal wear, to be seen only in the privacy of the home, and probably only in the boudoir. In 1716 Lady Mary Wortley Montagu wrote a poem satirizing fashionable life and mentioned this form of waistcoat:

I drank bohea in Celia's dressing-room:*
Warm from her bed, to me alone within
Her night-gown fastened with a single pin;
Her night-clothes tumbled with resistless grace,
And her bright hair played careless round her face;
Reaching the kettle made her gown unpin,
*She wore no waistcoat, and her shift was thin.***

Though other examples of quilted waistcoats do exist in Museum collections, they are relatively rare. This is because they were informal garments which were not usually put aside and kept. Most of these types of everyday clothes were worn until they wore out. We are lucky that this waistcoat has survived, particularly since the evidence of re-lining suggests that it was required to provide long service. This example is very decorative with its bright colours, pretty pink embroidery and matching lining. Other surviving quilted waistcoats vary from plain and simple to decorative embroidered examples such as this one. Though intended to be seen by very few people, functional, informal eighteenth century pieces were often embellished for the benefit of the wearer and her closest companions.

OBJECT NUMBER – MT.3042

*Bohea was a type of Chinese tea, at the date the poem was written it was one of the choicest grades available.

**Lady Mary Wortley Montagu, *The Complete Letters*, II, p.21; Town Eclogues, 1716.

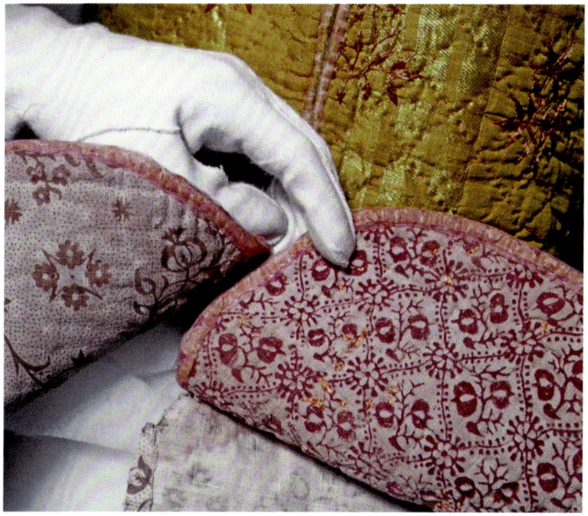

Lace

The early eighteenth century saw the emergence of beautifully delicate bobbin lace. Flemish lace was particularly sought after and much imitated. It was made using extremely fine linen thread, and this combined with complex and fluid designs made it ideal for the lighter fashions of the period. Flemish bobbin laces have been categorised into different types. These were named after towns such as Brussels or Valenciennes, though the lace was not necessarily produced solely in these areas. Although they carry the overarching label 'Flemish', the term refers as much to style and technique as it does to the area of production, particularly since some of the key lacemaking towns were absorbed into other states such as France or the Netherlands.

RIGHT Detail from a lappet of Valenciennes lace, 1730–1740 (see page 49).

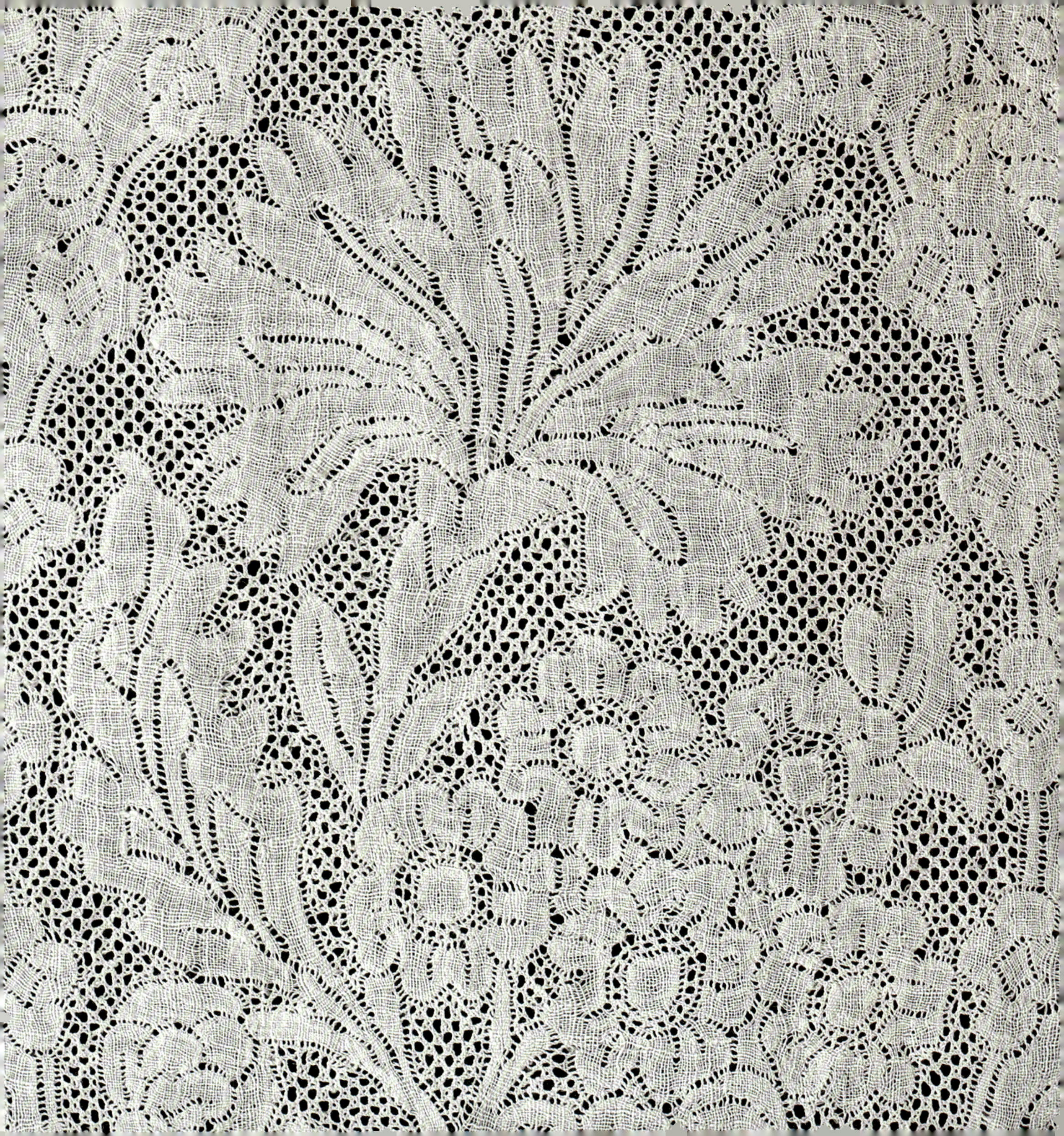

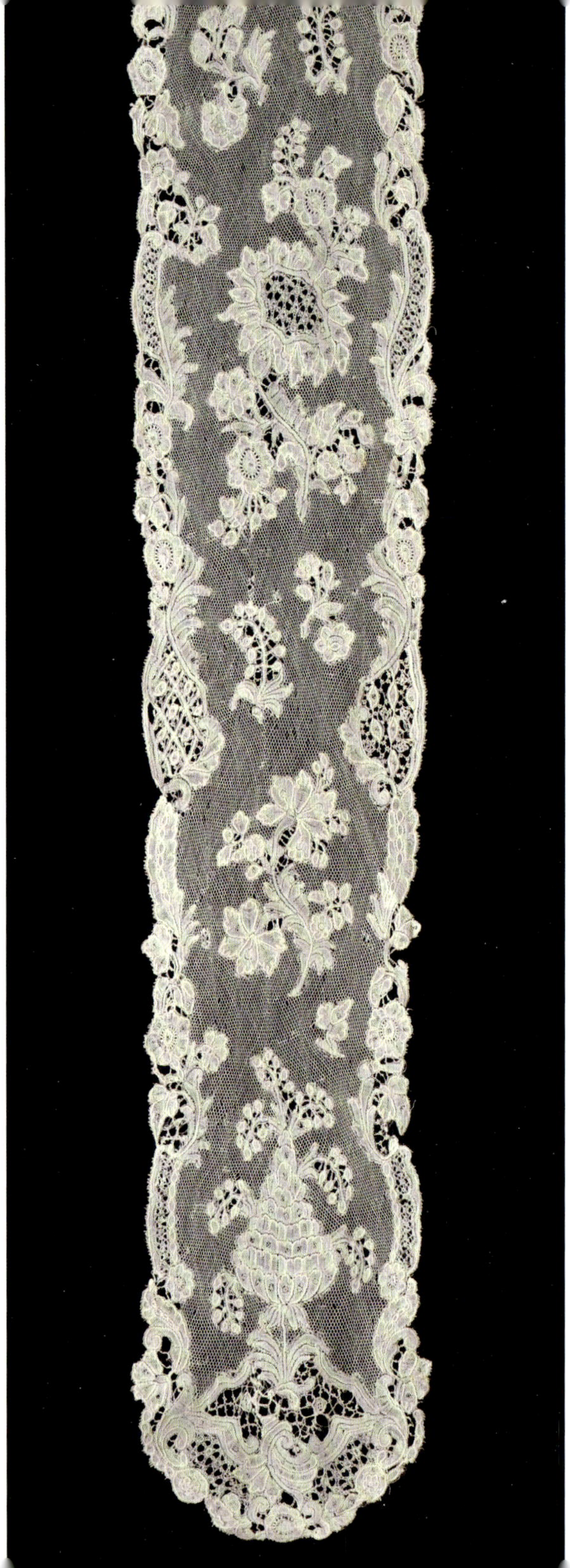

Lappet of Brussels lace, mid 1740s

This lappet is made from very fine Brussels lace. Lappets were attached to women's caps from the late seventeenth century into the nineteenth century, and they could be left to hang down at the sides of the face, or pinned up on top of the head according to fashion or personal preference. This example has a shaped picot edge formed by a border of flowers, leaves and ribbons, with floral sprays and a large flower centre piece made separately and mounted on a drochel or hexagonal mesh ground characteristic of Brussels lace. The meandering flowers and 'C' scrolls evident in this piece are typical of Rococo design, which lent itself beautifully to the delicacy of this type of lace.

OBJECT NUMBER – MT.1753

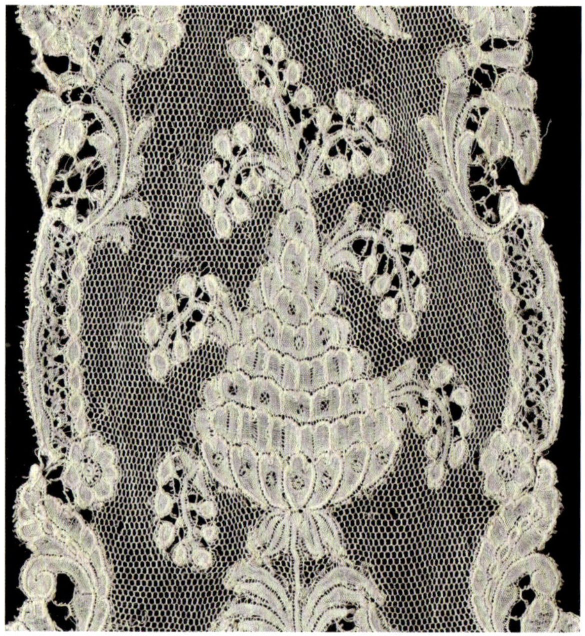

Lappet of Valenciennes lace, 1730–1740

A fine example of a Valenciennes lace lappet, with a shaped picot edge formed from a scrolling border. It has central flowers and cartouches with a crown at the end. The pattern is worked in very fine clothwork with pinhole borders and the ground is of the round Valenciennes type. Unlike eighteenth century Brussels lace, Valenciennes of this period is a straight lace, which means that it was worked in one piece rather than creating the pattern and ground separately and stitching them together. It was extremely time consuming to make, taking up to 800 bobbins to make a strip 10 centimetres in width. A pair of sleeve ruffles of the finest quality Valenciennes lace could take almost a year to produce, and as a result it commanded high prices.

OBJECT NUMBER – MT.1748

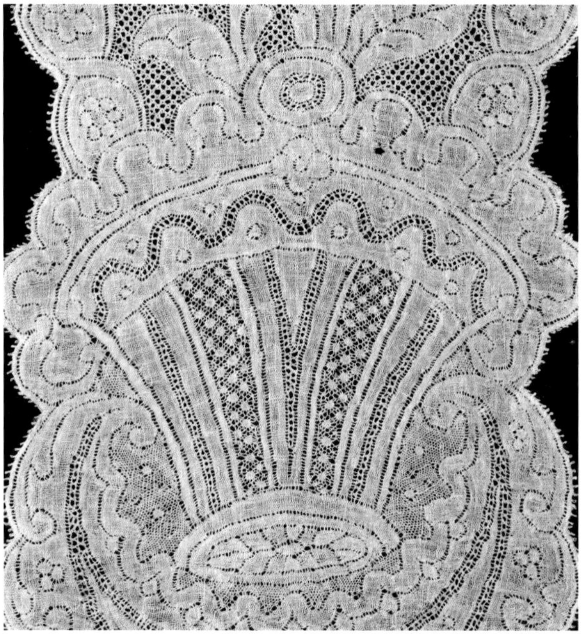

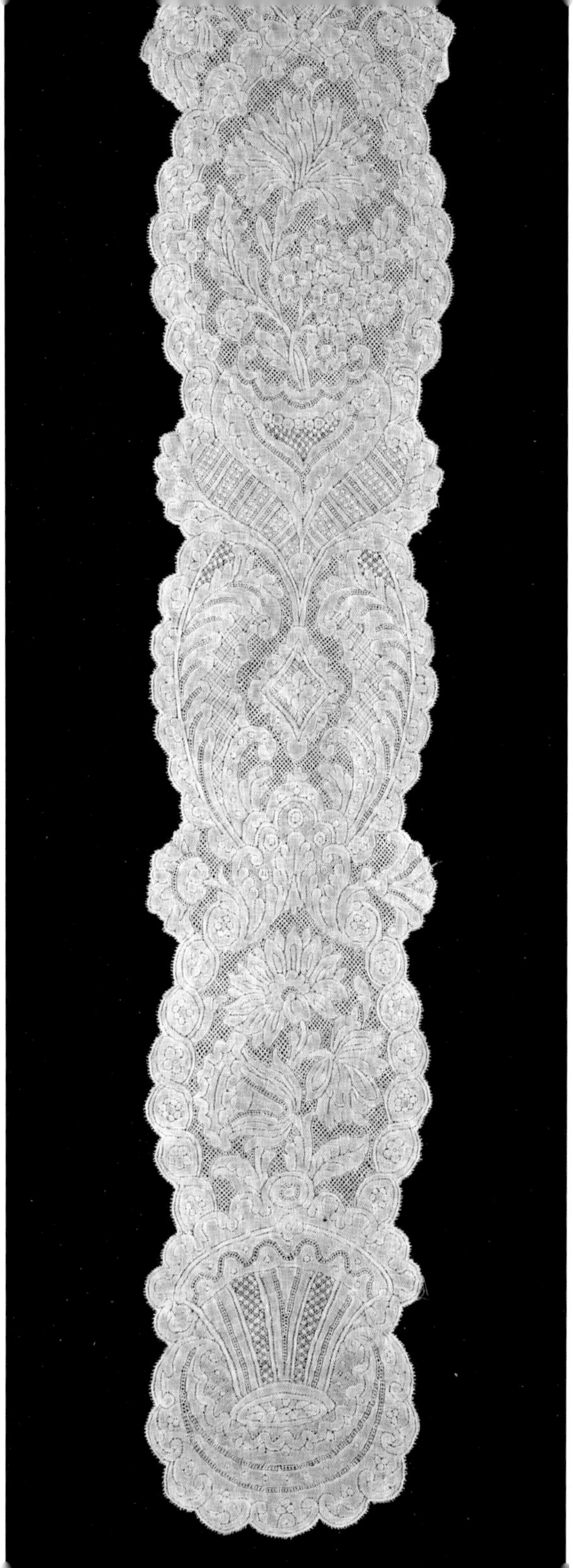

Woman's apron, 1740–1750

The apron is made from cream silk taffeta and the edges are shaped into broad scallops. It is lavishly embroidered in a bold, floral design using couched gilt metal thread and silks. The design owes something to both the formal styles of the early eighteenth century and to the more flowing, naturalistic forms that became fashionable from the 1730s. The symmetrical framework of the pattern is softened by the curling flower shapes as well as the meandering lines which embellish the two central leaves.

Aprons were worn by women at all levels of society, but this type was designed as a fashion accessory for formal occasions and served no practical purpose. The cut of the apron can provide clues about the overall look of the outfit it completed. The waistband finishes with short tabs and is designed to be pinned or stitched in place, avoiding the need for ties which might interfere with the line of the dress at the back. The apron dips to a point at the centre front matching the shape of the bodice or stomacher above, whilst the gathers at the top edge would have echoed the gathers on the dress waistband beneath, again helping to achieve a clean line. The fullness and width of the apron also tell us about the prevailing silhouette. During the 1740s skirts were growing wider. The apron was designed to complement that width; the stiff taffeta helping it to stay in position as it flared out to its broadest point.

OBJECT NUMBER – M.1994.45

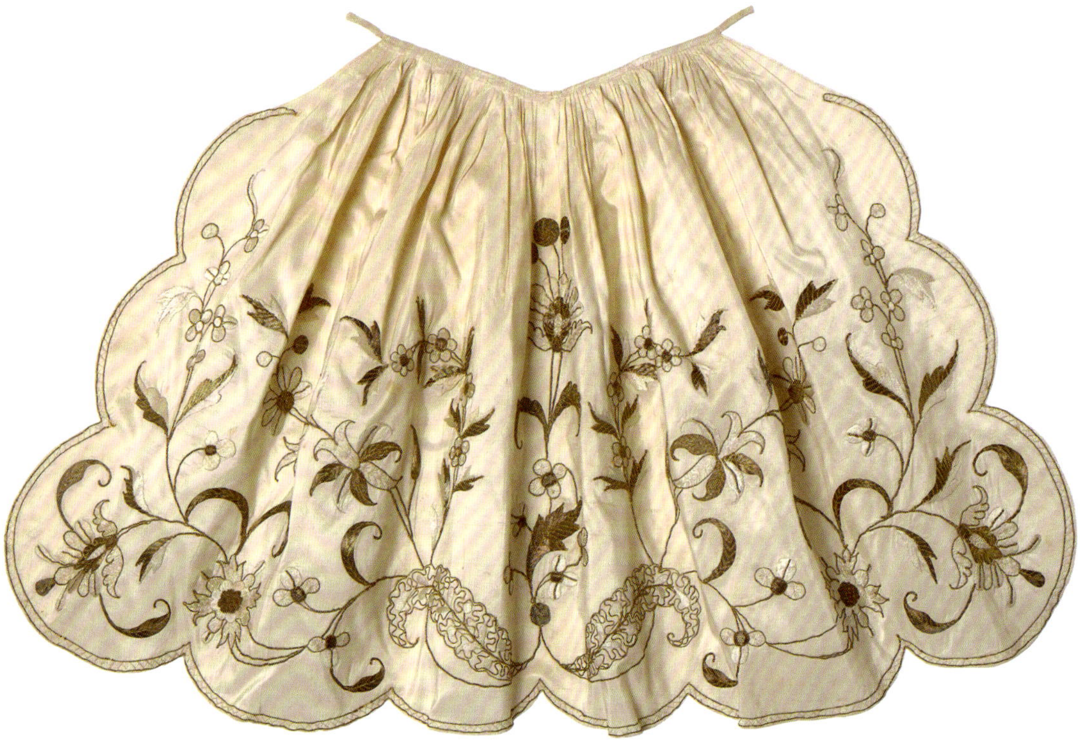

Women's shoes shown with clogs. Shoes, 1735–1745, clogs 1720–1740

A pair of silk brocade shoes with wide straps or latchets crossing over a high front tongue. The shoes are trimmed with gold lace and dark green silk braid. They are lined with cream suede, brown leather and cream silk satin. The latchets would have been fastened with a shoe buckle to keep them in place, and several of these are illustrated on pages 61–63. The clogs are of leather with shaped sockets to keep the heels in place. They have two wool-lined leather straps to fasten across the front and are covered with silk brocade similar in design to that of the shoes.

Clogs provided some protection for shoes when walking through muddy or dusty streets, preventing shoe heels from digging into the ground. Pattens were also worn at this time. They were similar in design to clogs, but gave greater protection as they had an iron ring or four-lobed hoop fixed to the sole, raising the wearer further above the dirt. These clogs and shoes are not an exact pair, but they are the same size and similar in style. Olive Matthews purchased the shoes from the Caledonian Road Market in London for half a crown. She was delighted when she found the clogs several weeks later at the same market.

OBJECT NUMBERS – MT.1923 AND MT.1922

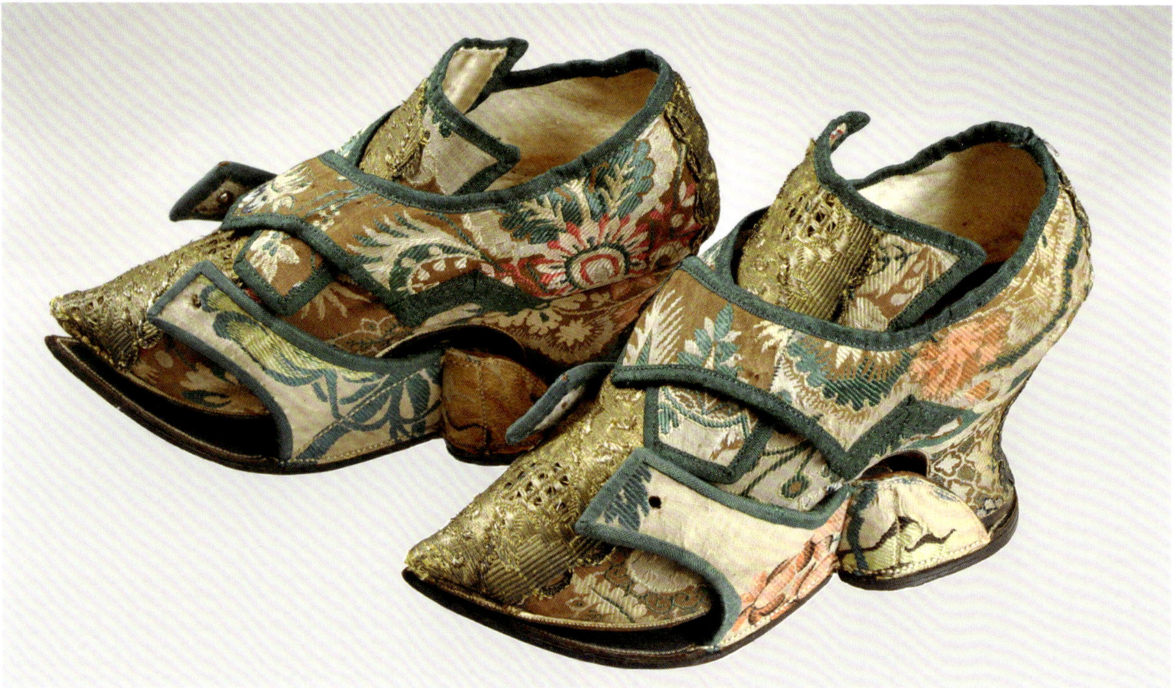

Silk brocade open robe, 1750–1760, silk brocade 1734–1735, shown with replica stomacher and petticoat

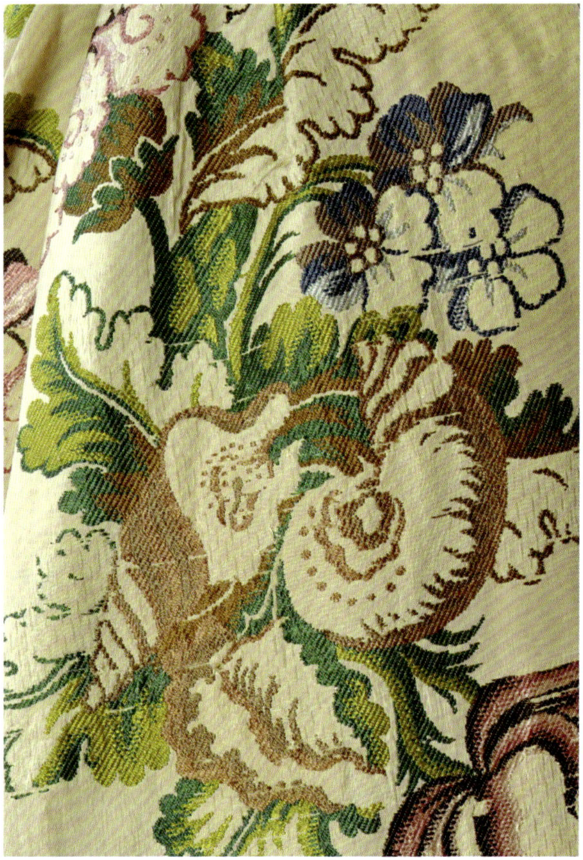

Dress of cream silk brocade with a large floral design. The fabric dates to around 1734, but the dress was remodelled during the 1750s.

The fabric of this dress was woven by hand on a draw loom by highly skilled artisans. It is likely to have been woven in Spitalfields – an area of East London well known for its skilled weavers. The main design is typical of the period with its large floral pattern on a light coloured background, and is reminiscent of work by the talented designer Anna Maria Garthwaite, many of whose patterns survive at the Victoria and Albert Museum. Upon closer inspection, it becomes clear that the dress is made up of three different brocaded silks. This was done quite frequently by the less well off as a means of gaining a fashionable look without the great expense of purchasing large pieces of woven silk. Cheap labour meant that it was comparatively inexpensive to have a dress made up at this time. Instead, most of the cost of clothes went on the fabric. This is the reason why the dress has been altered twenty years after it was first worn – a common occurrence, evidence for which is found in many surviving examples of eighteenth-century garments.

The cloth of this dress is an excellent example of the fashion for large, flowing botanical designs which followed on from the more rigid, stylised patterns of the earliest years of the eighteenth century. It is likely that this fashion was based on broader exploration of the wider world. Botanists returned from their travels with new and unfamiliar plant specimens; capturing the public imagination and inspiring a fashion for exotic designs which had to look as realistic as possible.

This craze for naturalistic plant designs was coupled with the development of new techniques in silk weaving. Jean Revel, a talented silk designer based in Lyons, France, is credited with mastering a method which allowed shading in silk patterns. Originally trained as an artist, he identified the need for a more realistic three-dimensional effect, and this was achieved by dovetailing different tones of colour: a technique called *pointes rentrés*. The secrets of this new method were quickly acquired by designers and weavers in other important silk weaving centres such as Spitalfields in London, and it can be seen in the silk of this dress. The use of this new weaving method closely coincides with an abundance of bold floral patterns, as designers celebrated the newfound realism that *pointes rentrés* allowed them.

OBJECT NUMBER – MT.2039

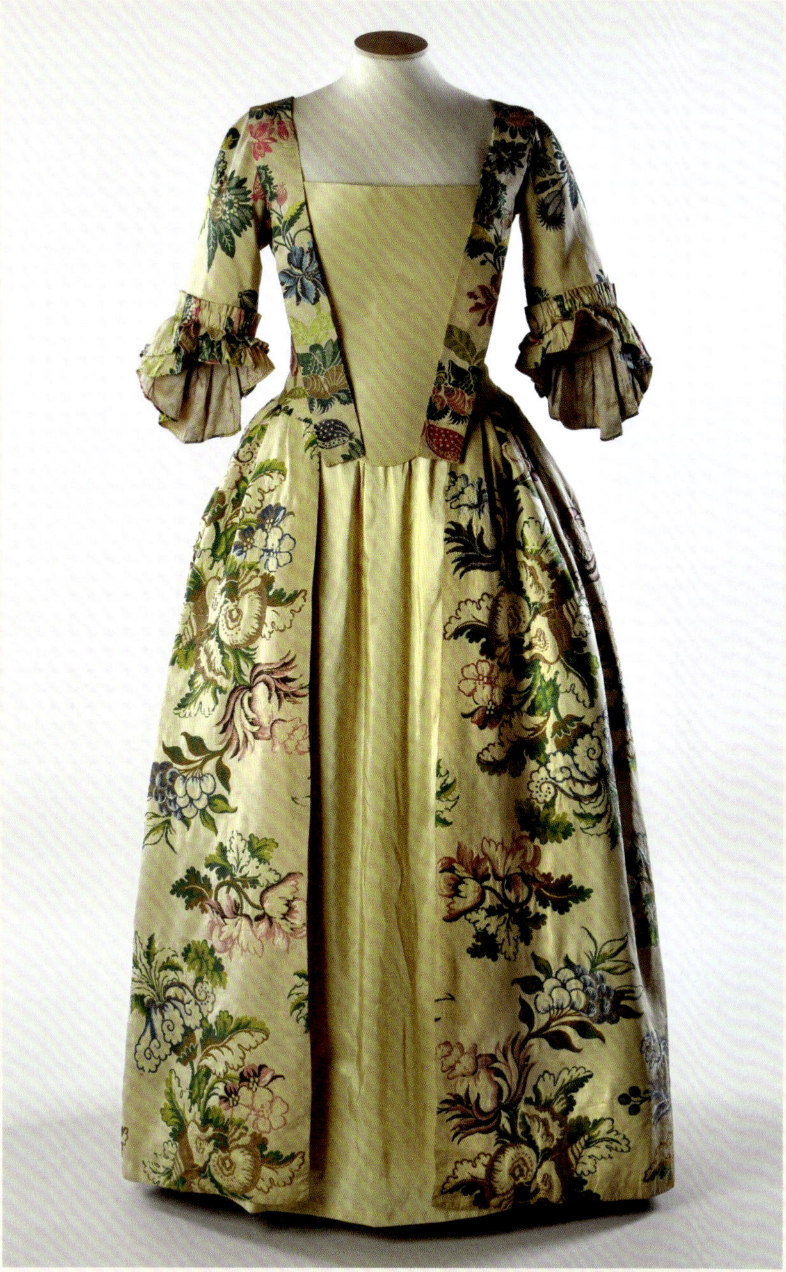

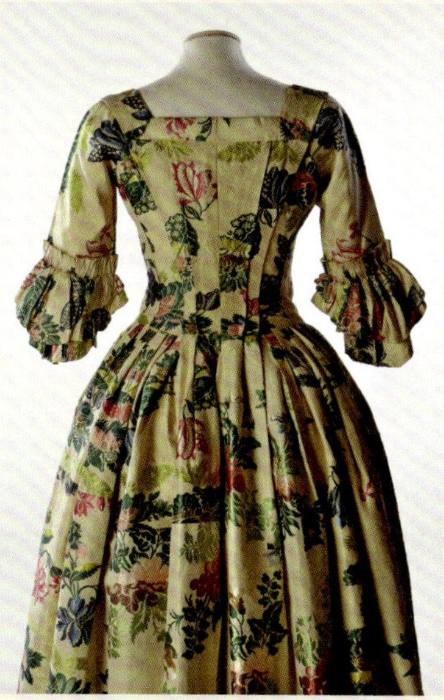

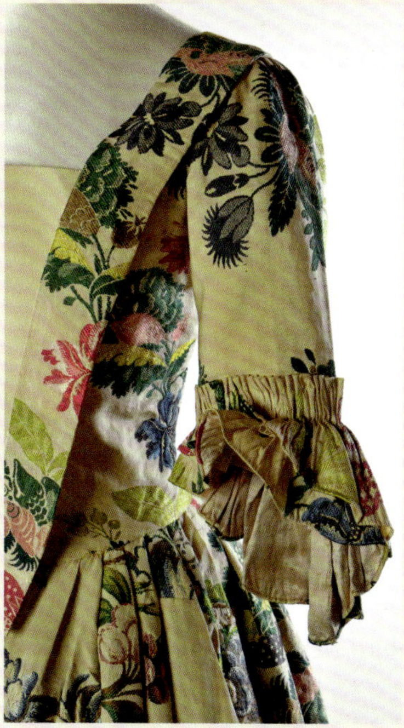

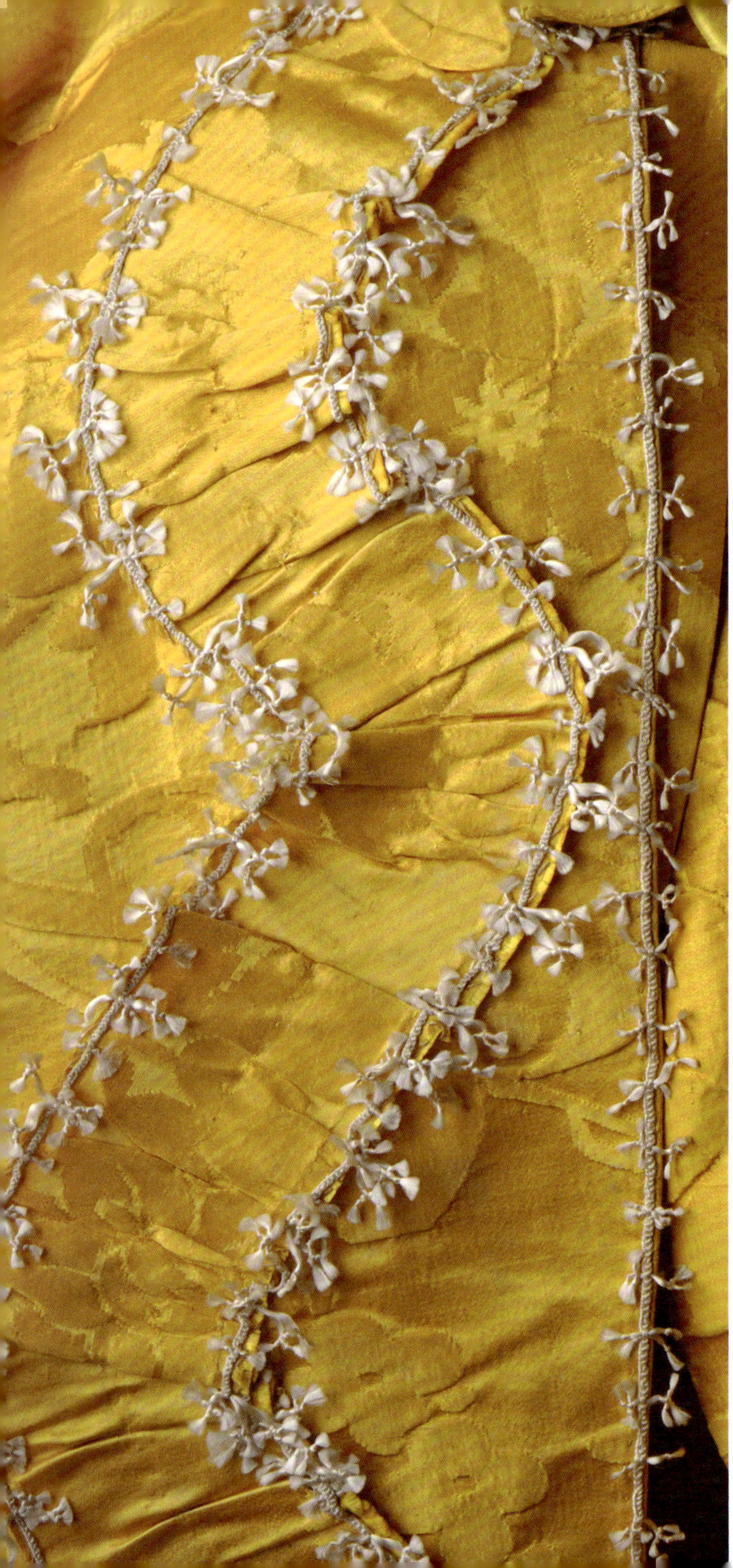

Sack back gown and matching petticoat, 1760–1770, silk damask 1740–1745, shown with replica stomacher

This stunning sack back gown is made from bright yellow floral silk damask. The name 'sack back' relates to the box pleated section of material that runs from the back of the shoulders to the hem. Sack back dresses were worn in varying forms for much of the eighteenth century. They were adopted as part of general everyday wear from the 1720s, but by the 1760s were worn only on the most formal occasions.

The silk damask of this dress was woven in the early 1740s and it is difficult to find an example which has retained its colour without fading. However, the construction and surface decoration of the garment now dates mostly to the 1760s. The double sleeve ruffles are typical of this period, as are the serpentine robings. Women's fashion was heavily influenced by Rococo designs during the 1750s and 1760s, with great emphasis on surface decoration and trimmings. These are further enhanced by the inclusion of white fly fringe decoration – a trimming which was particularly popular during the third quarter of the eighteenth century. It consists of braid made from cord and floss silk which is knotted to make it stand out, adding to the three dimensional effect of the dress.

It is rare to find a dress that has come down to us unchanged from its original state. The re-modelling of garments to bring them up to date was a very common practice during the eighteenth century. Silk was an expensive commodity, and for the less well off, the logical solution was to re-make an old garment to bring the cut up to date. This dress has also been altered more recently for fancy dress. Although disappointing, these changes probably ensured its survival; long after it was fashionable, and before it was deemed historically valuable, this garment found a new role which saved it from disposal.

OBJECT NUMBER – M.2010.01

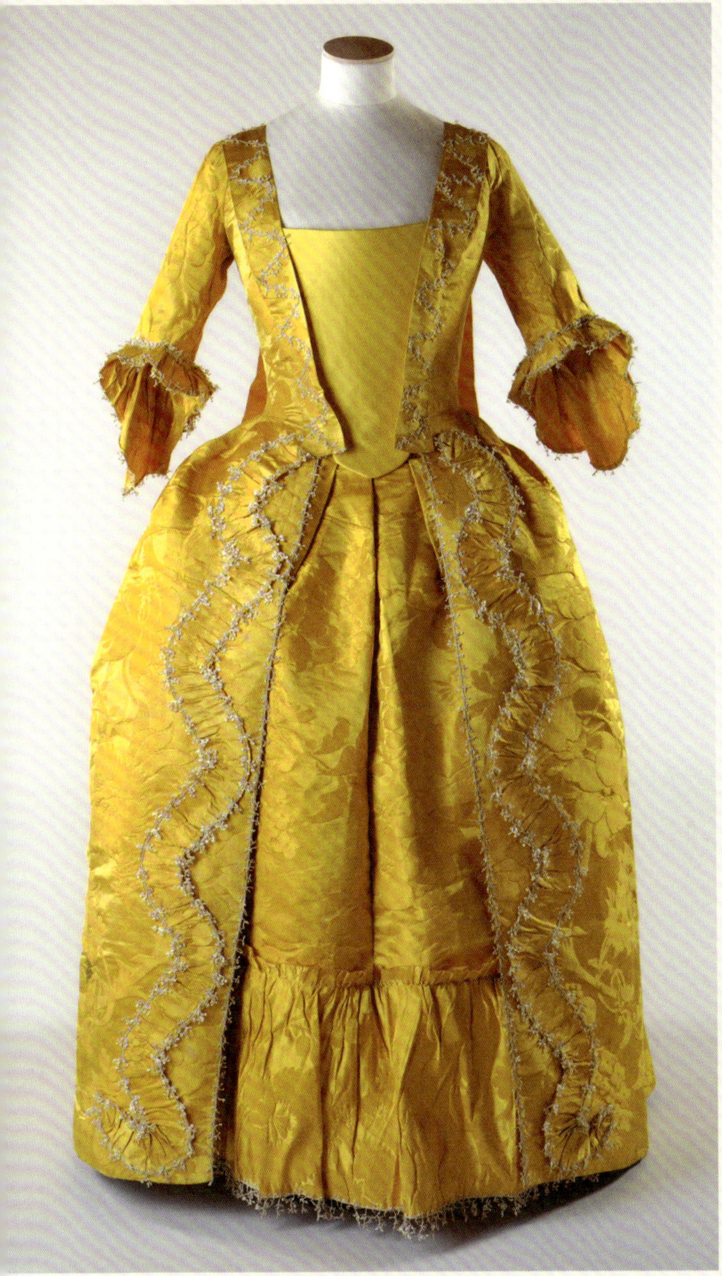

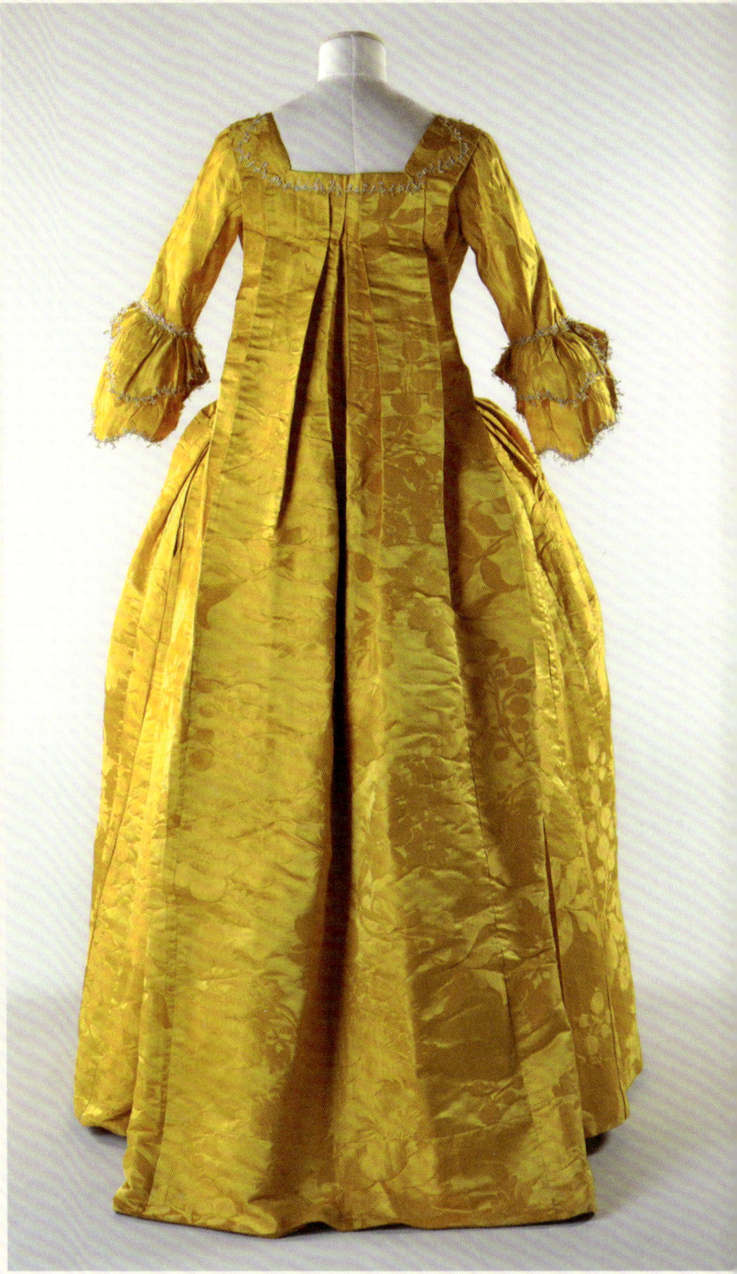

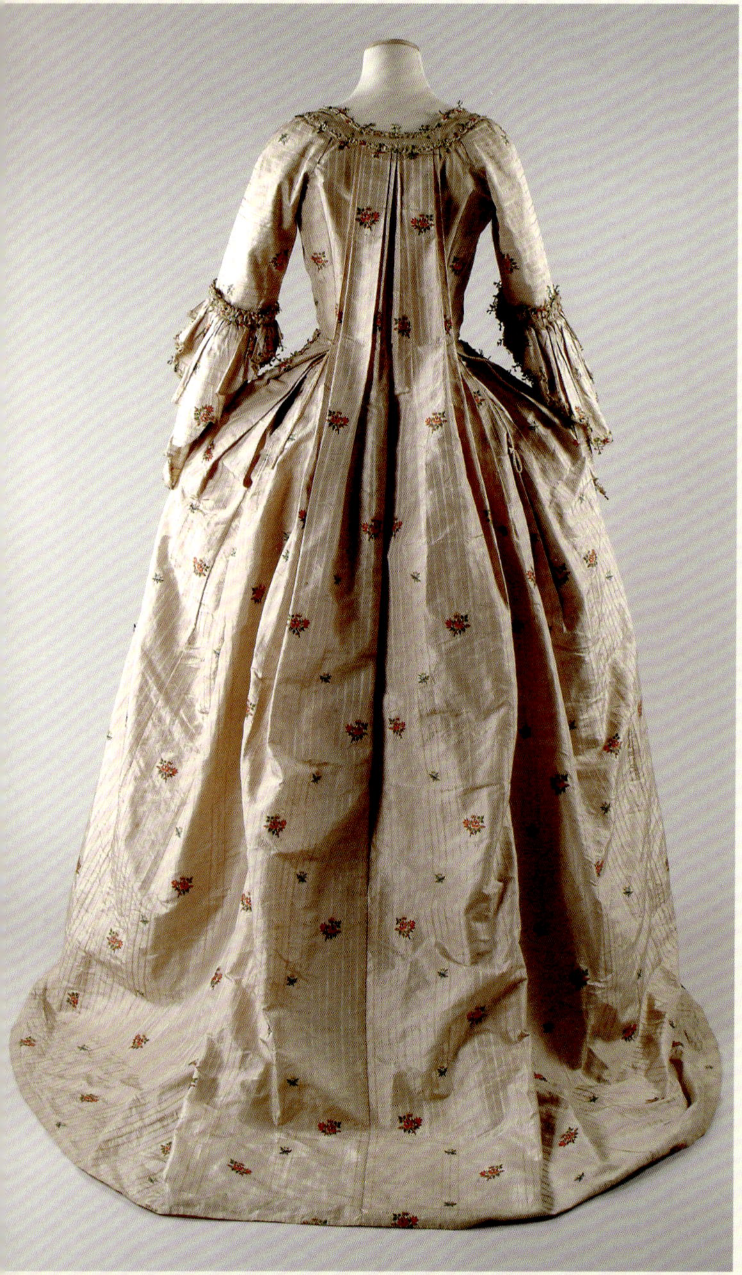
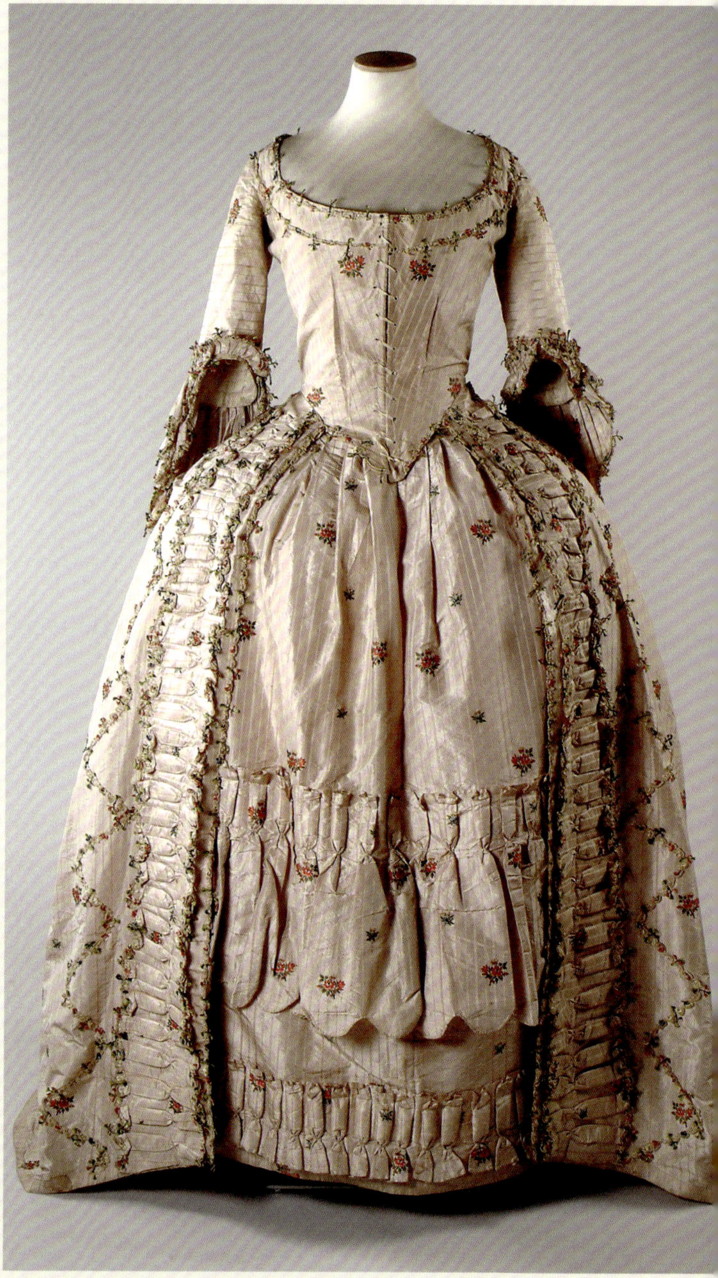

Sack back gown and matching petticoat, 1776–1778

This beautiful garment incorporates many of the traditional stylistic features of the 1770s. It exhibits the typical cut, delicate colours and complex decoration of the era. As a sack back gown of this period, it would have been reserved for *full dress* and only worn on the most formal occasions. The abundance of flowing material that the style required lends this gown a luxurious and extravagant air, which would have been accompanied by the rustle of the silk as the wearer walked.

Further features of the gown's construction include a boned bodice and wide skirts designed to incorporate side hoops. The dress could also be worn *à la Polonaise*. As the name suggests, this style had its origin in Polish dress, and was a fashion of the 1770s and early 1780s. The style could be achieved in a variety of ways, but for this piece the skirt was ruched up through plaited cords and held in place by fabric covered buttons on the outside of the bodice back. The style lent dresses a pastoral, shepherdess-like feel in keeping with the Arcadian ideals of the period.

The gown is made from silk brocade, probably woven in Spitalfields, East London, and the fabric design features small floral sprigs on a subtly striped background. Silk patterns altered significantly during the course of the eighteenth century, as floral designs gradually diminished from the oversized bold forms of the early 1700s, to sprigs which became smaller and smaller before disappearing completely. This silk is a good example of the transitional designs of the 1770s. The stripes woven into the background were soon to come to the fore as neo-classical style began to dominate during the 1780s. In addition, the robe exhibits many other decorative features. Cotton-wool padded robings have been added, as well as double sleeve ruffles and abundant fly fringe decoration, creating a beautifully textured three-dimensional effect.

Just like the yellow sack back gown discussed earlier, this piece has been modified for fancy dress or theatrical costume, probably during the nineteenth century. The bodice has been enlarged, and holes for front lacing have been added and crudely stitched. The petticoat has also been let out and re-stitched onto a modern tape waistband, but despite this, it retains its late eighteenth century character and elegance. Miss Matthews never owned a sack back gown, but had expressed a wish that one should enter the collection. She would no doubt have been delighted when this piece was added during the 1990s.

OBJECT NUMBER – M.1999.4

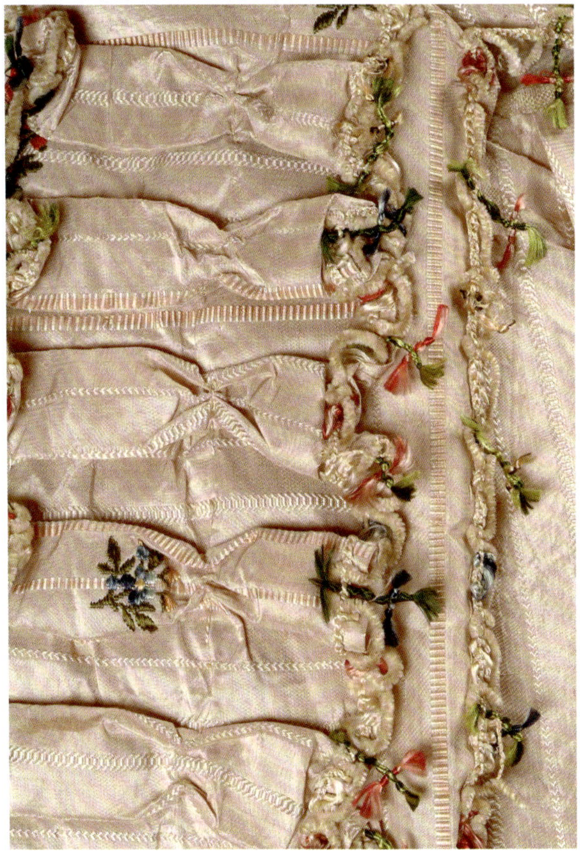

Hand painted silk fan, 1783–1787

This charmingly decorated fan has ivory sticks and guards inlaid with gilt metal and silver foil in classically inspired patterns. The front of the silk leaf is hand painted and embellished with silver gilt spangles (or sequins), while the reverse is simply painted with two flower sprigs. The fan features several vignettes containing flowers and birds. The central vignette shows a woman in fashionable 1780s dress posing with a bird cage. The fan was made in France and dates from around 1785, and as well as being an important example of an eighteenth century accessory in its own right, the depiction of a woman in fashionable dress adds a further dimension. The fashions help to date the fan, they also provide information about dress and hat styles, and just like a fashion plate they can show how these garments were worn.

The Olive Matthews Collection contains a number of fans from the eighteenth and nineteenth centuries, providing researchers with a broad range of different styles and media. Accessories of all kinds are just as important a part of the collection as garments. Their intricate and highly decorative nature appealed to Miss Matthews. They were also small, making them relatively easy to collect and store in large numbers.

OBJECT NUMBER – MT.1721

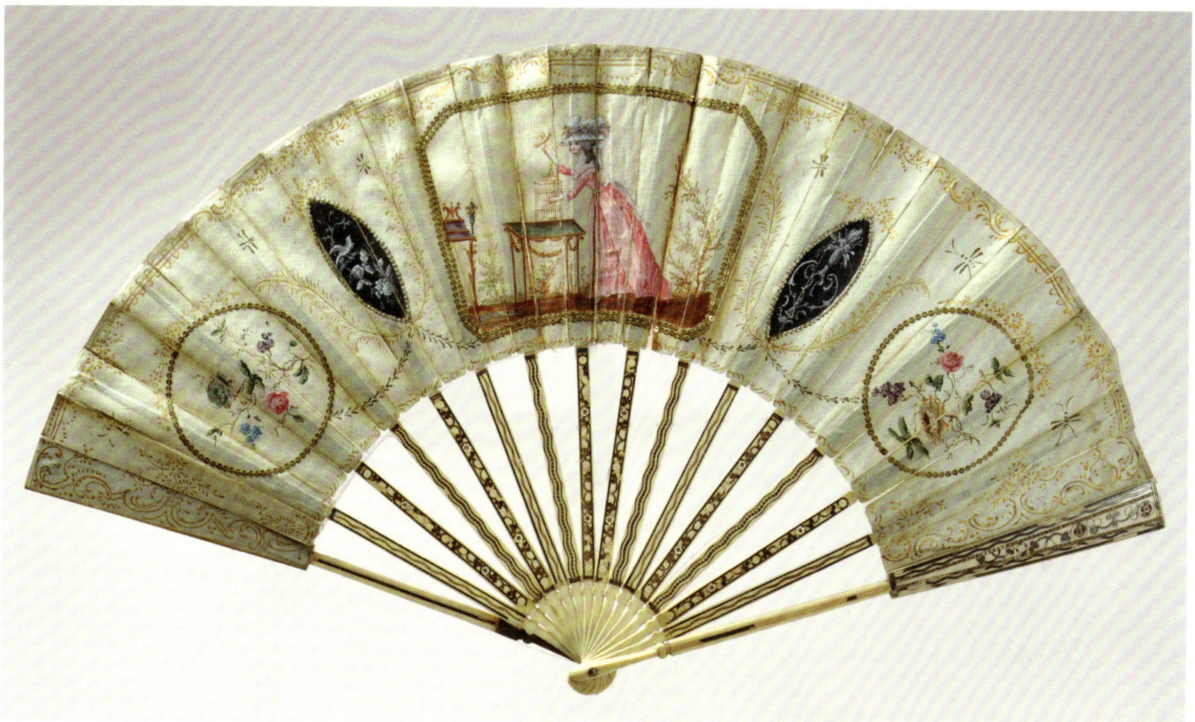

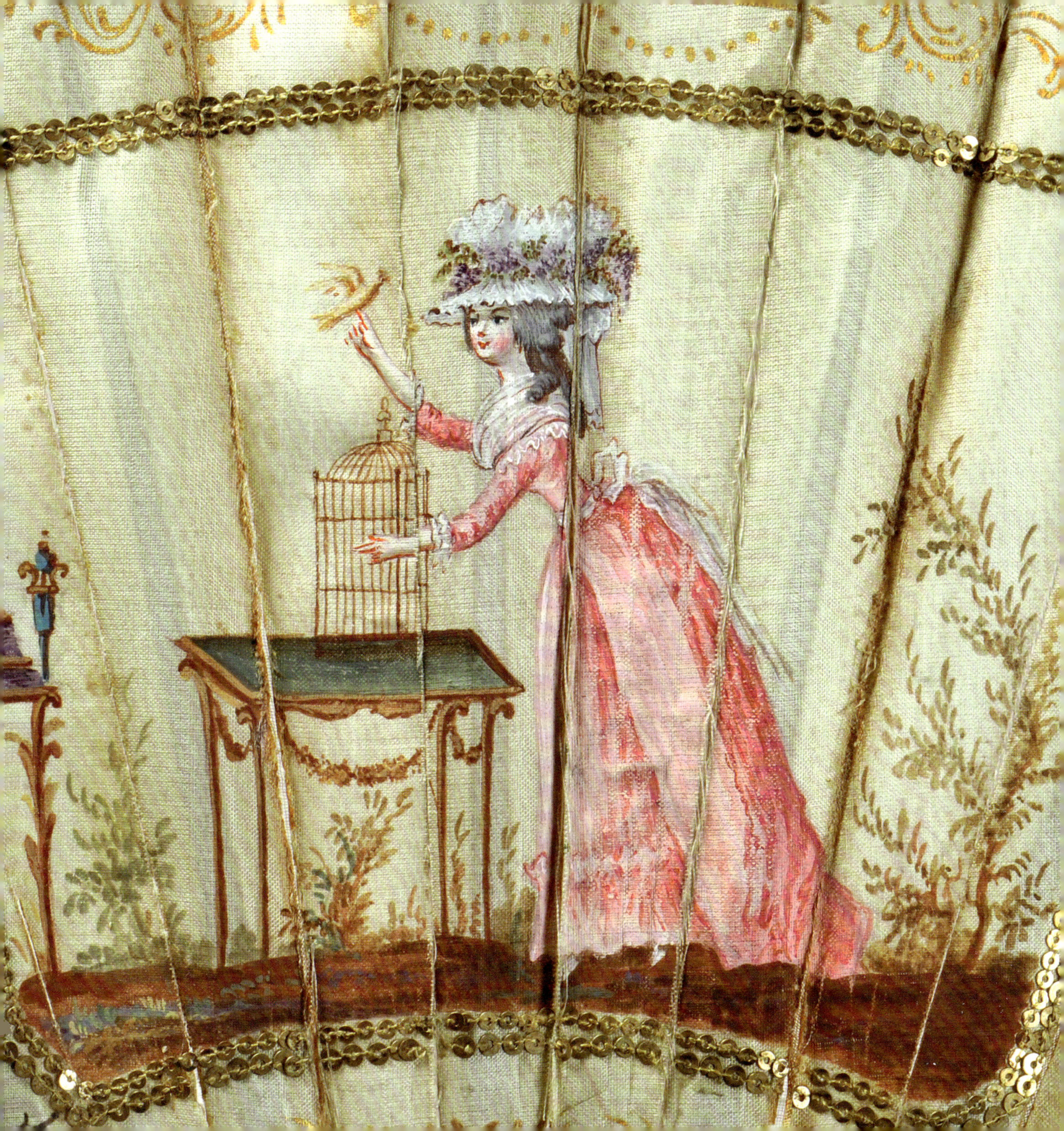

Group of shoe buckles

The Olive Matthews Collection contains a large and important group of eighteenth century shoe buckles. Many are made from silver, but the collection also includes buckles of other materials, and a number are richly decorated with paste stones. Miss Matthews managed to acquire some of the best examples, many with clear maker's marks and bold, imaginative designs.

Shoe buckles were extremely fashionable during the eighteenth century. They varied in size through the era, reaching their largest point in the 1770s. In Sheridan's play *A Trip to Scarborough*, 1777, Lord Foppington observes that though previously the buckle had been used to keep shoes in place, 'the case is now quite reversed, and the shoe is no earthly use, but to keep on the buckle'.

They were worn by both men and women, and their popularity is shown by the quality and variety of buckles which survive in collections such as this one. England was particularly famed for its production of shoe buckles, most of which were manufactured in the Midlands. Livelihoods depended on the industry and when the fashion started to wane, the buckle manufacturers petitioned King George III for help in maintaining the style, but with little success.

Shoe buckles are divided into two parts – the ring and the chape. The ring – the outer frame of the buckle, is the decorative part, designed to be visible when the buckle was worn. The chape is the inside, and consists of separate parts – the bridge or pin, the roll and the tongue. The roll holds the under latchet of the shoe by two lugs (the latchets are the straps which cross over the top of the foot). The tongue, which is shaped like a small fork, pierces the upper shoe strap and rests on the buckle ring. This holds the shoe tightly on the foot, and keeps the buckle ring in place.

RIGHT Silver shoe buckle, 1790–1800 (see page 63).

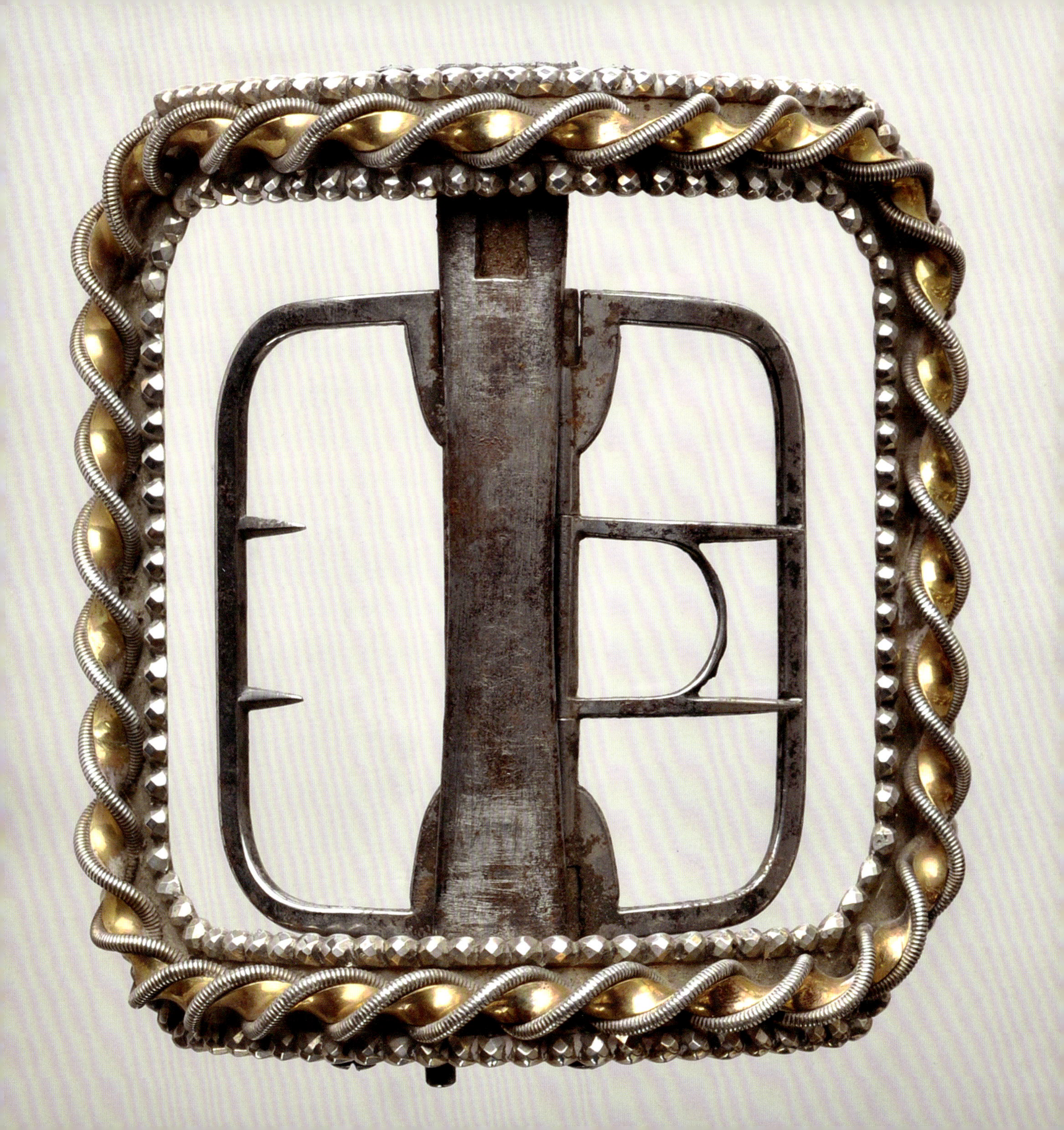

Silver shoe buckles, 1740–1770

Pair of arched oval shoe buckles. They are made from silver and are decorated with scallop shell and leaf motifs. They have steel pitchfork chapes and are hallmarked on the reverse with the maker's mark 'G.S' possibly George Smith. The shell was a key Rococo motif. It is found in many forms of decorative art from the middle of the century until the 1770s. The comparatively small size of the buckles also confirms their mid-eighteenth century date.

OBJECT NUMBER – MT.3115

Silver shoe buckles, 1770–1784

Pair of arched oval shoe buckles, cast silver with flower head roundels at the centre of each side between rows of engraved lines. The chape is made from silver, and they are stamped with the maker's mark 'I.L' for Joseph Lewis. They were made in London, and show how the delicate curving lines of the Rococo had by this date given way to much more solid forms. The design of these buckles is associated with the burgeoning fashion for classically inspired styles featuring bold stripes and symmetrical patterns. Clothing exhibiting these stylistic features had to be balanced with heavier accessories, so buckle designs followed suit.

OBJECT NUMBER – MT.3127

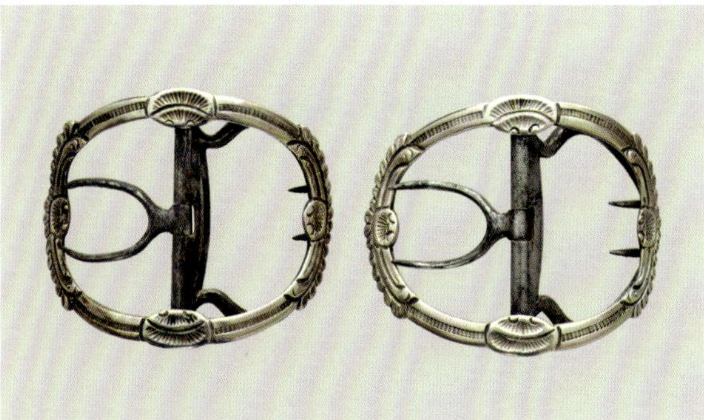

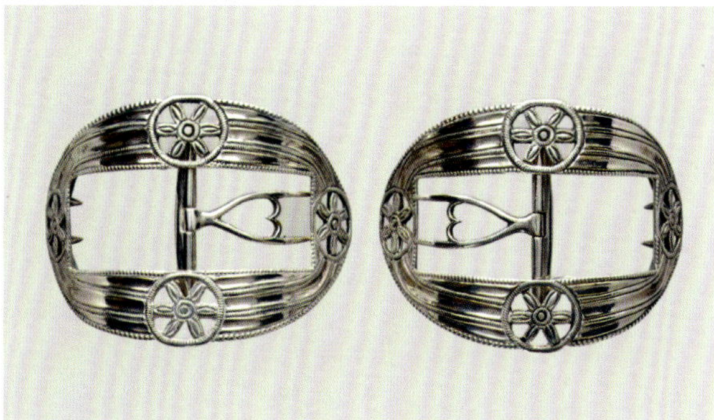

Silver shoe buckles, 1790–1800

Pair of arched square shoe buckles. They feature silver 'cut steel' style borders either side of twisted silver gilt central lines. Steel buckles were very fashionable during the late eighteenth century because cut steel had a particularly crisp, fresh look. Even though silver was a more valuable metal, the fashion was so widespread that silver buckles were made with decoration imitating cut steel. This pair are stamped on the sides with a George III duty mark, 'O 6' and the maker's mark 'W.E' for William Eley. They have a steel spring chape marked 'RIGHT' and 'LEFT' for the right and left foot and 'WE 1306 KK'. Partly as a response to the decline in the English buckle trade, buckle manufacturers began to take out patents for their designs from the 1780s. One of the most important was the spring clip which was invented by William Eley and patented in 1784. By pressing a button on the outer frame, the inner chape would spring back, enabling the wearer to put the buckle on his shoe easily before clipping the ring back into position.

OBJECT NUMBER – MT.3121

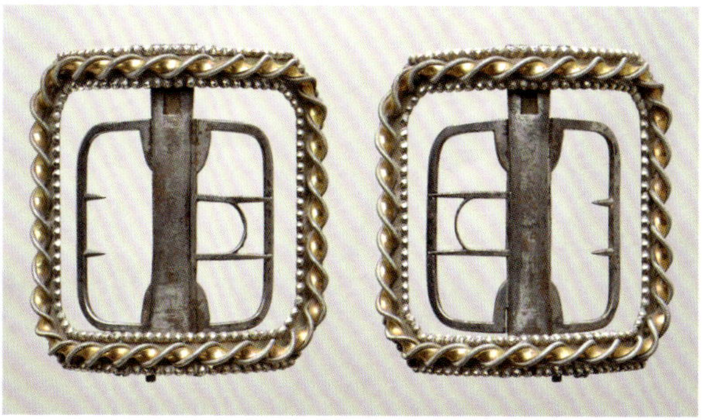

Shoe buckles set with pastes, 1780–1790

Pair of rectangular shoe buckles with rounded corners, set with one row of clear oval pastes. They have a stamped gilt copper inner bezel and a blued steel chape. Improved domestic lighting during the eighteenth century, and the creation of the brilliant cut, which sparkles well in candle light, meant that faceted gems became very fashionable. Diamonds were highly prized, and as new sources were discovered in Brazil, they were more abundant in the jewellery and accessories of the time. Since diamonds were not within the reach of most people, there was an increased demand for paste jewellery – imitation stones of glass. As well as being a fraction of the price, paste allowed people to have 'jewels' of whatever shape or size they wanted. There was also less concern about the possibility of theft. Since shoe buckles were so fashionable, it was inevitable that they should be adorned with jewels – whether real or imitation. This trend began in the 1740s and continued until the late 1780s.

OBJECT NUMBER – MT.1787

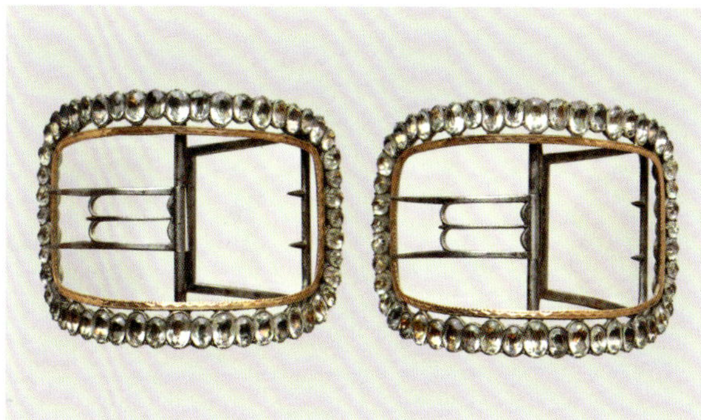

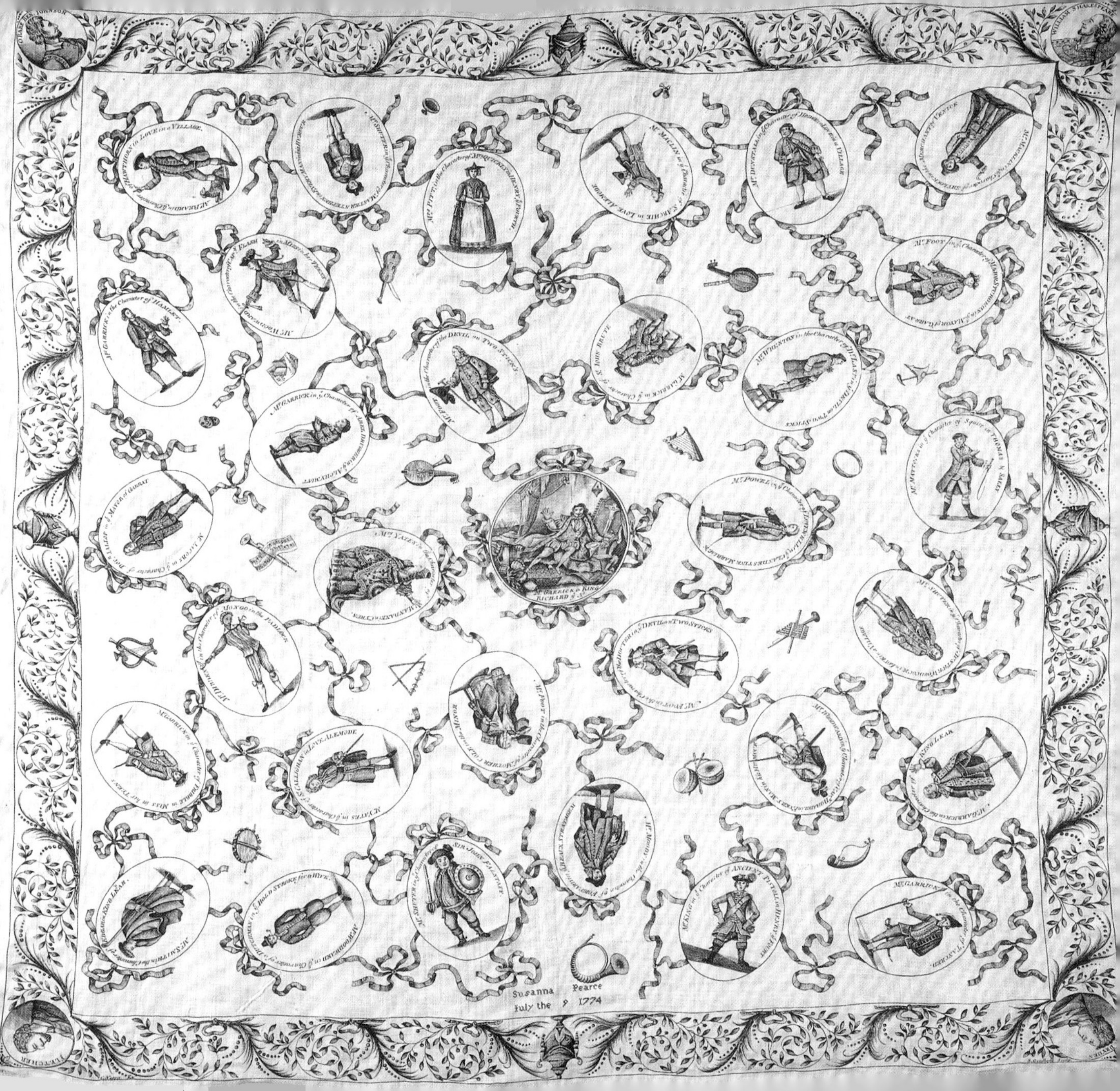
Susanna Pearce
July the 9 1774

The Garrick Handkerchief, 1774

This rare handkerchief is made from white linen, and has been copperplate printed in indigo. It features a central cartouche of David Garrick, the celebrated actor manager of Drury Lane theatre. He is shown playing Richard III in an image based on William Hogarth's 1745 painting of him. Garrick is surrounded by thirty one smaller ovals containing engravings of actors. Six depict him playing a variety of tragic and comic roles and sixteen further famous performers of the day are also featured, some of whom play several roles. Each image includes a note to tell us the actor's name, the character they are playing and the relevant play.* The playwrights William Shakespeare, Ben Jonson, John Fletcher and John Dryden are found in the corners of the handkerchief.

David Garrick managed his company at the Theatre Royal Drury Lane from 1742 to 1776. He had enormous influence over all aspects of the development of theatrical performance, as well as being one of the most outstanding actors of his generation. He was instrumental in the transformation of acting style, which became far more natural under his direction. He was also enthusiastic about the improvement of theatrical lighting. Garrick used large numbers of concealed candle lamps and mirrored footlights to illuminate the stage. This unobtrusive, sometimes coloured light was far more effective than the inflexible chandeliers that had gone before. He died in January 1779, and was buried in Westminster Abbey.

The handkerchief was purchased as a souvenir, probably after a trip to the theatre in London, and embroidered with 'Susanna Pearce, July the 9 1774'. Susanna was the great, great grandmother of Olive Matthews (for further information about Miss Matthews' particular attachment to this item, see pages 14–15). Printed handkerchiefs were very popular from around 1740 to 1840. Many were produced as souvenirs, particularly to commemorate important events. Others were printed with maps and served as convenient, lightweight travel aids, helping people to find their way around towns and cities. They would have been relatively expensive to buy, and were targets for thieves and pickpockets. Their large size is partly due to practical considerations as their popularity coincided with a peak in the fashion for snuff taking, which could induce violent sneezing.

OBJECT NUMBER – MT.4827

***See page 145 for a full listing of the actors featured on the handkerchief.**

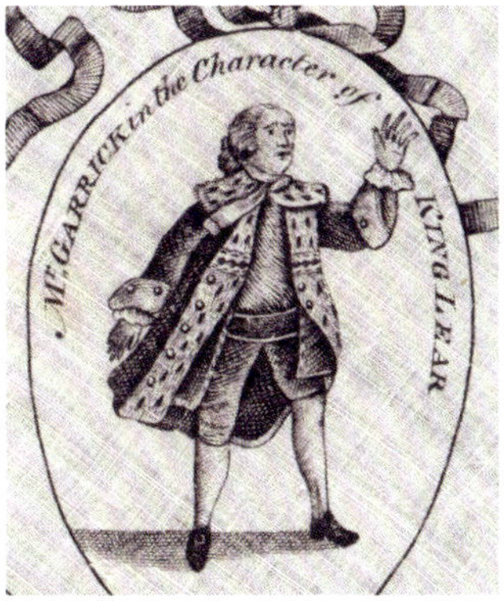

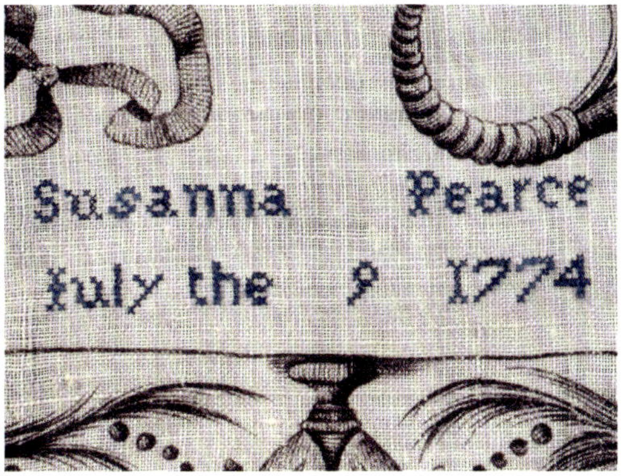

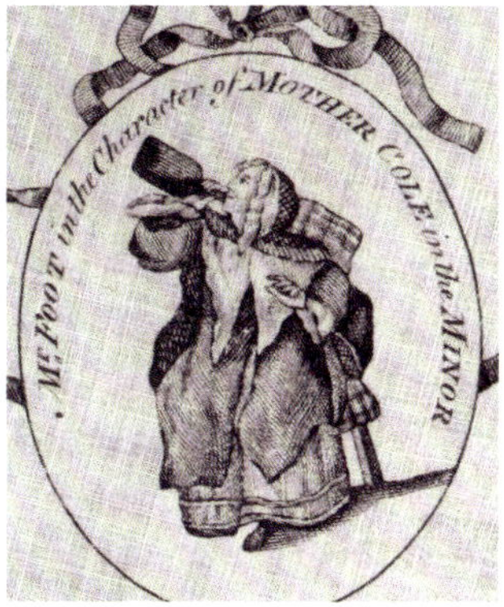

Wedding ensemble, 1780

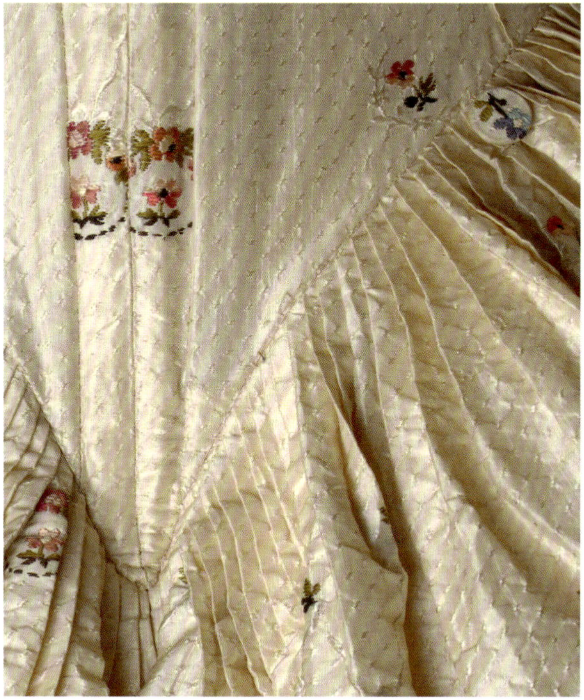

This important group consists of a dress, matching petticoat, hat and shoes. The dress has simple shaped cuffs and a square neckline. The back of the bodice is sharply pointed and boned, and the skirt is tightly pleated. Plaited silk cords are stitched into the inside at waist level, and these could be looped under the skirt and over buttons at the back of the bodice to achieve the 'Polonaise' style. The silk used for the dress is very light, crisp and fresh in appearance. The creamy-pink ground is woven at regular intervals with tiny cream spots. Small circular wreaths enclosing flowers with flowing ribbons are brocaded sparsely into the silk. The fabric is probably Spitalfields silk, and though the dress is dated to 1780, the silk brocade is likely to have been woven in the late 1770s. It may have been purchased a few years in advance of the wedding, or bought from a provincial supplier whose stock was a little out of date.

The *bergère* style hat is made from plaited straw covered in cream silk, and the outer edge trimmed with cream lace. The hat is decorated with cream silk ribbons and padded with cotton wool to give a soft, three-dimensional effect. It would have sat slightly forward on the head over a soft, broad hairstyle of frizzed, powdered curls. The shoes are made from cream silk satin. They have leather soles and white kid lining and the heels are wedged. The shoes have been modified to resemble a newer slip-on style – the latchets, or straps over the top of the foot, are stitched in place in the centre rather than held together with a buckle. A peaked tongue extends above the latchets as seen on the latest fashion plates of the time. They were probably ordered from a maker who was trying to achieve a fashionable look without deviating from a familiar shoe construction.

It is extremely rare for a complete outfit such as this to survive, but it is even more exciting that we also know the names of the bride and groom. The clothes were worn by Miss Jane Bailey on the occasion of her marriage to James Wickham Esquire. The couple were married in Holy Trinity Church, Wonston, Hampshire, on the 9th November 1780. They were both twenty four years of age at the time of their marriage, and went on to have four children; William, James, Jane and Mary, all of whom survived into adulthood. The families on both sides were landowners and gentry farmers from neighbouring parishes, and it seems likely that this was a marriage of equals in terms of social standing. When James died, aged 78, in 1834, he was able to leave behind considerable sums of money and parcels of property. He died three years after Jane who passed away aged 75 in 1831. Jane's wedding ensemble was fashionable without being cutting edge, but beautifully made from the best quality fabrics. Given the date of the marriage and the social circumstances of the couple, it is exactly what one might expect for a bride from a wealthy family living in a small village in rural Hampshire.

OBJECT NUMBERS – MT.4838, MT.4839, MT.4829

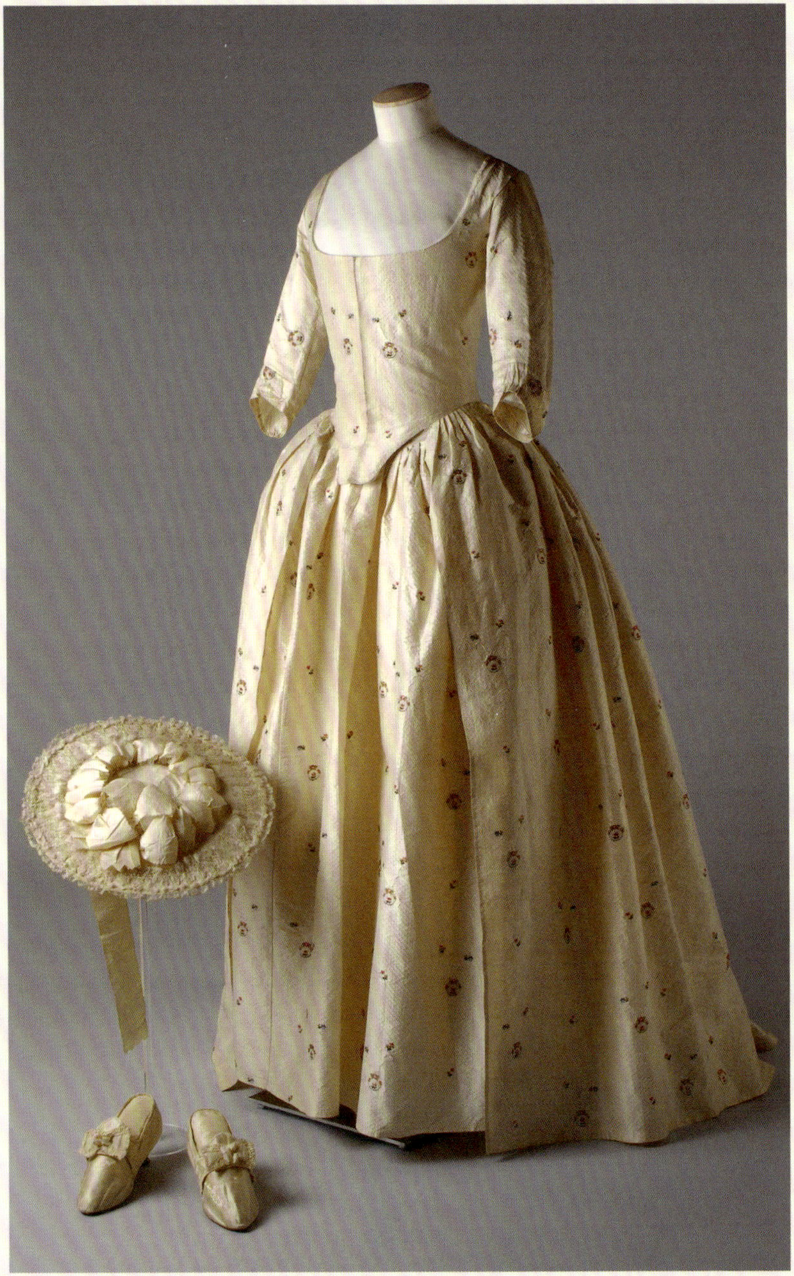

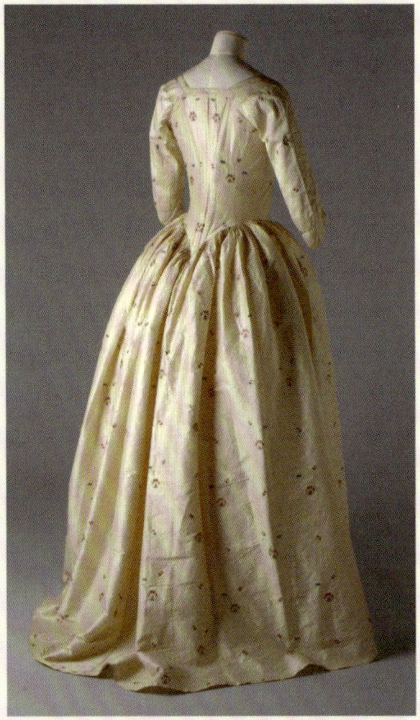

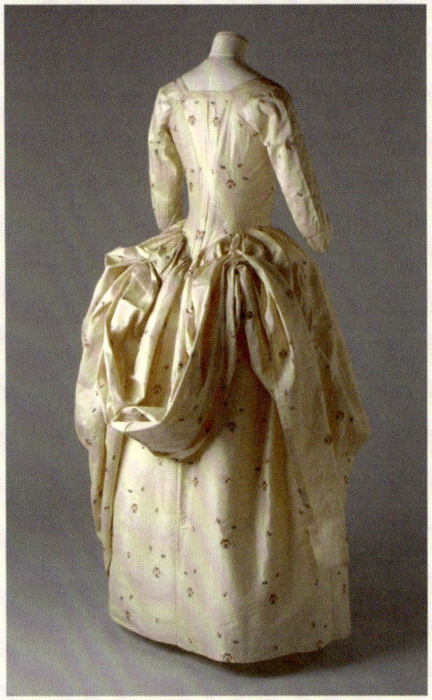

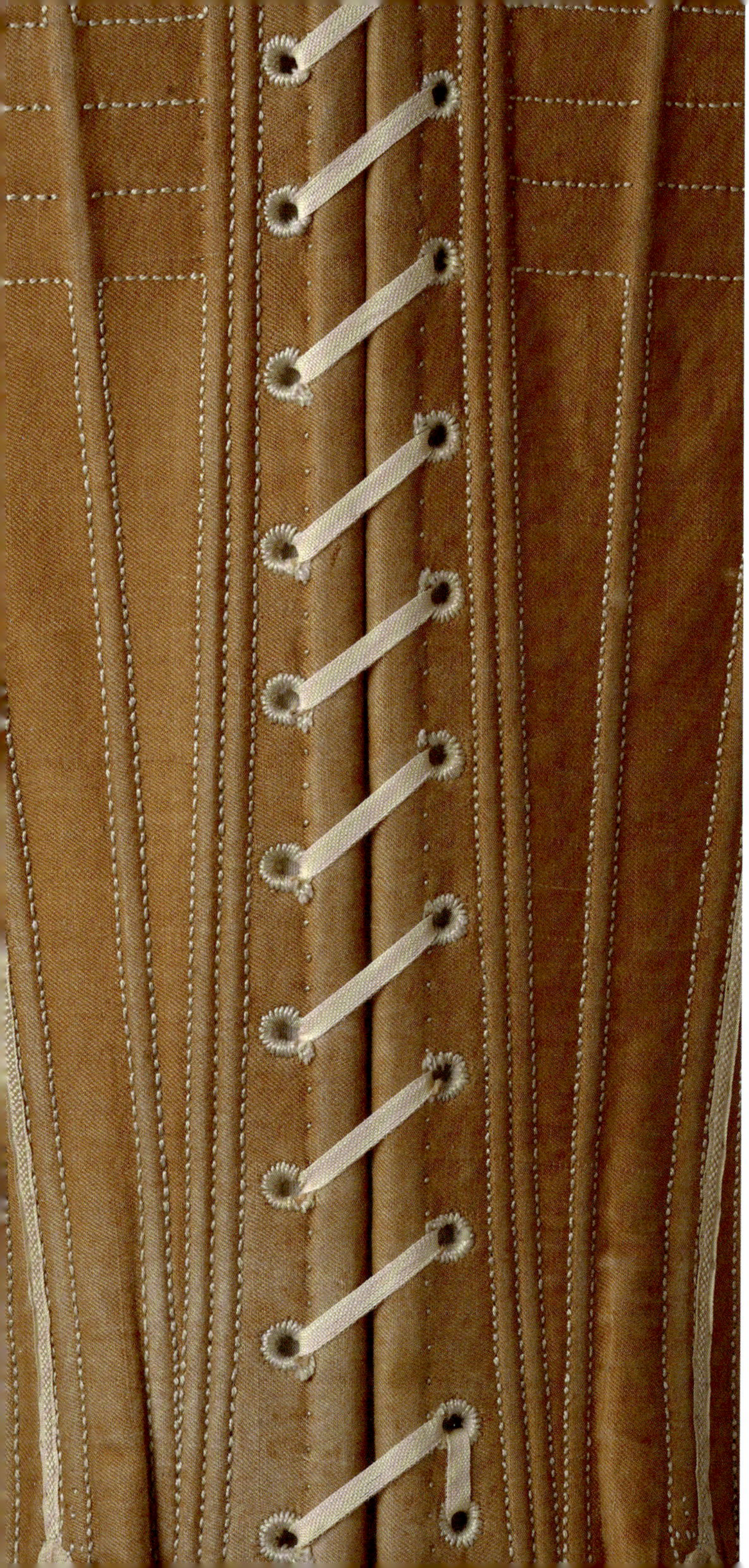

Pair of half-boned stays, 1785–1788

They are made from brown twill weave cotton, lined with natural linen and boned with strips of whalebone. The term half-boned is used because there are some gaps between the whalebone pieces. In full-boned stays there were no gaps, and the stays would have provided even greater figure control. It is possible to date these stays because of the relatively high waistline. The basic structure of stays did not alter greatly through the mid to late eighteenth century, but the waistline rose with that of fashionable dress from the mid-1780s. The famous and fashionable Georgiana, Duchess of Devonshire published a novel (anonymously) in 1778 entitled *The Sylph* in which she mentions the wearing of stays. This excerpt can give us some idea of what it might have been like to wear them:

> *My dear Louisa, you will laugh when I tell you that poor Winifred … broke two laces in endeavouring to draw my new French stays close. You know that I am naturally small at bottom but now you might literally span me. You never saw such a doll. Then, they are so intolerably wide across the breast, that my arms are absolutely sore with them; and my sides so pinched! – But it is the 'ton' [meaning fashionable society] and pride feels no pain.**

Stays, or corsets as they were later called, formed an indispensable part of women's wardrobes and were crucial to the fashionable look of the period. They were designed to mould the body into a cone shape, flattening and pushing up the bust, smoothing the torso and emphasising the slimness of the waist. They were worn from childhood, and some were even worn at night to try to mould the growing body into the correct shape and posture.

The most common material for achieving the desired shape was whalebone. Whalebone, as used for stays, was not from the main skeleton of the whale, but a horn-like substance called baleen. It is found in the roof of the mouth, sticking out much like the teeth of other mammals, and serving to filter plankton while the whale swims. Once brought ashore, skilled workmen boiled the whalebone to make it malleable. They then cut, dressed and finished it to the standards required for stay making.

Stay making in the eighteenth century tended to be a male profession. Women were not deemed strong enough for the hard physical work required, and male involvement in the fitting process of this most intimate of garments did cause comment at the time. Layers of fabric were stitched by hand with channels into which whalebone pieces of varying widths were pushed. The stays were then pressed with a warm iron to mould them into the correct shape. The malleability of whalebone was one reason why women tended to prefer to keep their stays for long periods. Over time, the heat of their bodies would mould them to the figure, making their stays more comfortable to wear, and even wealthy women had their 'broken in' stays altered or mended rather than ordering a new pair.

OBJECT NUMBER – M.2008.53

*Quoted in Steele, Valerie *The Corset a Cultural History*, (Yale University Press, New Haven & London), p.25.

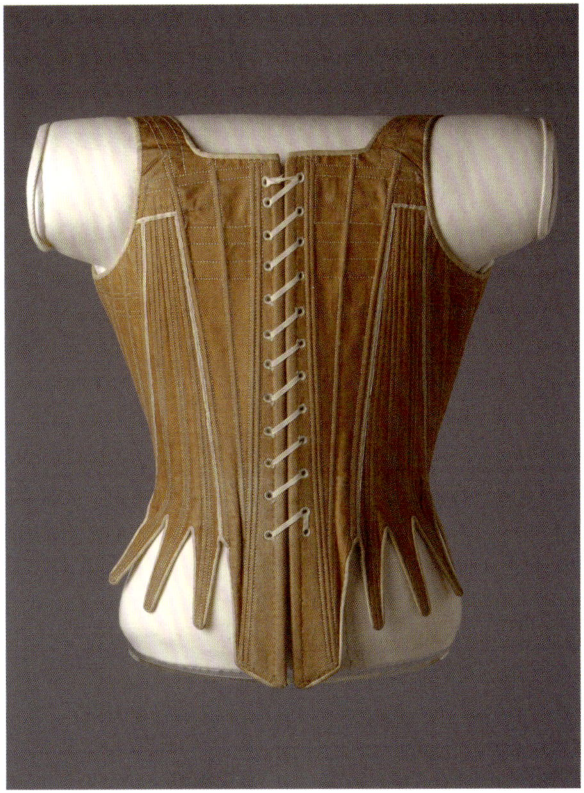

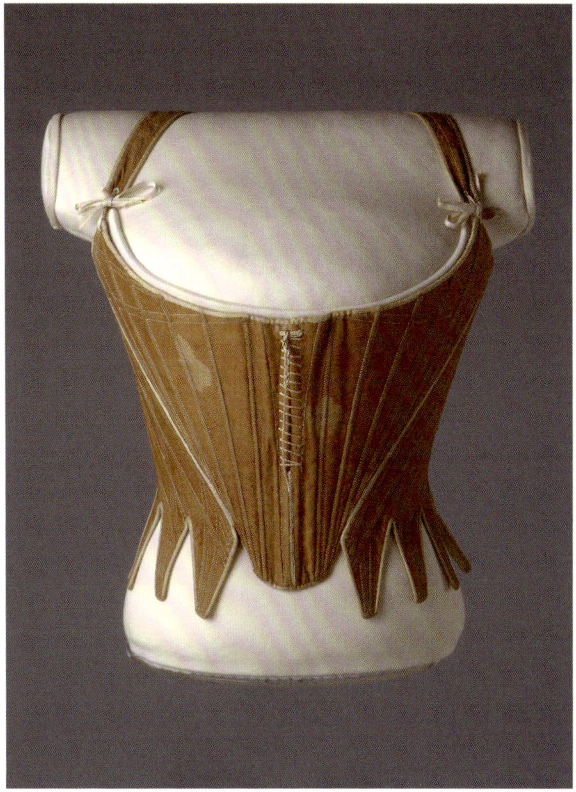

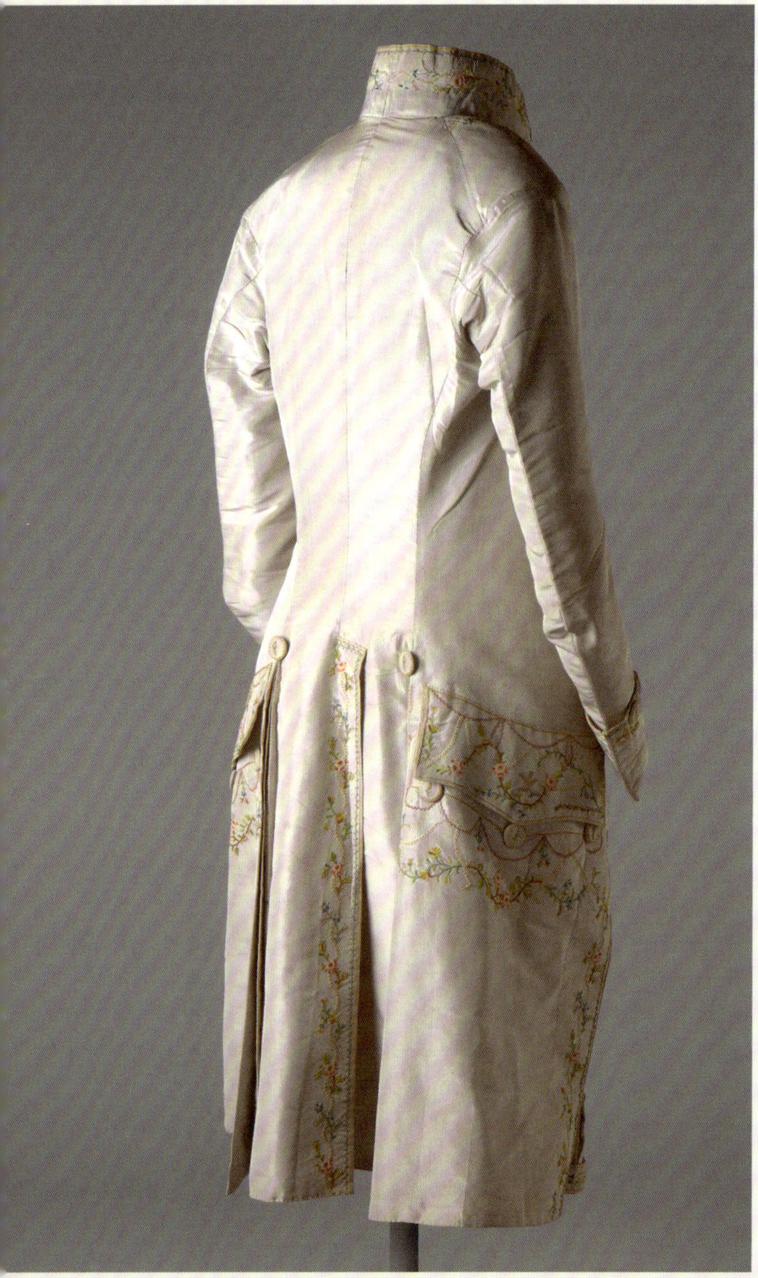

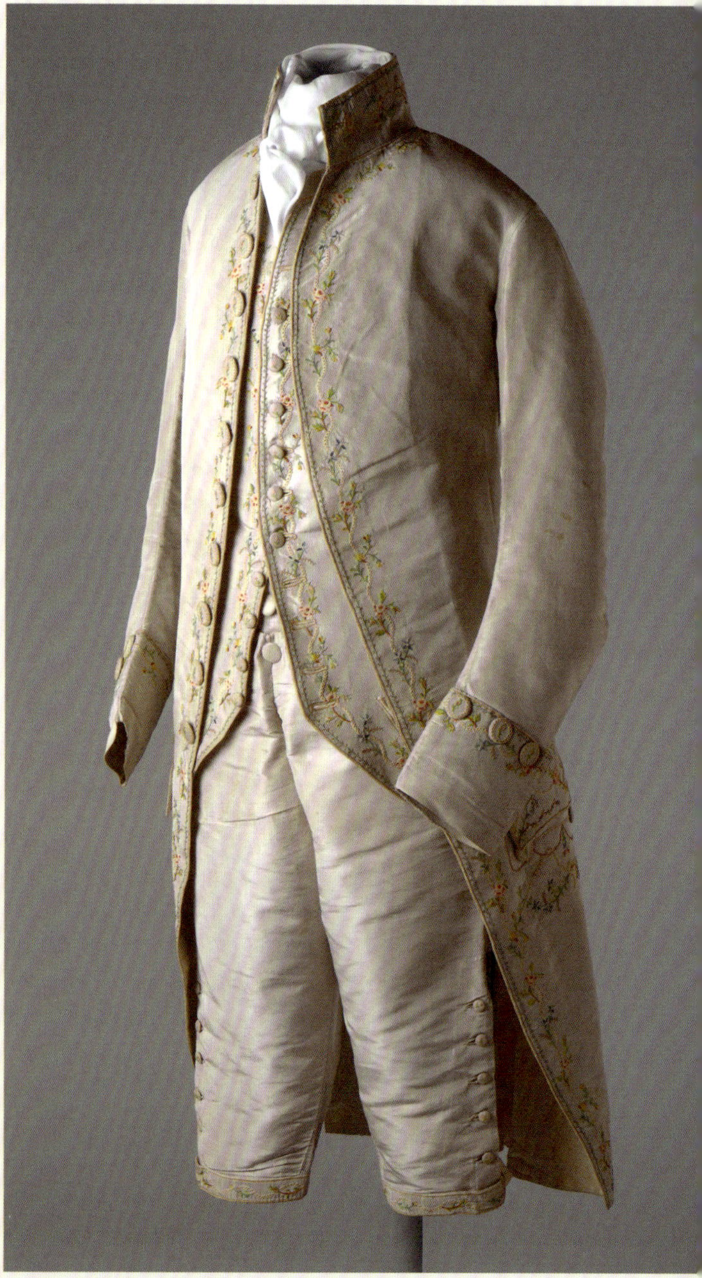

Man's three piece suit of dove grey silk, 1780–1788

This suit consists of matching coat, waistcoat and breeches, made from grey ribbed silk and embroidered with trailing flowers and swags. They are all lined with ivory silk and natural linen. The coat has a high stand-up collar. Collars of this sort began to be added to coats from the 1760s, when they were quite modest in size. They gradually became taller, reaching their highest point in the 1790s. Another new style development is evident in the coat fronts. Still cut in one with the body at this date, they curve away to the back so that the skirts have almost transformed into tails. The back of the coat has three vents with pleats surmounted by fabric covered hip buttons, and there are two large shaped pocket flaps with buttons beneath. These and the buttons along the edge of the coat are purely decorative, as they have no corresponding buttonholes. The coat is closed at the centre with hooks. The long narrow sleeves have generous turned back cuffs with three decorative buttons. The breeches have wide fall-fronts and four pockets. There is a buckle at the back of the waistband for adjustment of fit. As with all eighteenth century breeches, the fabric is gathered at the back of the waistband to allow room to sit down. The breeches are long and quite tight, with five buttons fastening the knee vents whilst the knee bands are buttoned below the knee. The waistcoat is straight fronted, but cut away at the lower edge. It has two hip pockets with pocket flaps, and each has three embroidered buttons.

The suit has been hand embroidered with a delicate floral design in tambour work. Tambour work is an extremely intricate chain stitch embroidery which is done with a small hook. The technique was introduced into Europe from India in the 1760s. The fabric to be embroidered was stretched over a circular frame and the hook was passed through in order to draw a loop of silk thread up onto the surface to form the tiny chain. The work on this suit was undoubtedly done by a professional embroiderer, probably in France, but tambour work also became a popular pastime for wealthy ladies.

This suit was definitely worn for formal occasions, and possibly at Court. It would have been very expensive, particularly as the embroidery was time consuming to complete. It may be French in origin, as highly decorated suits were more commonly worn by French men at this date. Unless attending very important events, late eighteenth century English men wore quite plain suits, with emphasis on fine tailoring and quality fabrics rather than lavish decoration. This garment has both, and was a particular favourite of Olive Matthews. It has survived in remarkably good condition; the crisp silk and the intricate embroidery making it a really excellent example of its type.

OBJECT NUMBER – MT.4832

Painted cotton gown, 1790–1795, shown with a replica petticoat

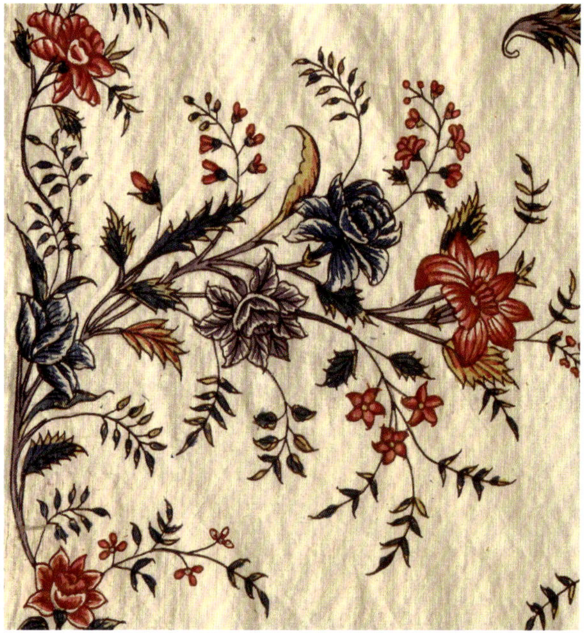

This long, flowing open fronted cotton dress is decorated with a trailing floral design. It has a wide train, and the bodice front and sleeves are of green silk taffeta lined with white linen. The back of the bodice is carefully pleated to fit closely to the waist and then left loose to provide fullness to the skirt. The cut is designed to show off the fabric, which was imported from India and highly sought after. At first it appears to be printed, but tiny differences in the repeat of the pattern indicate that it was in fact hand painted or 'pencilled' – the word used to describe the hand painting of mordants or dyes onto cloth. All the colours except the blue have been applied in this way. The indigo for the blue has been resist dyed.

Fashion in women's clothing moved towards lighter fabrics as the eighteenth century drew to a close. Indian cottons first became popular in the seventeenth century when the East India Company started to export them, but by the mid-eighteenth century there was a thriving European industry with cottons being printed in France, England, Holland and Switzerland. The native English silk weavers felt threatened by the popularity of printed cottons, and successfully lobbied the government for a ban on the import, manufacture and sale of printed cottons (though it was not strictly adhered to). In 1774 the ban was finally lifted and the industry thrived.

Printed fabrics were popular with working women as they were relatively cheap to buy and easy to keep clean. However, during the 1760s and '70s they were also taken up as fashionable undress – that is informal clothing for everyday wear. By the 1790s they had virtually taken over from silks in all but the most formal clothing. The change was partly connected to the freer social and political attitudes of the time which made a strong impact on fashion. People began to favour lighter, more comfortable garments over the stiff, formal silk clothing of a decade before. Although cottons produced and decorated in India were designed for the Western market, the patterns on printed and painted cottons and linens still owed something to their Far Eastern origins. Even when manufactured in England, printed fabrics retained elements of the swirling floral motifs of Indian design, with their bright reds and yellows. Chinese-inspired themes were also popular and Western styles with Eastern touches struck the right balance between the familiar and the exotic.

This type of gown is a rare survival because the style is transitional. The fitted nature of the bodice, the way that the sleeves are set back at the shoulders and the inclusion of some silk are reminiscent of the formal silk dresses with boned bodices common for the majority of the eighteenth century. However, the higher waistline, the cotton fabric and the flowing lines were relatively new and would soon develop into the even higher waisted white cotton muslin dresses that became fashionable at the end of the 1700s and into the early 1800s.

OBJECT NUMBER – MT.2023

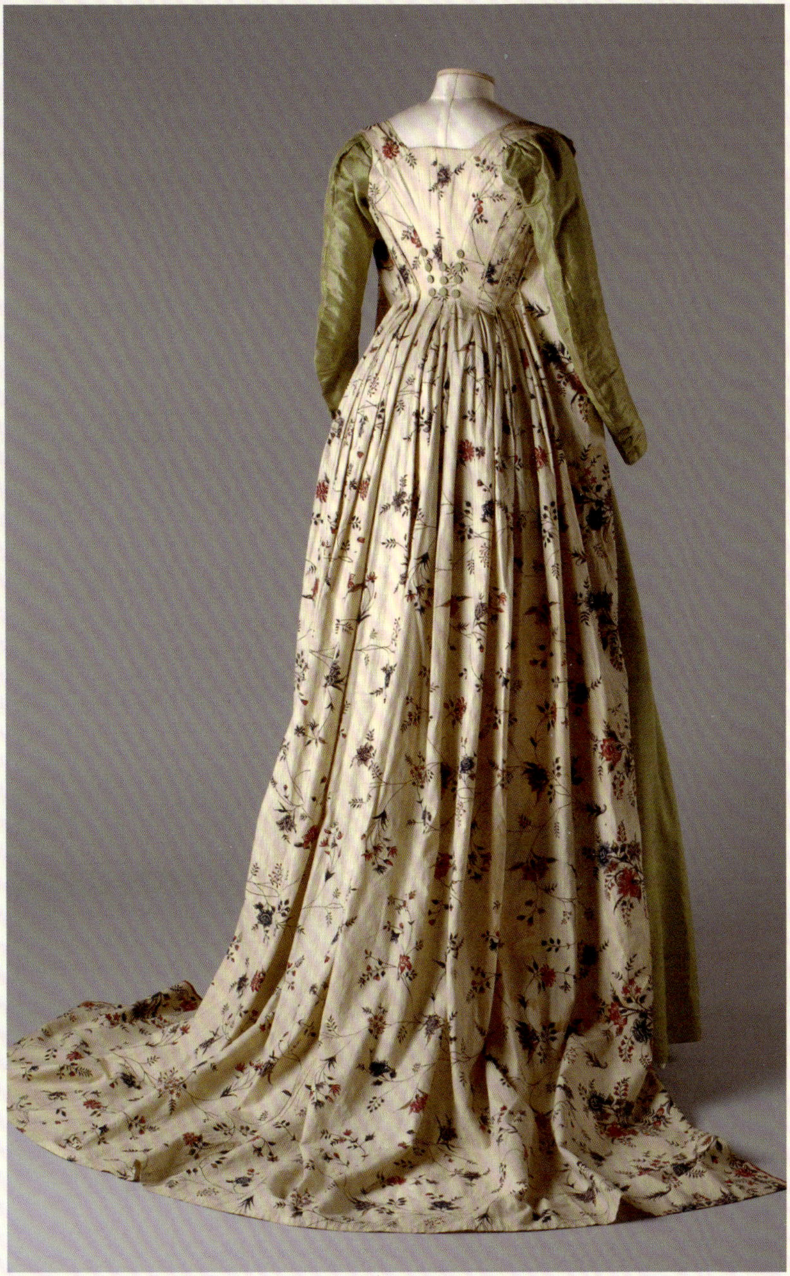

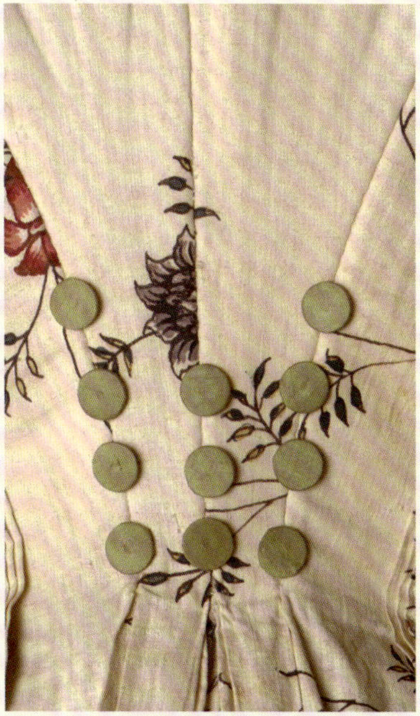

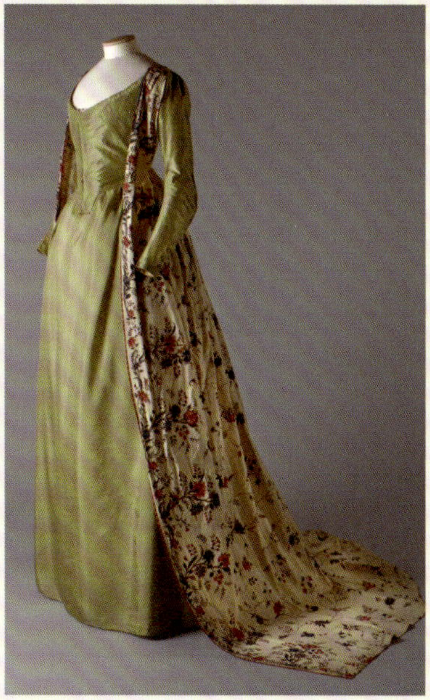

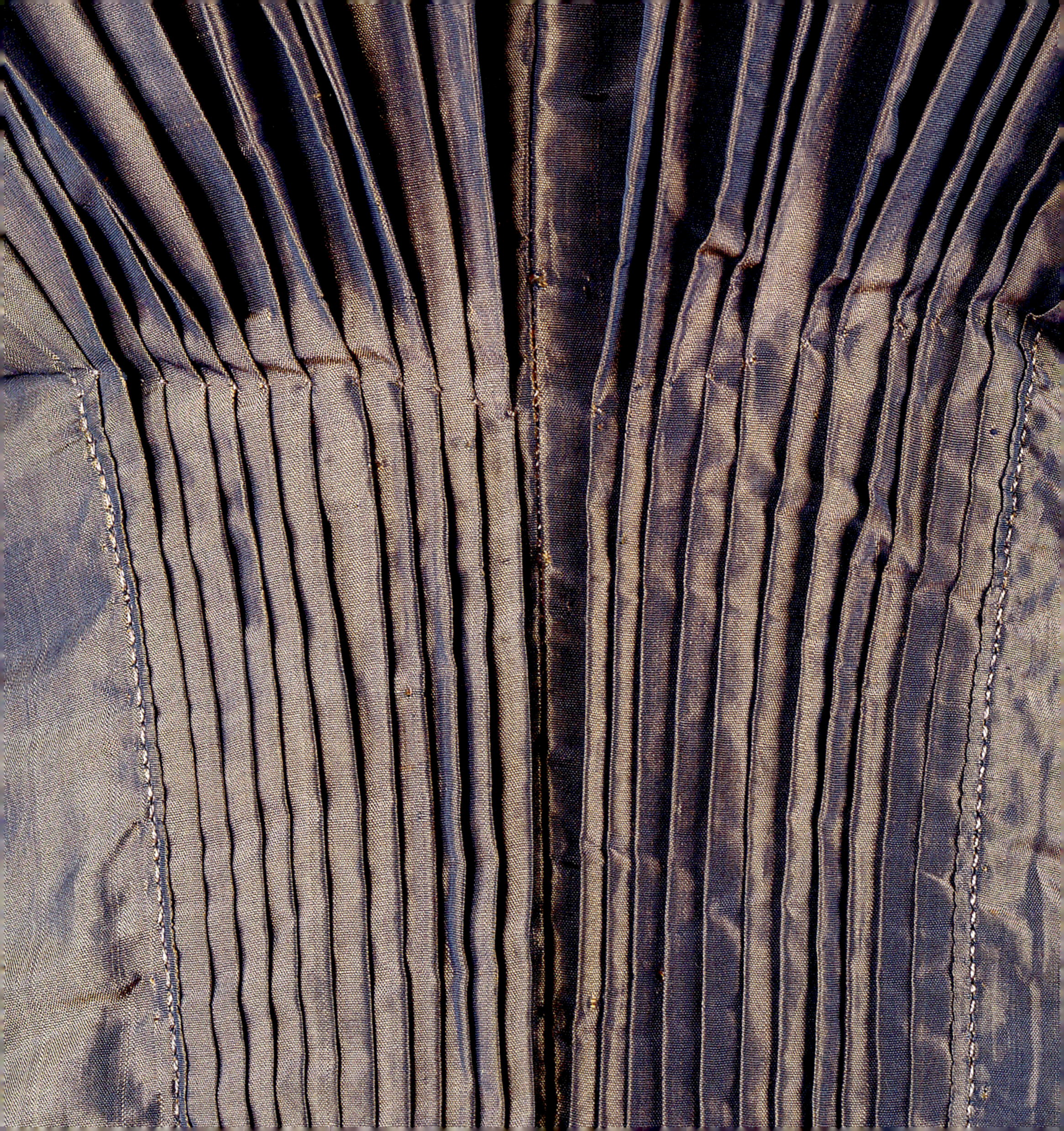

THE NINETEENTH CENTURY

*'No sooner has she acquired the desired form than fashion demands another . . .'**

In fashion terms the nineteenth century was an exciting period of incredible richness and variety, particularly in women's wear. Although contemporary commentators noted that fashions moved increasingly swiftly as the eighteenth century progressed, this pace would accelerate rapidly during the hundred years that followed. Excellent examples of key styles from the entire span of the nineteenth century are now contained within the Matthews Collection and some of the best pieces are discussed here. However, the collection was not always so comprehensive and very few pieces dated later than the 1850s were contained within the original group. In the previous two chapters the garments and accessories included were collected by Miss Matthews, or have a direct link to her known preferences. Miss Matthews was quite clear about her feelings on items from the nineteenth and twentieth centuries. In a letter to the Museum dated the 22nd of April

* 'Luke Limner' (John Leighton), *Madre Nature versus the Moloch of Fashion*, (1870) quoted in Gernsheim, Alison, Fashion and Reality (London 1963), p.60

LEFT Detail from a shot silk day dress, 1845–1850 (see pages 94–95).

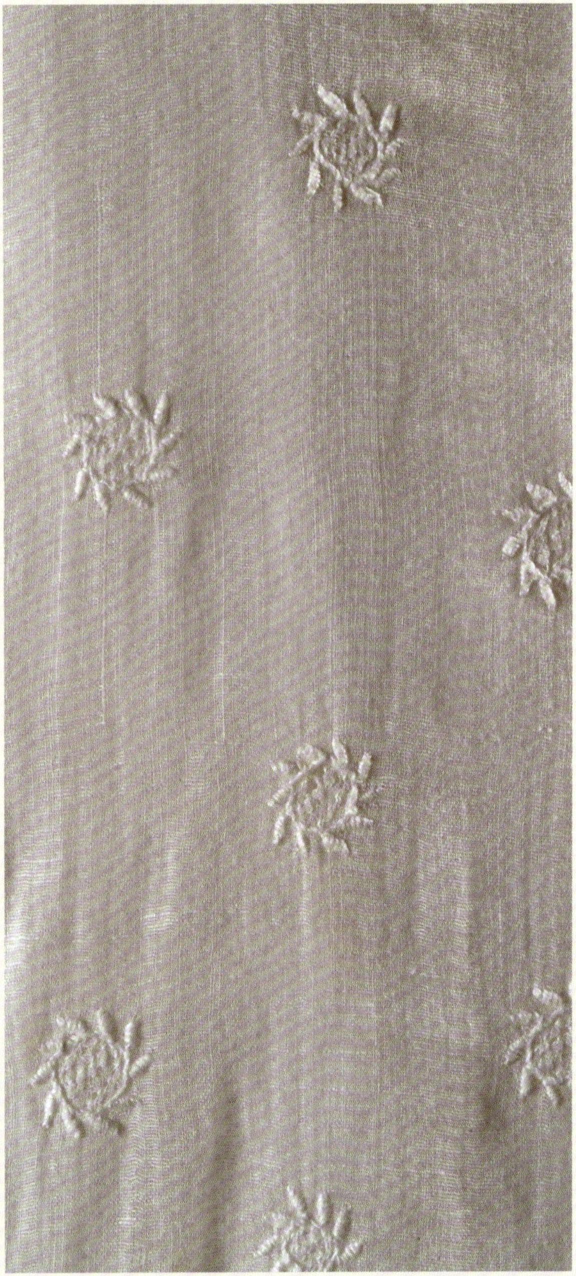

1974 she stated 'I am interested in costumes up to about early Victoria ... Styles that I knew and wore I don't care about. They are not antiques to me'. Although the process of collecting from later periods is at odds with the original ethos of the collection, the decision has since been made to bring it up to date by carefully selecting suitable items when they have become available. It was felt that the collection needed to be relevant to the needs of today's users. Since the majority of fashion education courses now cover the nineteenth century, the collection has adapted and grown in order to accommodate these requirements. The character of the original group of pieces and the nature of Miss Matthews' preferences are well documented and made clear to visitors, but the collection has gained some extremely important additions which only serve to make it stronger and more adaptable, now and in the future.

Dress, 1803–1805

Made from white cotton, this delicate Indian muslin dress is hand embroidered all over with rosettes, and the long narrow tubular skirt has a short train. The bodice features small puffed sleeves gathered with drawstrings and a very high waist. It is cut in the 'apron' style – a bib section is stitched to the waistband, similar to the front of an apron, which covers the bust. The bib would have been pinned or stitched in place just below the top of the shoulders. A plain cotton support structure is located beneath the bib front and would have been stitched or pinned together to give uplift under the bust. At the back of the bodice the sleeves are set very far back, exhibiting a truncated version of the standard bodice structure found in dresses from the eighteenth century. The muslin is also tightly gathered into the small of the back to give the dress a soft, rounded appearance fashionable at the time. This rather over-complicated structure and variations of it are very common in dresses from the early nineteenth century. It is evidence of dressmakers struggling to create the new and radically different fashion silhouette, but not yet knowing how to achieve it in the most practical way. Instead they have modified existing bodice styles and married those with construction derived from practical work wear.

The style of this dress falls into the category of neo-classical. Fashions such as this were inspired by the clothing of ancient Greece, and had associations with the liberal teachings of philosophers such as Rousseau. In addition, these classically inspired fashions had their roots in the perceived democracy of the ancient Greeks, and their popularity can be seen as a response to the overthrow of the old aristocratic regime during the French Revolution in the early 1790s.

OBJECT NUMBER – M.2003.21

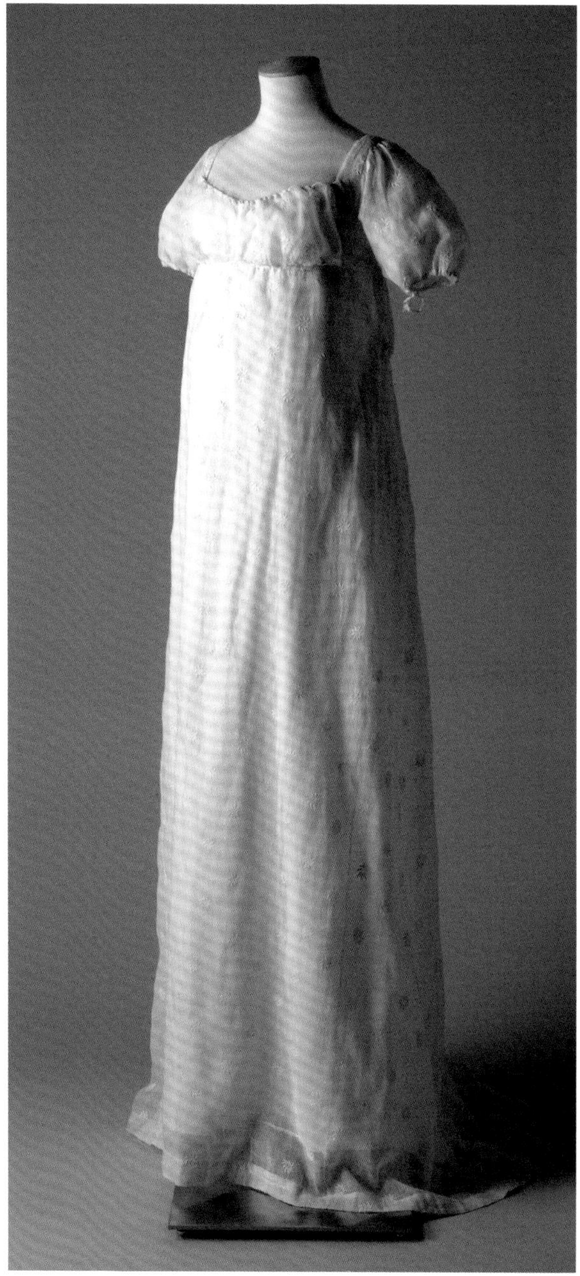

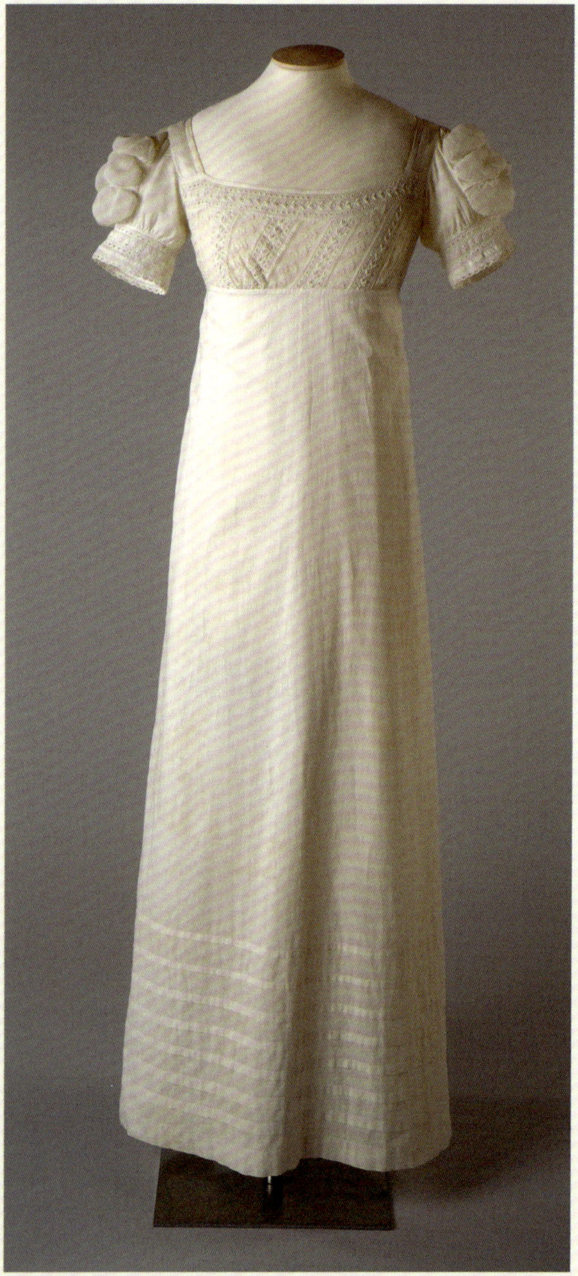

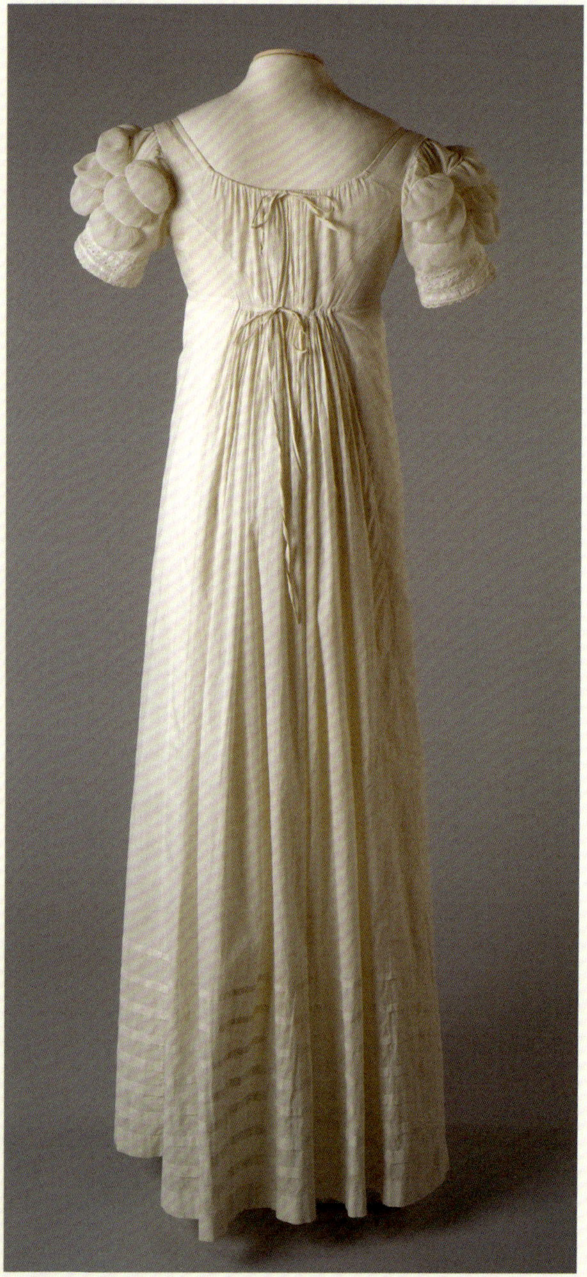

Dress, 1810–1815

This dress retains the high waist which had been fashionable from the late eighteenth century. However, simple neo-classically inspired clothing was now being diluted by other influences. The piece embodies a number of emerging trends, and in particular it exhibits decorative details associated with the *Gothic*. In this period Gothic inspired fashions were loosely based on medieval, sixteenth and seventeenth century costume, and we can see this influence in the puffed sections on the sleeves. These were intended to imitate the slashed garments of the Tudor era, when the undergarments beneath were pulled through the holes. However, the raw edges seen in sixteenth century doublets were not copied during the nineteenth century. Instead the openings were carefully finished with piping.

The bodice features white work insertions with drawn threadwork edging and needle run bobbin lace stitched in diagonals across the bodice. As well as the inclusion of muslin puffs, the short sleeves are trimmed with white work embroidery. It is interesting to note that unlike the 'apron front' dresses of the earliest years of the nineteenth century, the construction of this dress has been simplified. It fastens at the centre back with drawstring ties at the neckline and waist, making it much easier to put on. The skirt is A-line in shape – a style which would shortly become more pronounced. A pocket slit has been added to the right hand side of the skirt – allowing access to a hanging pocket worn beneath. This is a return to an eighteenth century dress feature. A hanging pocket would have ruined the line of the lightest muslin dresses worn a few years earlier, and is further evidence of the emergence of stiffer, more structured styles. The skirt also features tucks which become gradually closer together towards the hem – another reference to a burgeoning fashion, this time for hem decoration which would become increasingly bold during the 1820s.

OBJECT NUMBER – MT.2024

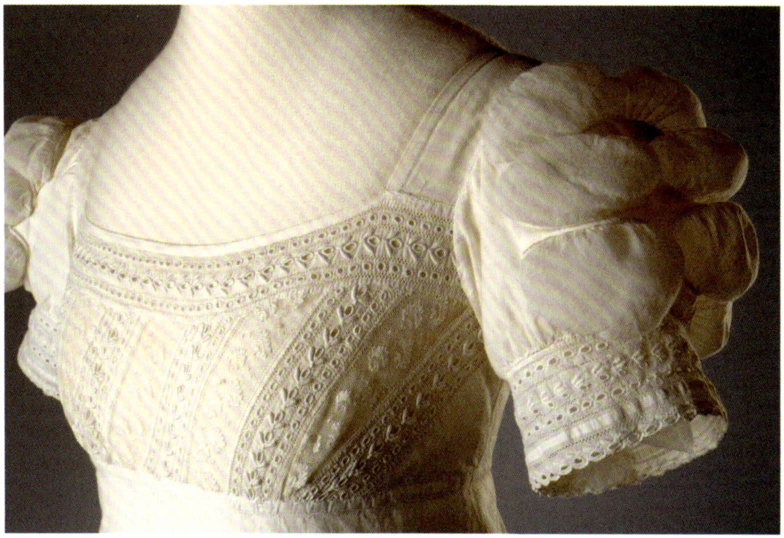

Spencer, 1815–1817

This beautiful pink silk Spencer is a key piece from Miss Matthews' original collection. It incorporates the intricate and skilled workmanship that she actively sought out. Covered in complex hand-worked decoration, it is made from silk taffeta, lined with white cotton and embellished with complex applied decoration of rouleau loops and leaf shapes edged with piping. The Spencer was originally a form of men's wear, first worn during the late eighteenth century, and named after George, second Earl Spencer (1758–1834). By the early nineteenth century Spencers had found their way into the female wardrobe, taking on a form which closely followed the high waisted bodices of the period. They were usually worn over the white muslin dresses which were so fashionable during the early part of the nineteenth century.

Part of 'Walking Dress' until the mid 1820s, the Spencer was often made from coloured silk. This silk fabric provided a more structured contrast to the soft flowing muslin of the dress beneath, as well as giving a little protection from the cold. Fashion plates of the period usually illustrate Spencers with matching hats or bonnets.

The epaulettes and decoration at the cuffs give this Spencer a slightly military feel; a patriotic fashion inspired by the uniforms of soldiers who were fighting in the Napoleonic wars. The style was particularly popular around the period of the Battle of Waterloo in 1815.

OBJECT NUMBER – MT.2043

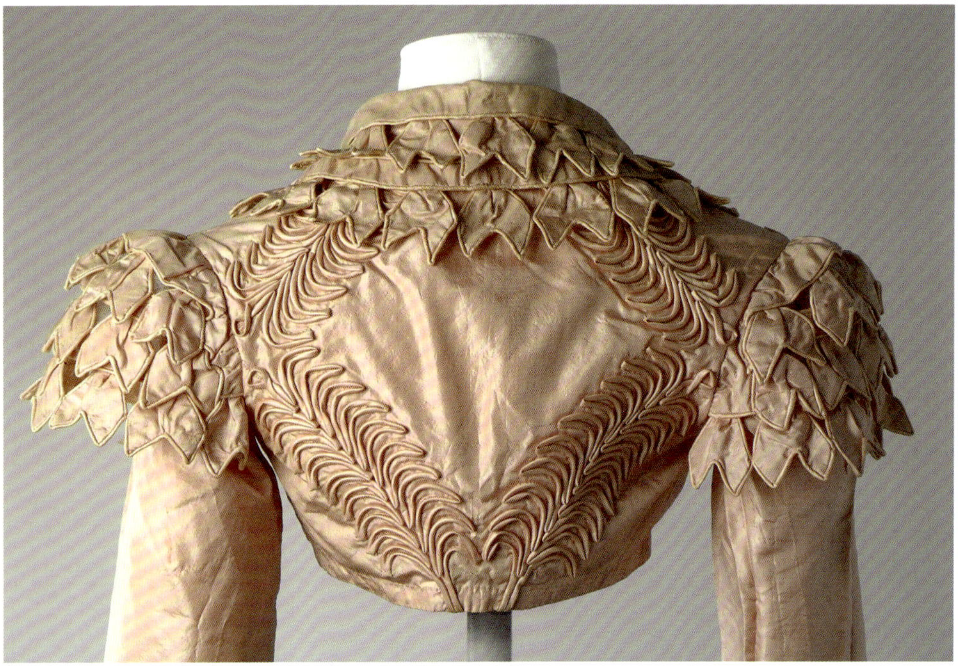

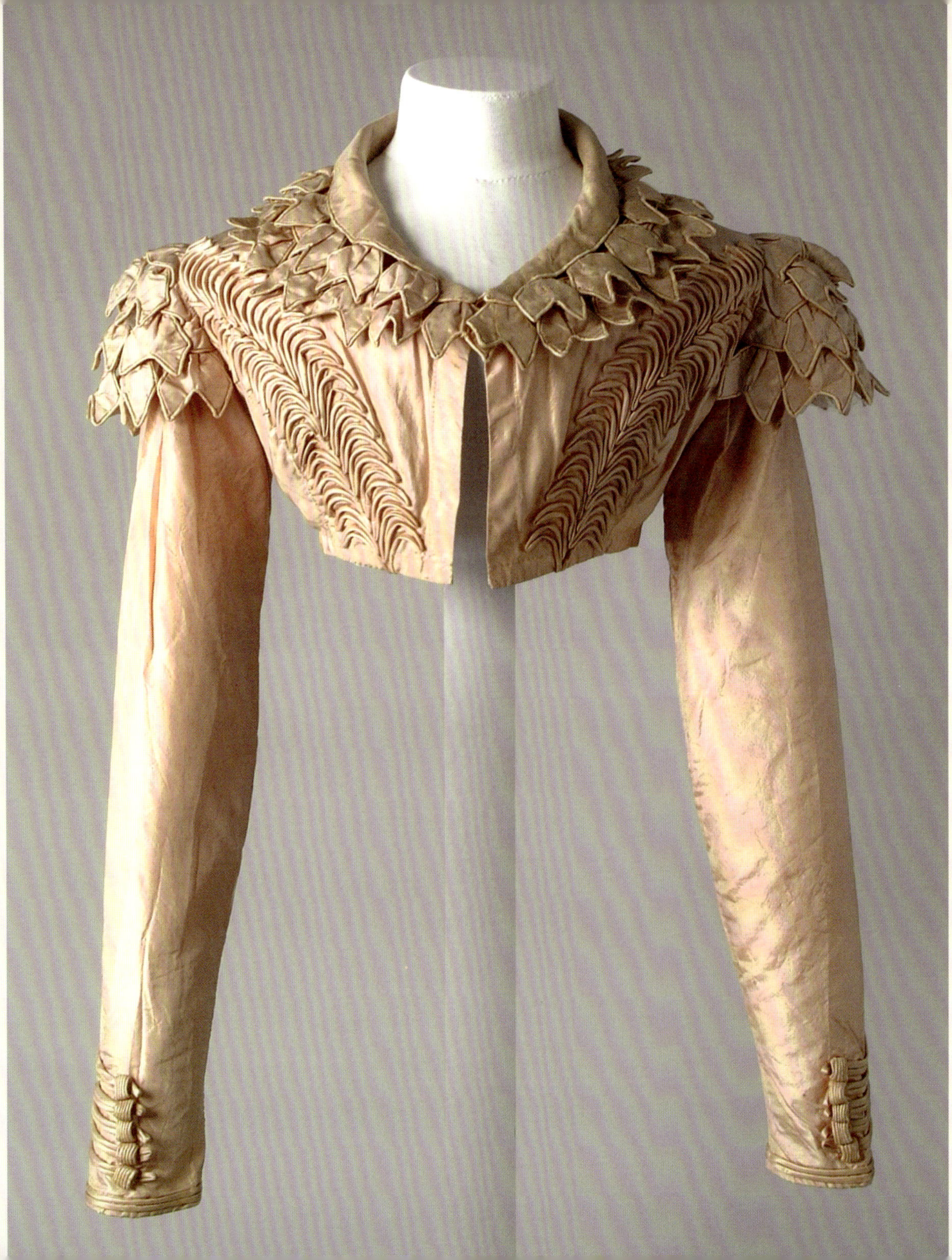

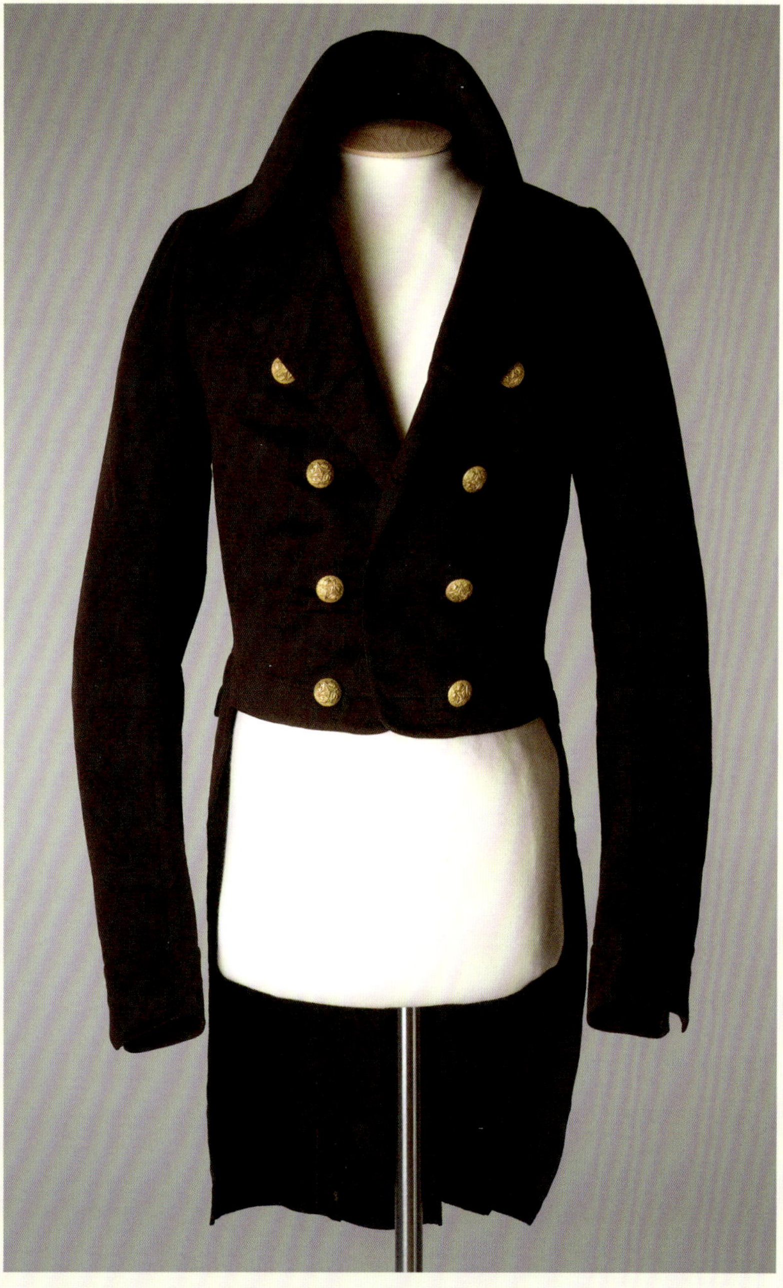

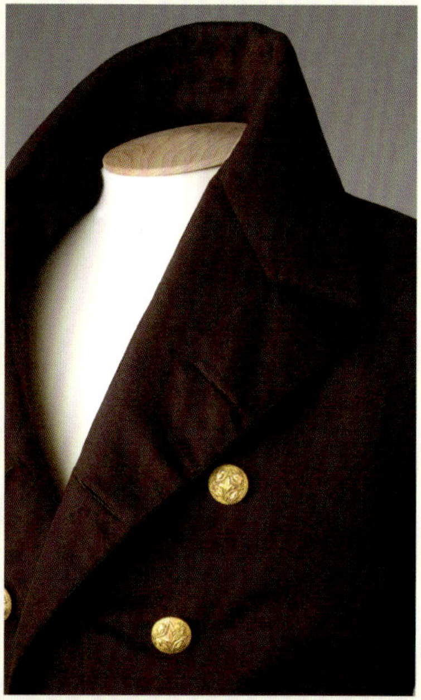

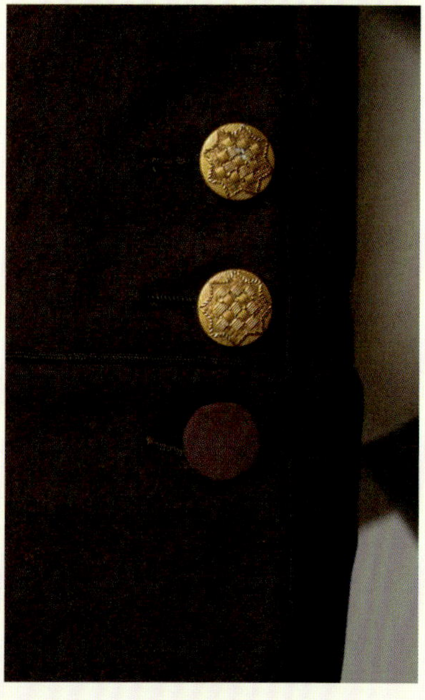

Morning dress coat, 1837–1840

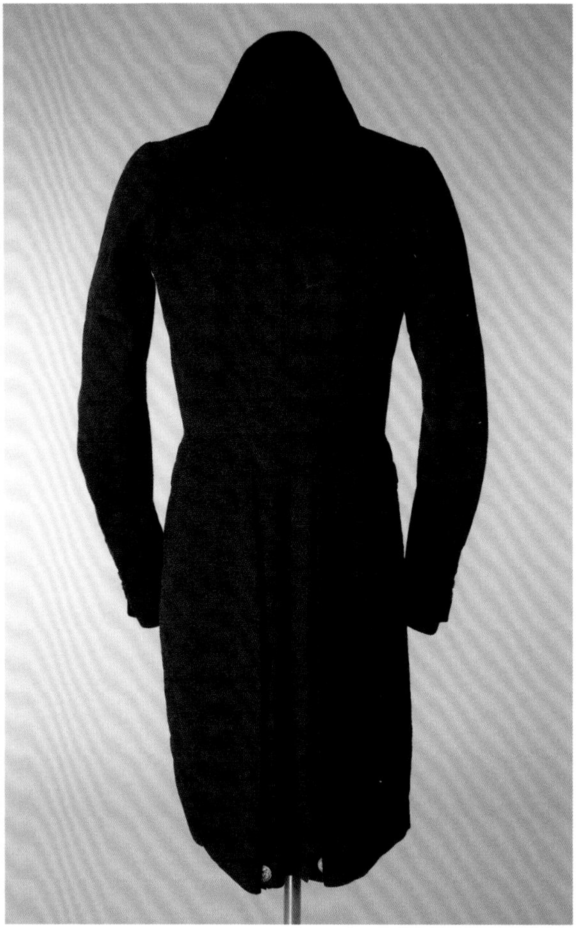

This beautifully tailored double-breasted tailcoat is made from rich dark claret coloured milled facecloth (a very fine type of plain weave wool). It has a high rolled collar with V-notches at the point where the lapels and collar meet. The collar is stiffened with an interlining of canvas, moulded underneath by means of graduated 'padding stitches' which link the layers together. The lower front edge is cut horizontally, and the rounded tails are stitched to the main body at the waist seam rather than being cut in one with the body – a technique which began in the 1820s. There are flap pockets at the top of the tails and the edges are bound with narrow silk braid. The sleeves are set in flat at the shoulders. They are long and tapered, and the corners of the slit cuffs are chamfered off, echoing the notches at the collar. The main body of the coat is lined with black silk, the sleeves with white cotton and the cuffs with brown silk velvet. There are also padded sections within the lining at the chest and back – a technique used from the early 1800s to make coats hang well and to give a pigeon-chested look. By the 1830s the effect was becoming more subtle.

English tailoring had a well deserved reputation for quality and cut. The later eighteenth century had seen tailors perfect their cutting skills to the point where the French, normally leaders of fashion, had adopted styles associated with the tailored English riding coat – a trend that was christened *Anglomania*. The fashion for beautifully cut cloth was inspired by the sartorial choices of English aristocrats who spent much of their time on their country estates. By the 1780s their outerwear – practical coats made from woollen cloth in muted colours – had become mainstream fashion for all but the most formal occasions. Innovations in the practice of cutting and fitting during the first half of the nineteenth century led to further refinements in men's tailoring. Tape measures were developed and used for the first time during the early 1800s, leading to a more scientific approach based on geometry and human anatomy. This prompted the publication of a number of complex guides and handbooks for the quality tailor. However, perhaps the greatest development of the era lay in the art of construction and fitting. The subtle use of interlinings, padding and shaping meant that coats followed and sometimes enhanced the line of the body in a new and far more flattering way. These techniques were used in conjunction with the tailor's iron, which shaped and stretched the pliable woollen cloth to the required silhouette.

OBJECT NUMBER – M.1994.19

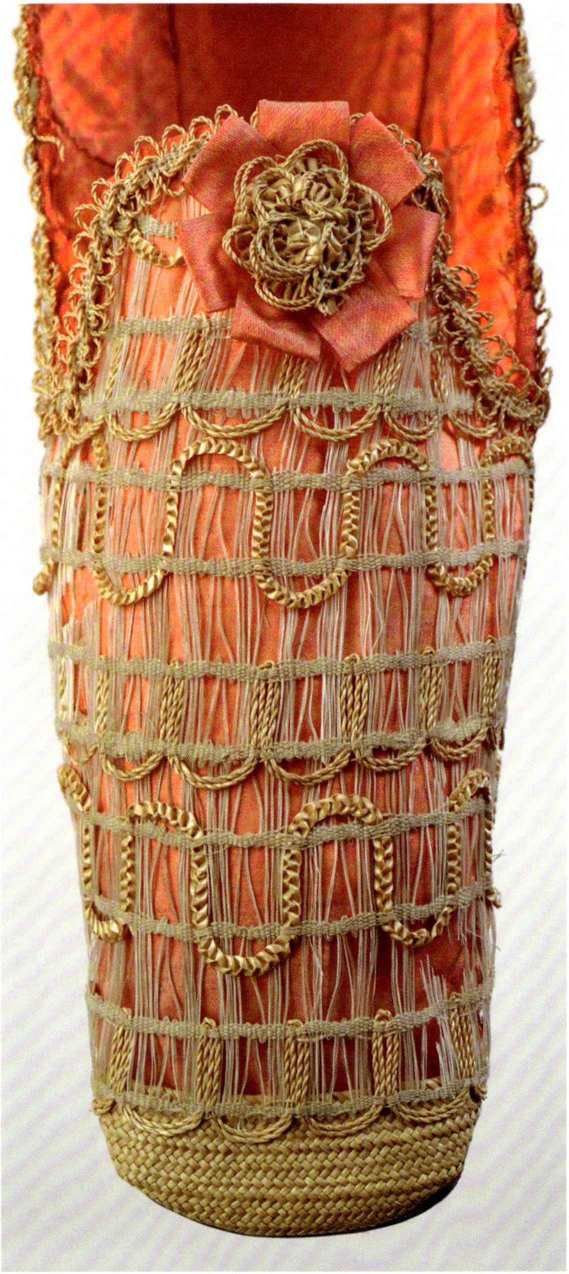

Pair of women's shoes, 1830–1840

Lined with red silk, the toe caps and counters are made from natural coloured plaited straw, while the uppers feature braids of straw and horsehair in an undulating pattern. A rosette of red silk and plaited straw has also been added, and the soles are made from brown leather. The shoes are straights, meaning that they are identical in shape rather than being modelled to fit the right or left foot. This method of producing women's shoes was almost universally used until the mid-nineteenth century, and some continued to be made as straights until 1900.

This is a fine example of plaited straw work – as well as being used for making hats this craft was harnessed for use in other fashionable garments and accessories from the eighteenth century through to the 1870s. Straw work shoes seem to have been particularly fashionable during the 1830s. A few examples are found in other museums – a very similar pair survives in the collection of the Kyoto Costume Institute in Japan. All have red silk lining, and exhibit the Leghorn plaiting technique in which fine straw plaits are joined together with tiny ladder stitches. Plaited straw of this kind was produced in Tuscany and was mostly used for making hats of the highest quality. However, this diversification into other accessories shows how versatile the technique could be.

OBJECT NUMBER – MT.1934

Beaded drawstring bag, 1830–1850

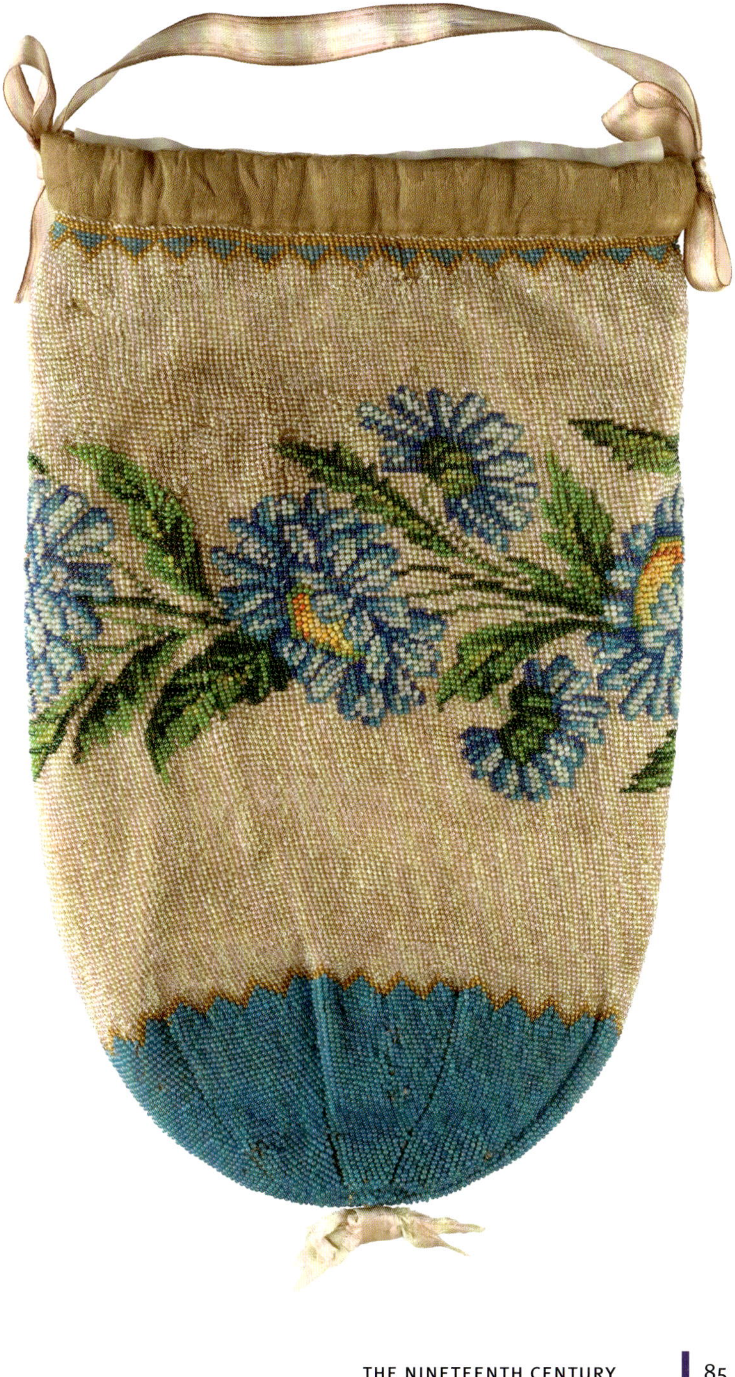

Worked all over with tiny glass beads, a band of blue flowers winds around this large and handsome drawstring bag. The flowers are set off by a white background, and a cream silk ribbon bow finishes off the bottom section. It is lined with un-dyed cotton, and cream silk has been used to bind the drawstring opening at the top.

Beadwork has a very ancient history. Beaded items have been found in Egyptian tombs and we know from surviving examples that beads embellished English medieval ecclesiastical vestments. Beadwork is also strongly represented in many Native American and African works of art and craft. In England the seventeenth century saw beads being used in embroidered samplers, caskets, accessories such as bags, and to decorate clothing, but the nineteenth century was the era when beadwork really came to the fore. Many techniques were used, including threading, stitching and couching, but in this example the bead knitting method has been employed. Beads were threaded on to each stitch to make a complete beaded fabric. The size of the beads used can indicate the age of an item since they got larger through the nineteenth century. In this case the beads are relatively small, suggesting that the bag dates from the 1830s or '40s. Beadwork was a popular amateur craft during the nineteenth century, but the quality of the work seen in this piece suggests that it may have been professionally made.

OBJECT NUMBER – MT.1523

Evening gown, 1818–1824

It is made from a fabric woven with alternating semi-transparent and figured silk satin stripes in olive green and cream, and has a wide neckline decorated with three ivory satin rouleau bands. The bodice is lined with glazed cotton and the short puffed silk satin sleeves have piped cuffs. The sleeves were originally overlaid with transparent silk gauze, probably in the style of a sleeve cap, but only fragments of this remain at the shoulder seams. The skirt, which is attached to a high waistband, is gathered at the centre back and falls in an 'A-line' shape. Above the padded hem it is decorated with silk triangles, fringing and rouleau bands. This evening dress is a rare survival from a transitional period in fashion. The waistline which had been so high since the late eighteenth century is now beginning to descend to its natural level, but has not quite reached it. The puffed sleeves, A-line shape, bold colour and exuberant decoration towards the hemline are nascent examples of the highly exaggerated styles which emerged in the late 1820s; an era which saw women dressed in wide cone-shaped gowns with three-dimensional hem decoration and vast puffed sleeves. As well as indicating the direction of future fashions, this dress also incorporates a feature which was very much of its time – the use of silk net or gauze in evening gowns – a style which was prevalent from around 1817 through to the early 1820s. Worn over lustrous silk petticoats it produced a muted but shimmering effect as the wearer moved (the original petticoat does not survive, so a replica is shown here).

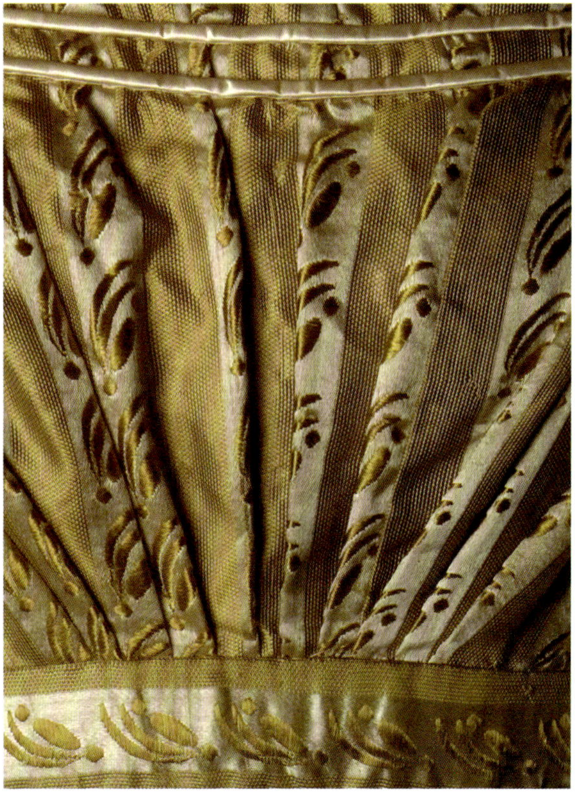

The wearer of this dress would also have benefited from a new development in fastenings – an early example of a myriad of new innovations in clothing construction made during the nineteenth century. Rather than using drawstrings or lacing, brass wire hooks and eyes have been stitched to the back opening. Though hook fastenings appear in clothing long before this date, this was the first time they had been used for fastening bodices in this way. It was a reliable and secure closure method which would continue to be used in women's wear until the advent of the zip fastener in the 1930s.

OBJECT NUMBER – MT.2038

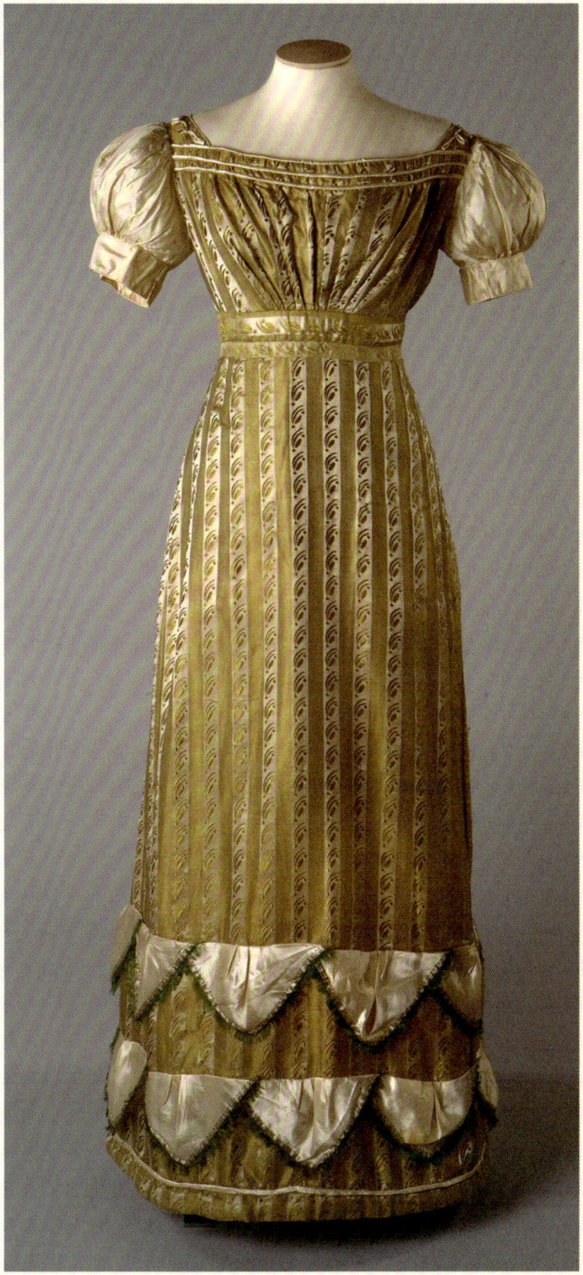

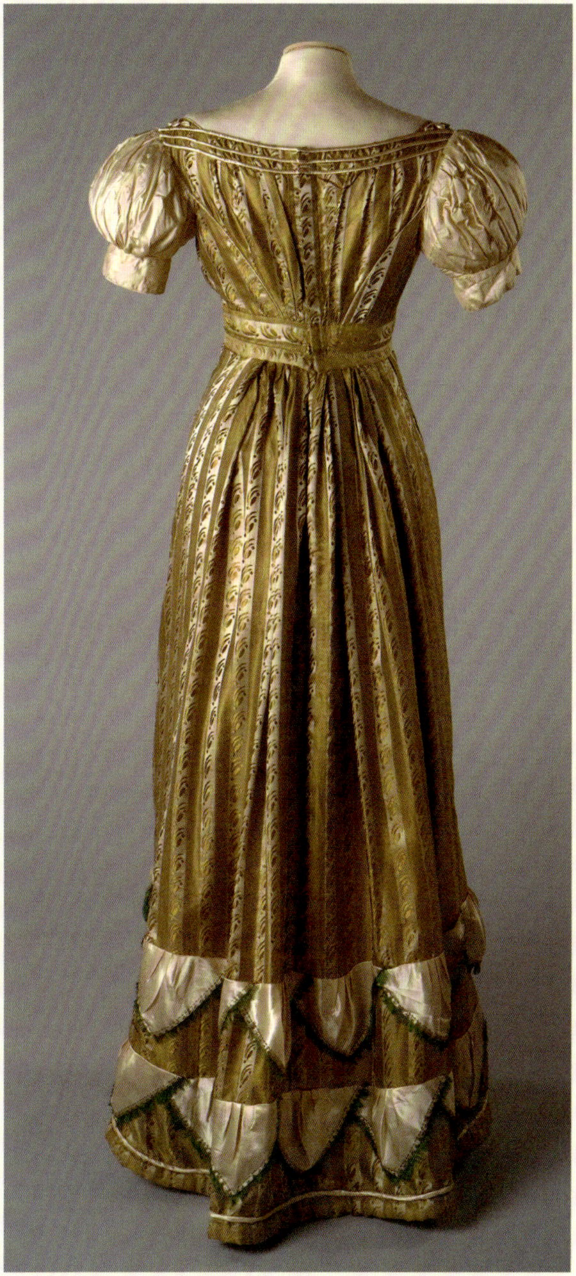

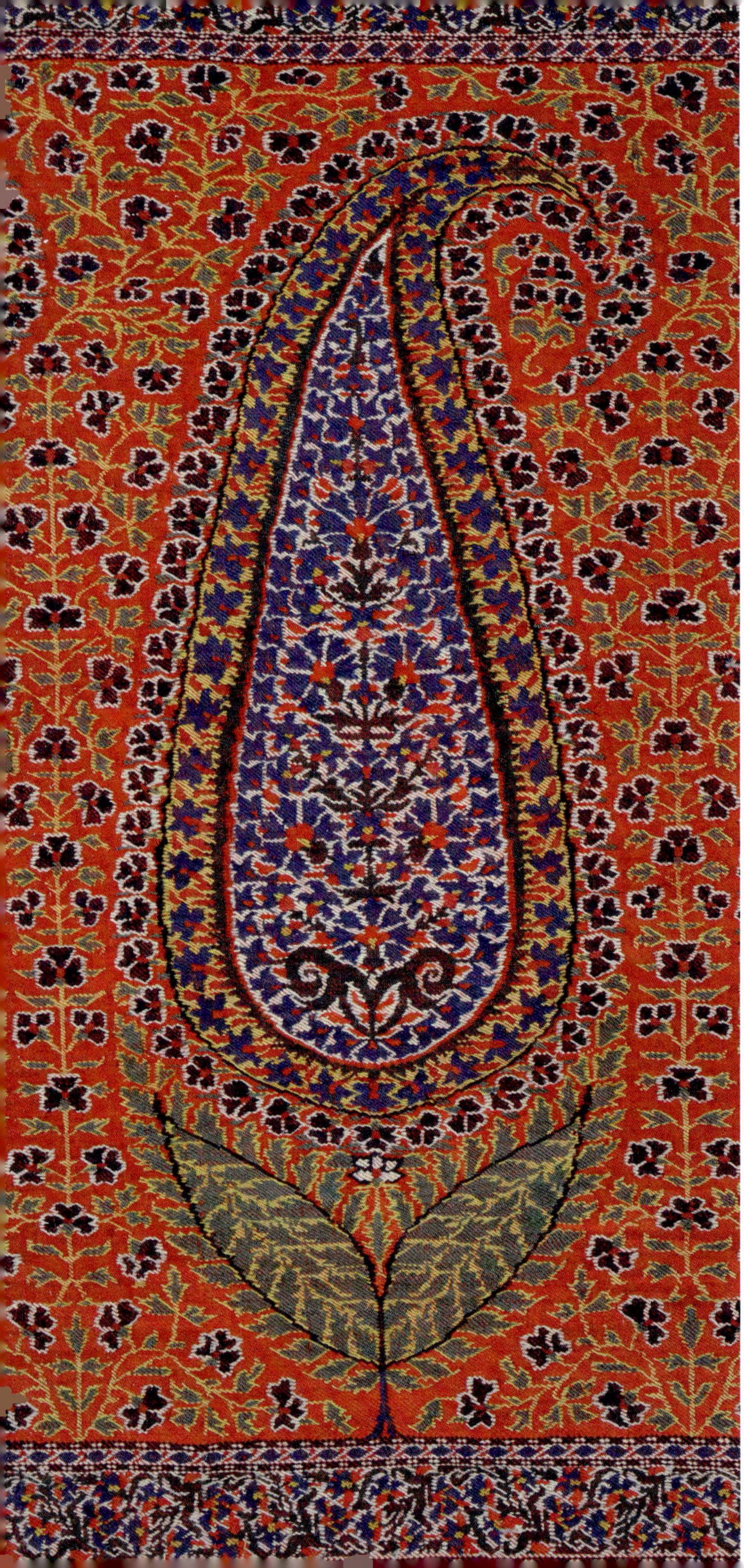

Wool shawl, 1820–1830

This bold red rectangular wool shawl is decorated with deep patterned borders featuring nine *botehs*, or pine motifs. An embroidered mark likely to be a maker's mark or an inventory label, has been added to one corner of the plain red ground. Referred to in Europe as *Kashmirs* since many were made in the Kashmir region, now a disputed territory between India and Pakistan, shawls became very fashionable in the West from the late eighteenth century. Exported by the East India Company, or brought home as souvenirs, they were expensive and highly desirable items. The best shawls were made of the extremely fine, soft and lightweight wool from wild goats (*Capra hircus*) which live on the high plateaux of the Himalayas in Tibet and Central Asia. Wool from domesticated goats was almost as fine and was also used as the industry grew.

Kashmiri weavers used a painstaking method of production, resulting in stunning designs and good durability. The patterned parts were produced using the twill tapestry technique. The reverse of the shawl (opposite below) shows this distinctive technique as it appears from behind. Each coloured section was separately hand woven only as far as was necessary for the pattern and interlocked with the rest of the textile. Until the early nineteenth century shawls were made entirely in one piece; the best examples taking up to three years to produce. By the time this shawl was woven efforts had been made to speed up the process, and they were made in at least two parts simultaneously on separate looms then 'invisibly' joined together. This shawl has indeed been made in two sections.

Shawls were adopted as part of women's dress from the late eighteenth century. Featuring cream backgrounds and subtle colours at first, but progressing to brighter colours as fashion dictated, the elegant draperies of the shawl were ideally suited to the new narrow muslin gowns. They enhanced the neo-classical look, and provided much needed warmth, as well as a touch of the exotic. This trend was fuelled by their image as a luxury item and their enthusiastic adoption by leaders of fashion. As early as the 1790s manufacturers in both Britain and France were attempting to capitalise on this fashion. In Britain

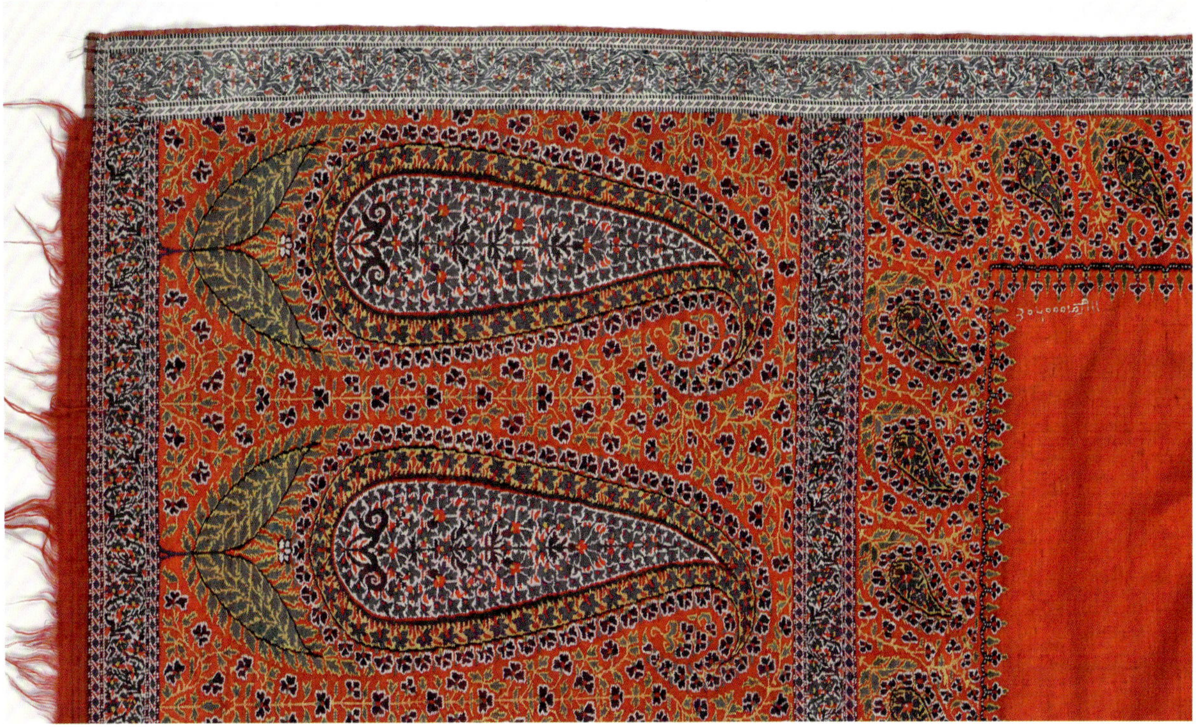

the centres for shawl weaving were Edinburgh, Norwich and later Paisley (the name was to become synonymous with the distinctive pine motif originally developed from Asian decorative art). They could not achieve the fine lightness associated with the Kashmir raw materials and technique, but many beautiful examples were produced, often incorporating silk to lighten the weight and improve sheen. The industry flourished, particularly in Paisley, and shawls remained fashionable throughout the first half of the nineteenth century. They became more affordable with mass production, and achieved a final burst of popularity during the 1850s and '60s when wide crinolines allowed for the display of shawl patterns to their best advantage.

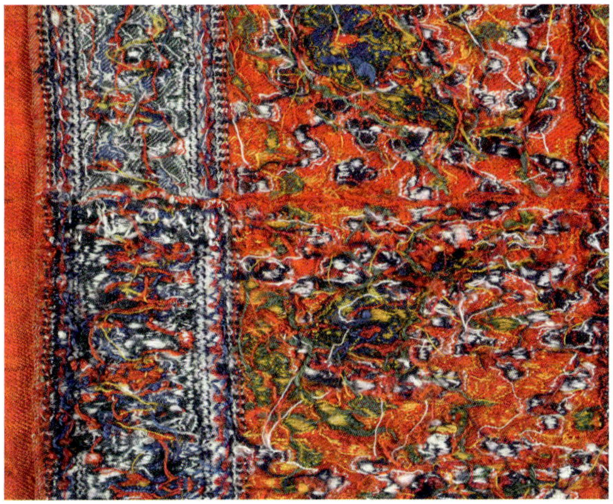

OBJECT NUMBER – MT.3988

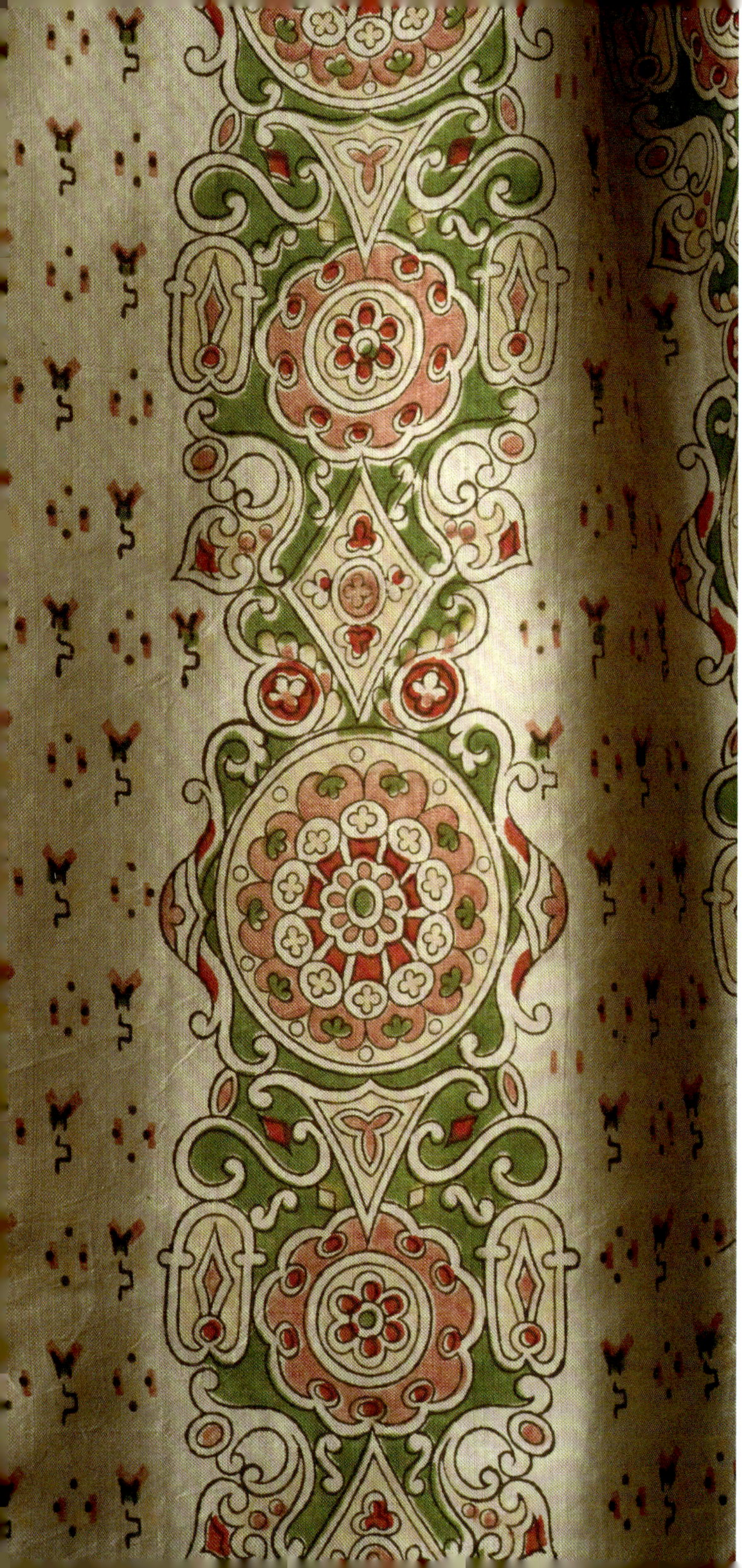

Printed day dress, 1837–1839

This attractive summer gown incorporates a number of key details of fashionable day dress from the 1830s. The skirt, with its padded hem, is tightly pleated to the waistband at the back and sides so that the volume of fabric required for the newly fashionable fullness can be incorporated. The bodice, which is lined with white linen, is closed with hooks and eyes at the back. It features a wide boat-shaped neckline, open almost from shoulder to shoulder, and the waistband is very near to the natural level. The style of the sleeves, with their pleating to the upper arms and billowing width below the elbows, represents the last gasp of nearly two decades of fashionably wide puffed sleeves. After reaching extraordinarily wide proportions during the 1820s and early '30s, the style was now being toned down. Here the top of the sleeve is pleated and held in place by green piping, and is decorated with frills. Pleats are again used to catch the sleeves into deep cuffs. By releasing the sleeve width below the elbow a drooping, muted effect is achieved which draws the eye down towards the lower half of the garment.

The dress is block printed with a colourful pattern designed to look like stained glass. Once again the influence of the Gothic revival is strongly in evidence – a trend which had begun to invade virtually every aspect of design. Few could mistake the homage to medieval ecclesiastical architecture in this clever and quirky print, while the use of lightweight silk and bright colours serves to counterbalance an essentially conservative historical theme.

The return to natural waist levels and full skirts had further implications for the fashion conscious. Small waists were again seen as an important feminine asset, with corsets and stiffened petticoats now becoming essential underwear components. In addition, new innovations in corset production pushed the boundaries much further than before. During the late 1820s metal eyelets were used on corsets for the first time. They prevented the fabric from tearing and fuelled the fashion for ever tighter lacing.

OBJECT NUMBER – MT.2036

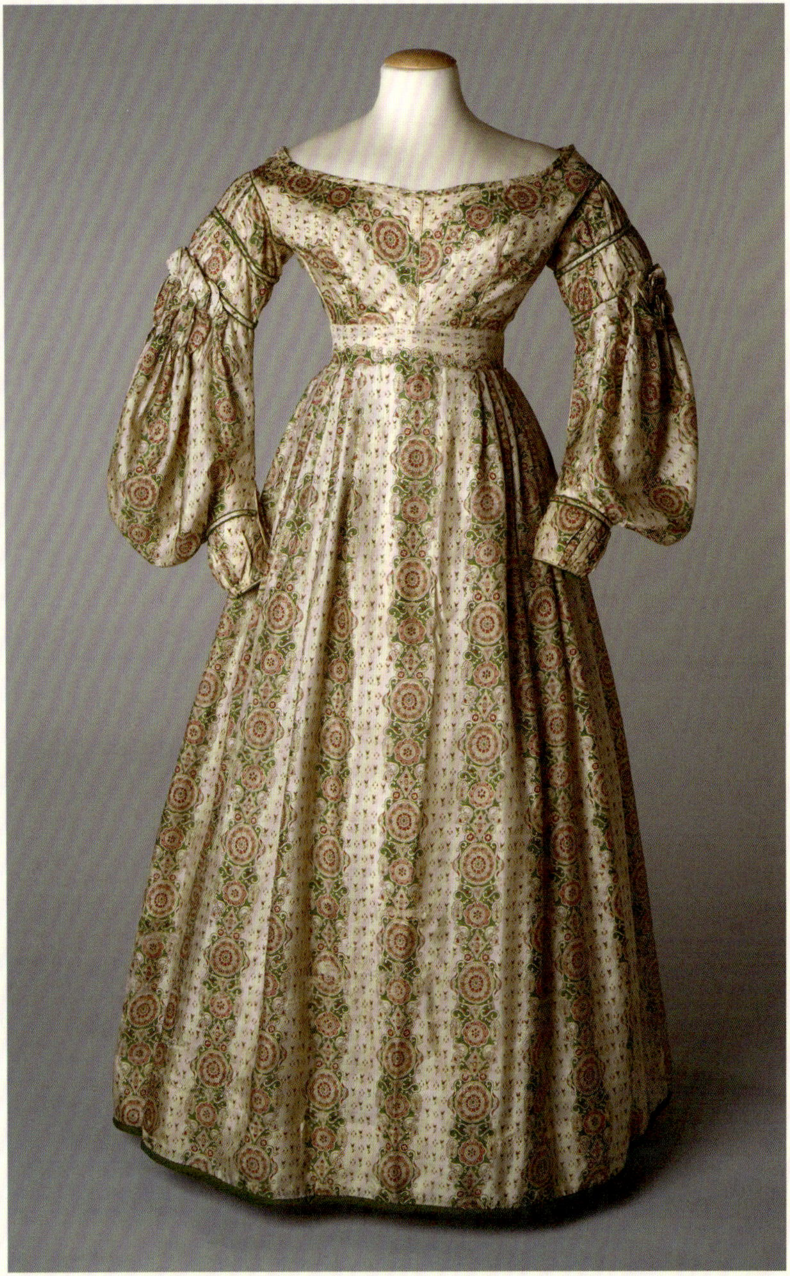

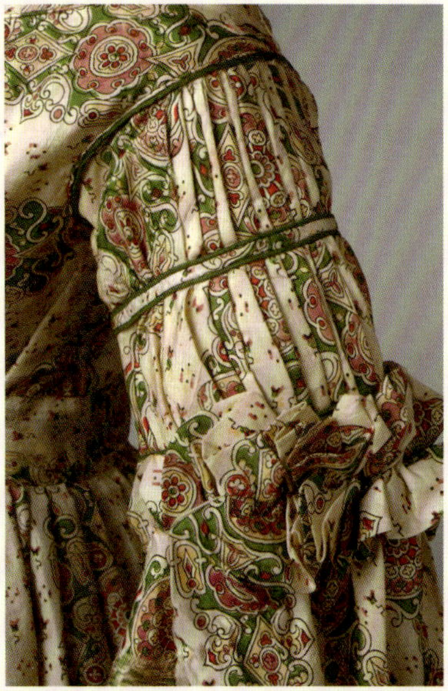

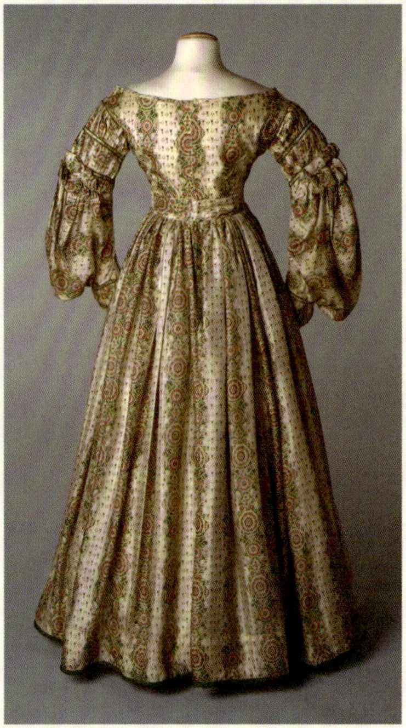

Man's waistcoat, 1840–1845

Single breasted with a shawl collar, this fashionable waist length man's waistcoat is made from silk velvet. The bright blue silk satin ground can clearly be seen where the dark claret red velvet pile has been hand trimmed or voided to create the elegant floral design. Two horizontally cut pockets have been added, as well as a crescent shaped watch pocket. The lining is of cream cotton and two strips of leather protect the waistcoat fronts from wear. The back is made from dark grey twill weave cotton with a gusset and two sets of tapes stitched to the centre back to allow for size adjustment.

While nineteenth century women's fashion galloped through a myriad of styles featuring ever more elaborate decorative devices and bright colours, men's clothing became more and more sober and plain. By the 1840s waistcoats were one of the few articles of male clothing that retained any decorative qualities, and even these were soon to become plainer, often being made to match the sombre colours of trousers by the 1850s. This beautiful example, owned by a young or very slight man, would have caught the light as the wearer moved, changing the colour emphasis from red to blue and back again and achieving a subtle yet opulent effect.

OBJECT NUMBER – MT.2252

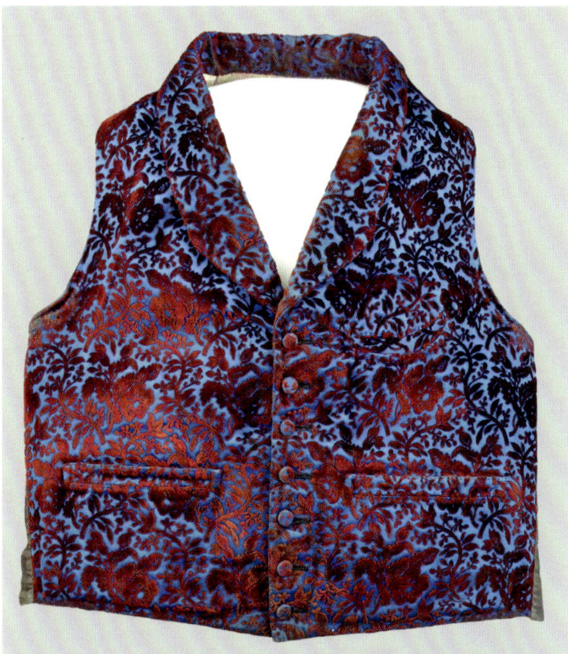

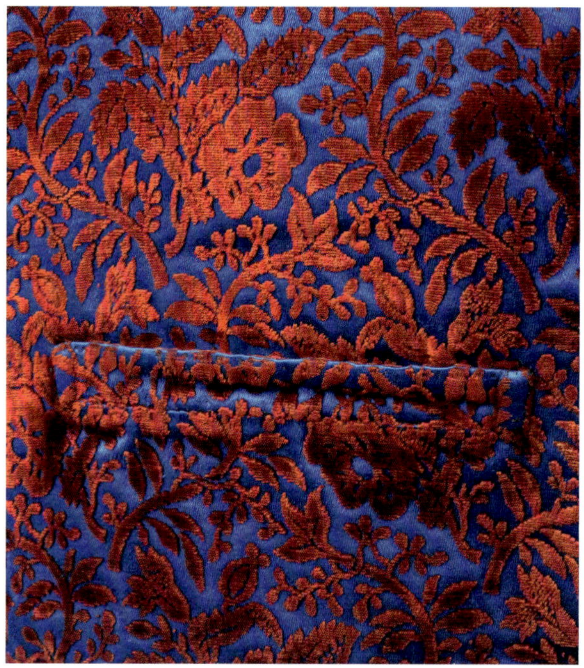

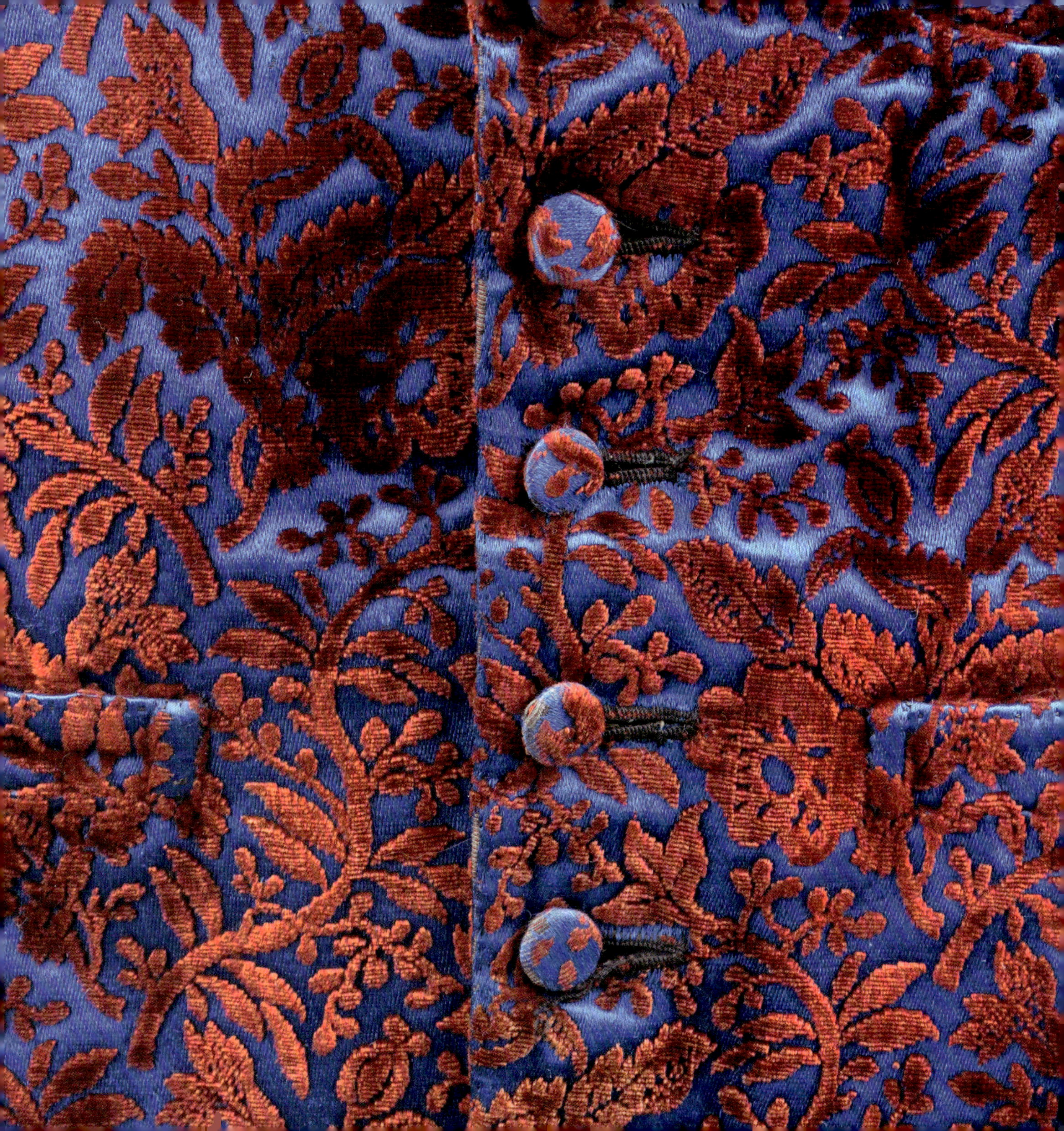

Shot silk day dress, 1845–1850

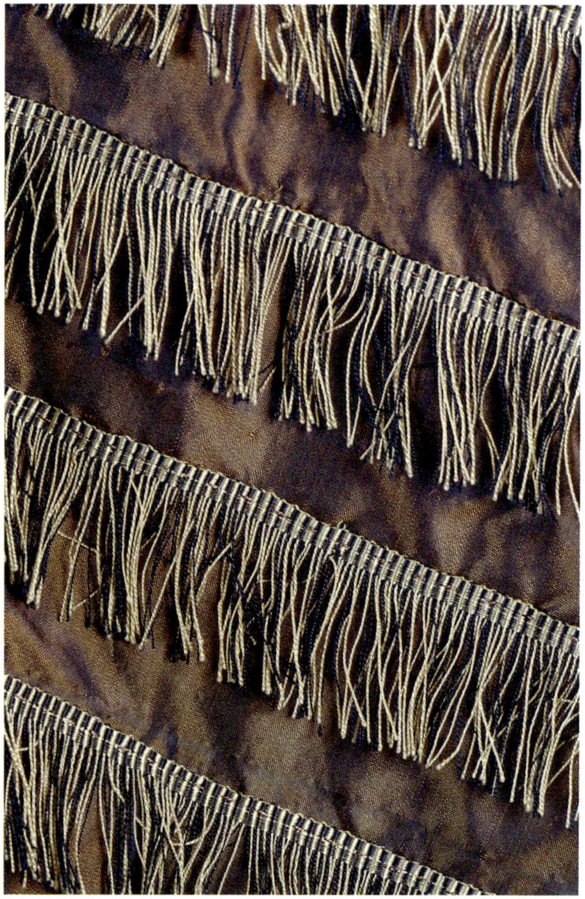

This one-piece shot silk gown has a small round neckline and long sleeves decorated with lines of fringing. The sleeves are set low on the shoulder, flaring out into an attractive bell shape below the elbow. They were known as pagoda sleeves and this new fashion would continue to gain popularity with sleeves growing ever wider through the 1850s and '60s. A considerable volume of pleated fabric provides an attractive central focus to the dress. Broad pleats start at the shoulder line and extend down the length of the bodice, becoming smaller as the waist narrows and emphasising the slimness of the figure. Known as *revers en pelerine* at the time, they are stitched down below the bust and taper to a point at the centre front somewhat below the natural waist level. The effect is that of an inverted triangle which draws the eye downwards and elongates the torso. The bodice fastens at the back with hooks and eyes. It is lined with brown and blue glazed cotton, and boned with whalebone. The full dome-shaped skirt is gauged to the bodice using relatively broad pleats at the front and cartridge pleating at the centre back to incorporate more fullness. It would have been supported by a number of petticoats, at least one stiffened with horsehair, which would rustle as the wearer walked and made women's clothing particularly hot and uncomfortable in warm weather.

The shot silk of this dress, with its purple, almost bronze hue, was immensely popular during the 1840s, and examples of very similar gowns survive in other collections including the Kyoto Costume Institute and the Museum of London. It was sometimes called *changeable silk* or *taffeta glacé*, and was created by weaving blue vertical (warp) threads with pink horizontal (weft) threads. The result was a beautiful sheen that appeared to change colour as the wearer moved.

As with pieces discussed earlier in this chapter, this garment also betrays the influence of the Gothic revival, but this time it is very much the cut rather than the textile decoration that links it to this immensely fashionable and influential design movement. The long pointed bodices of the 1840s, with their strong downward-curving lines, have been likened to the pointed arches of Gothic architecture. It was also fashionable at this time for women to wear their hair parted at the centre, mirroring the point of the arch below, with sections looped over the ears. The overall effect of hairstyle and outfit was muted and subdued and lent the wearer a rather meek, submissive demeanour; a style only too relevant to the extremely limited lives of many women at the time.

OBJECT NUMBER – M.1993.217

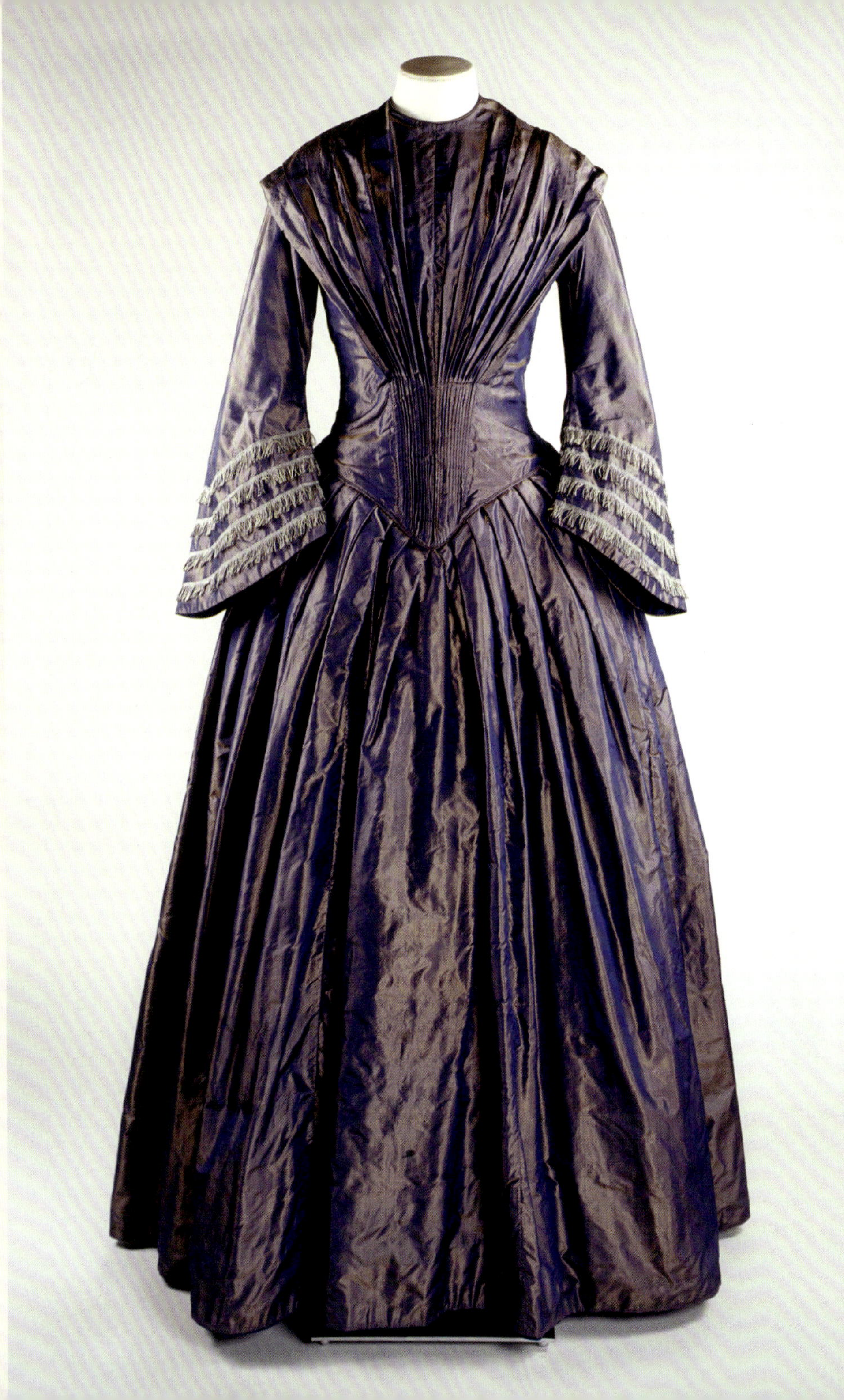

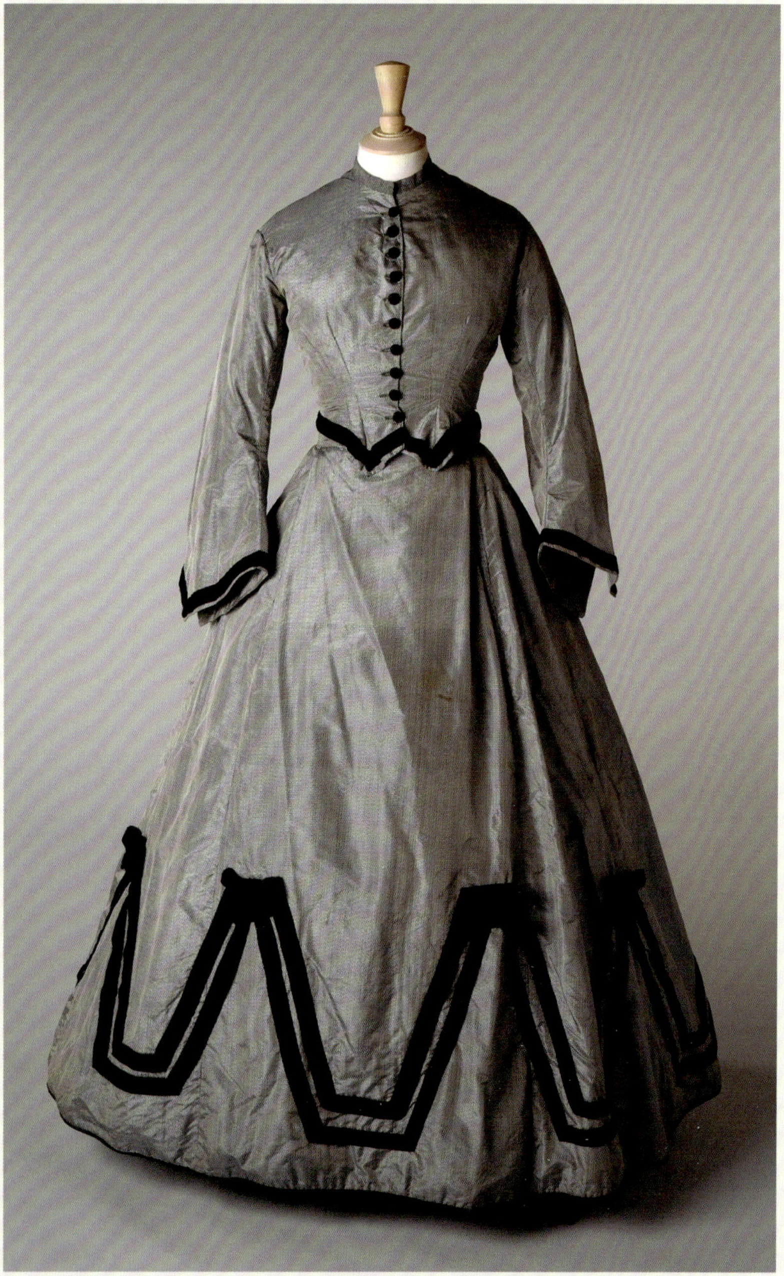

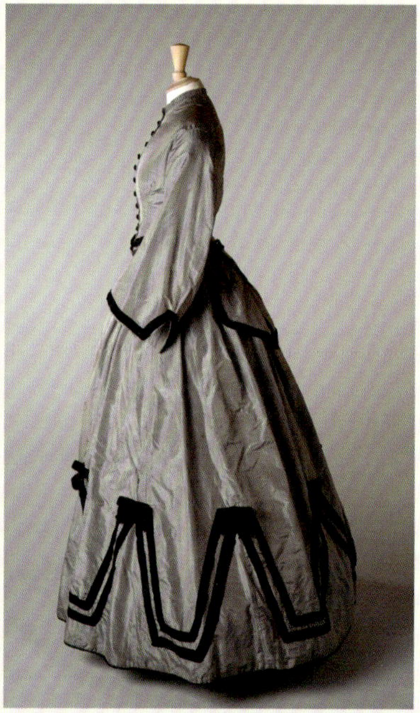

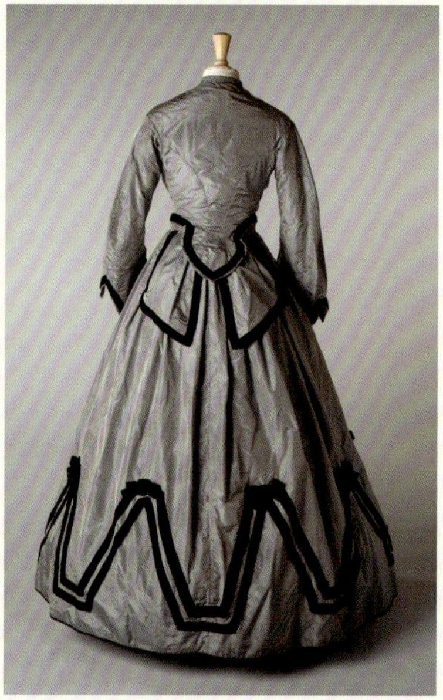

Silk day dress, 1862–1865

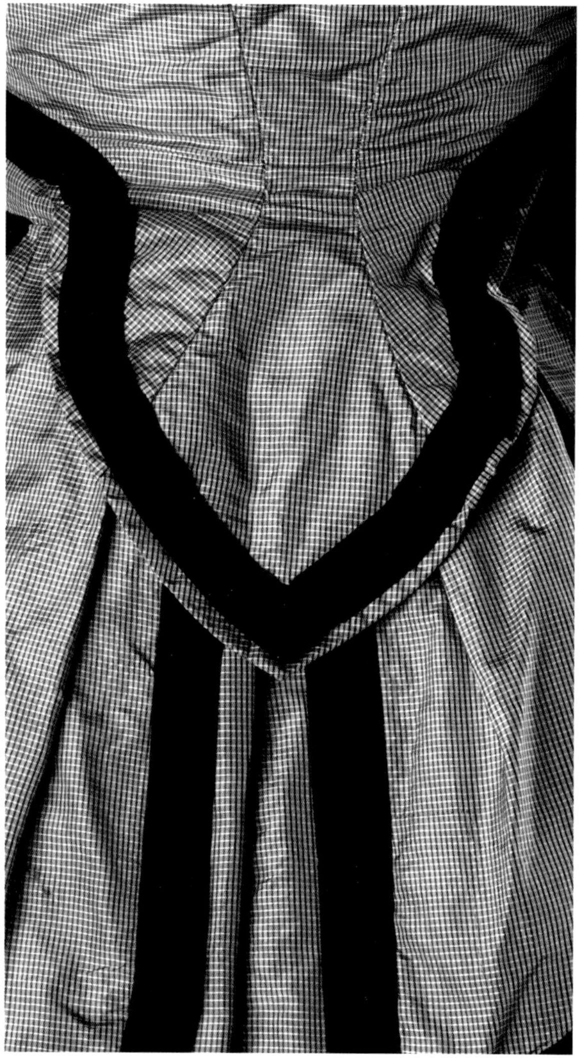

A crinoline dress consisting of a separate bodice and skirt, it is made of blue and white silk woven in a tiny check pattern. The bodice has a high round neckline and bell-shaped sleeves with short slits at the wrists. It opens centre front and is fastened with faceted imitation jet or Vauxhall glass buttons. A 'fish tail' or small basque extends at the back, which is cut in one with the bodice. Six bones have been inserted into the bodice and it is lined with white linen. The skirt is also lined with linen, gored and pleated. Cartridge pleating has been used at the centre back to give fullness behind. Two tabs have been added to the waistband at the back and combine with the fish tail to make an attractive feature. The dress is boldly trimmed with black silk velvet ribbon.

Despite being of quite modest width, this dress dates from the height of the crinoline era when skirts could be many yards in circumference. The fashion for wearing crinolines began around 1856, and they provided welcome relief from the many layers of hot, itchy petticoats previously worn to give skirts fullness. They swung attractively from side to side as the wearer moved, and were to prove almost universally popular. Most crinolines were of the cage variety with their hoops connected by cotton tape. The earliest examples were made from cane or whalebone but sprung steel was more generally used, and mass production by firms such as Thomson's made this fashion accessible to a wide cross section of the female population. Mass production was assisted by the advent of the sewing machine during the second half of the 1850s. Indeed the long seams of this dress have been machine stitched, though the more complicated areas have been hand sewn.

Though worn with a crinoline, this piece is an example of how the silhouette had recently changed. Until around 1860 crinoline hoops were perfectly round and held skirts out in a dome shape which grew wider and wider in circumference through the '50s. Perhaps due to reasons of practicality the 1860s saw hoops begin to flatten in front. As seen in this garment, skirts were gored to follow the new shape and soon the front was left flat and pleat free. The detail at the back of the dress also serves to highlight this shape – a new emphasis which would develop further as the decade advanced.

OBJECT NUMBER – M.2005.06

Cotton dress, 1868–1870

This attractive summer dress made from purple cotton muslin is an excellent example of a fashionable garment made on a budget. It consists of three separate pieces; a bodice, skirt and overskirt. The jacket bodice is lined with white cotton and features a return to narrow pagoda shaped sleeves – a fashion revival from the 1840s and '50s. It fastens at the centre front and has the new higher waistline finished with silk ribbon. There is a particularly flattering arrangement at the small of the back where the fabric below the waist has been gathered and curves down into two points. The bodice extends over the overskirt, and the latter is shaped so that it appears to be caught up above the skirt by further silk bows. The dress is generously trimmed with white cotton frills. By this date the crinoline was disappearing from fashion. Instead the skirt fits over an early form of bustle called a crinolette. This is made of white cotton and has a small hoop at the bottom with several half hoops behind to form the bustle shape.

The trimming is the first and most obvious clue to the likelihood that this garment has been produced on a budget, and probably at speed. The printed lace pattern on the white frills provides the effect of lace without the expense and this type of trimming could be bought readily and cheaply from a haberdasher's shop. From the loose and slightly erratic machine and hand stitching it appears that the dress was run up rather hurriedly, possibly by a home dress maker working from a fashion plate. However the colour of the dress – perhaps its most striking feature – is its most obvious link to the greater affordability of fashionable clothing for a broader cross-section of society. This vibrant colour has previously been incorrectly identified as *Perkin's Purple* – the first ever man-made dye. It nevertheless forms part of the new generation of affordable aniline dyed textiles.

Perkin's Purple was created by Sir William Henry Perkin, who christened it 'Mauvine' or mauve for short. Perkin discovered mauve (pronounced 'morv' by the Victorians) by accident in 1856 while trying to produce man-made quinine from aniline; a distillation of coal tar. He lodged a patent, and began to produce 'Mauvine' for the dyeing industry. It was hugely successful, and the fashion for Mauve lasted until around 1861. By this time further aniline colours were being created by Perkin and other chemists, who were quick to pick up on the financial success of such dyes. Upon further research, the colour of the cloth of this garment appears to be much closer to the violet shades that were produced in the ten years after *Perkin's Purple*. This fits with the date of the dress, and the colour is likely to be a 'Hofmann's Violet' (named after its creator, Professor August Wilhelm von Hofmann, who was teaching Perkin chemistry when he discovered mauve). Man-made dyes such as these revolutionised the fabric dyeing and printing industry. They also made bright colours cheaper and much more attainable for larger sections of the population.

OBJECT NUMBER – M.1986.19

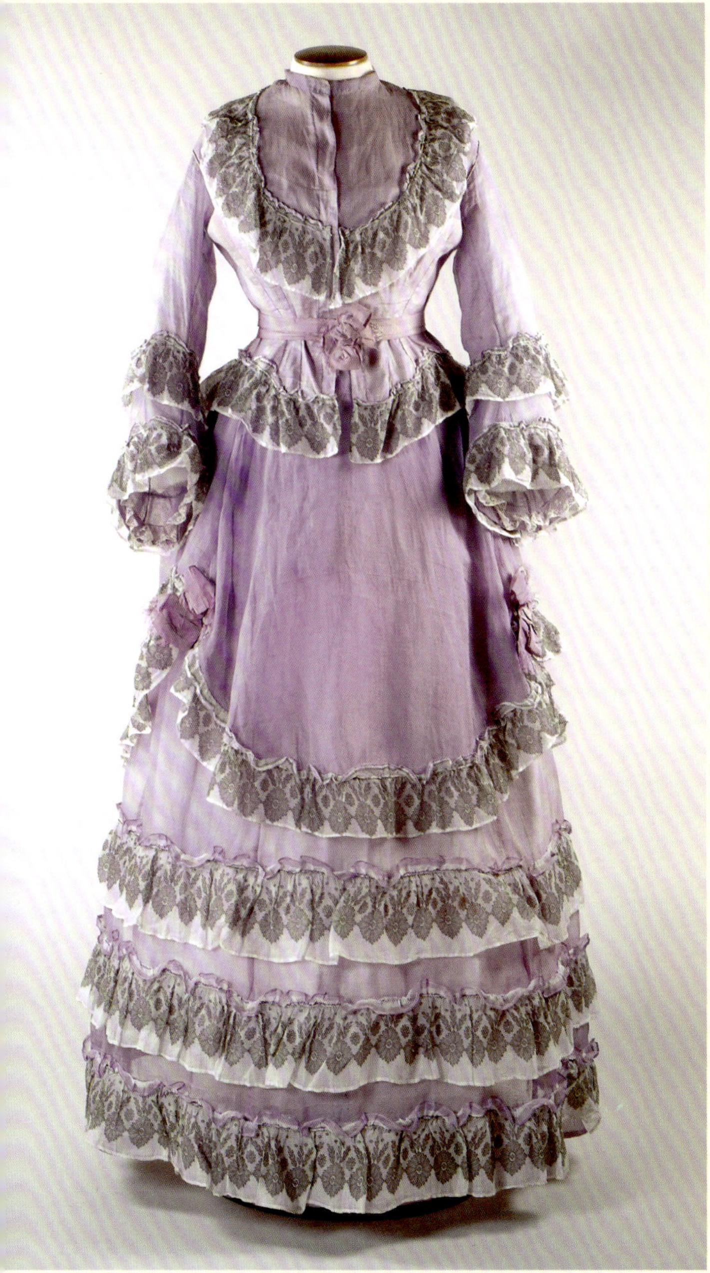

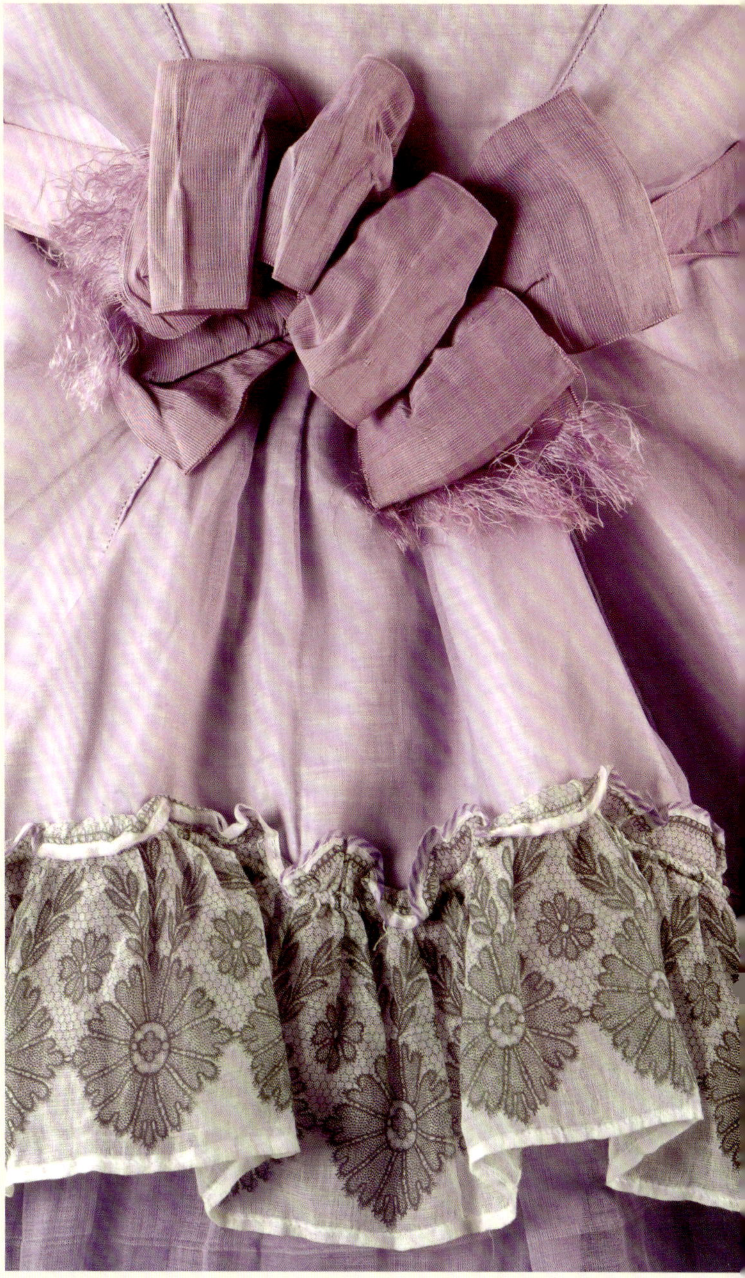

Day dress, 1879–1881

Made from a combination of worsted wool and figured silk satin, this day dress features an elaborate combination of textures, colours and trimmings. The dark blue of the wool is juxtaposed with the lighter colour and weight of the silk fabric, whilst the riot of ruching, pleats and gathers is exactly in keeping with the prevailing fashions of the time. The advent of the sewing machine has been cited as one reason for the increasing complexity of women's fashions, and indeed this dress is made from a combination of machine and hand stitching. The ease and speed with which seams could be run up appears to be counterbalanced by the addition of as many trimming, cutting and stitching devices as possible. The perceived value of fashionable women's wear during this period – which can conceivably be linked to the time and skill it took to make a garment well – could be maintained by clear evidence of intensive labour. This trend for complicated dress began during the early 1870s, when the most over-elaborate examples were created. However, by the late '70s slightly more subtle and cohesive garments such as this one were being produced.

The dress has a long, slender silhouette and exhibits the princess-line; being cut in one with the skirt and made without a waist seam. Both this form and the equally fashionable cuirasse bodice utilised a number of shaped panels to hug the figure and tightly follow the contours of the body to well below hip level. This caused corsets to lengthen, and to be laced much tighter in order to achieve a fashionably small waist. Tight lacing had not been prevalent during the crinoline era as the wide skirts made waists seem narrow by comparison, but now a significantly smaller waist was necessary to compensate for the loss of this optical illusion.

In order to maintain the narrow, tubular shape of the skirt cotton tapes have been stitched into the lining. These were tied behind the legs so that the fabric could be stretched tightly across the front. The rear view reveals elegant and complex back draperies extending into a train. The fashion for trains as part of day wear lasted until around the end

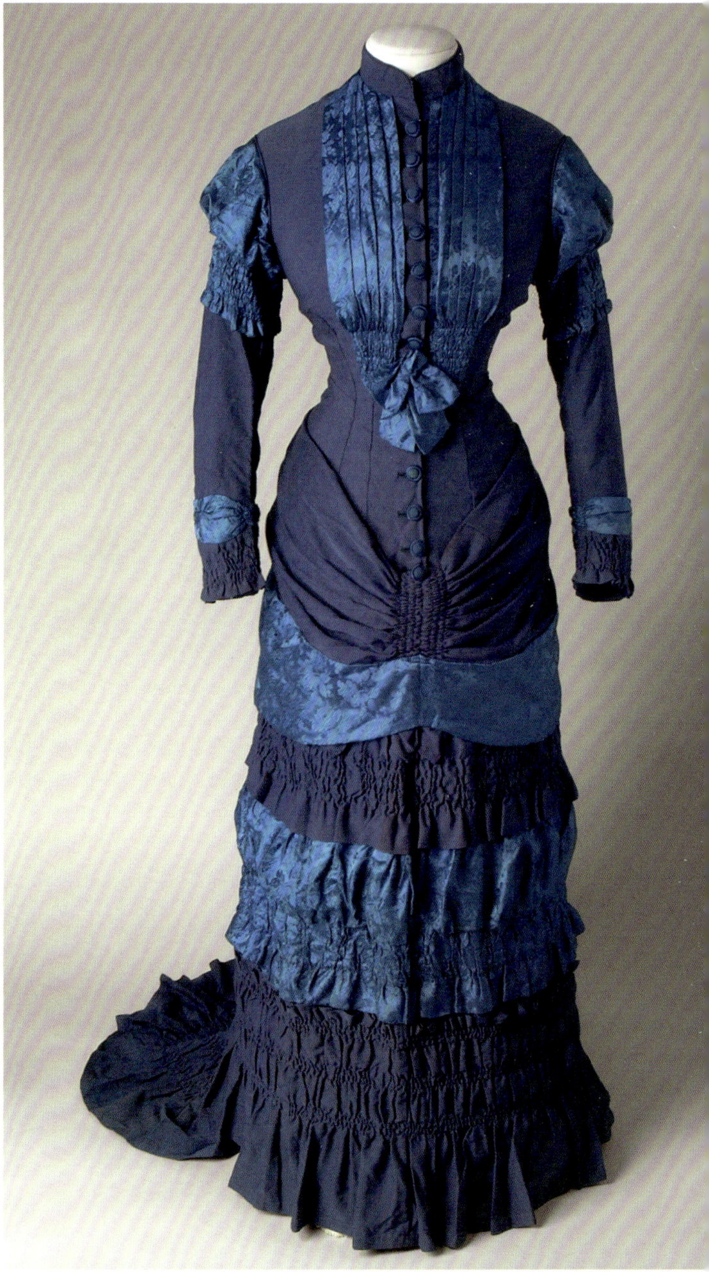

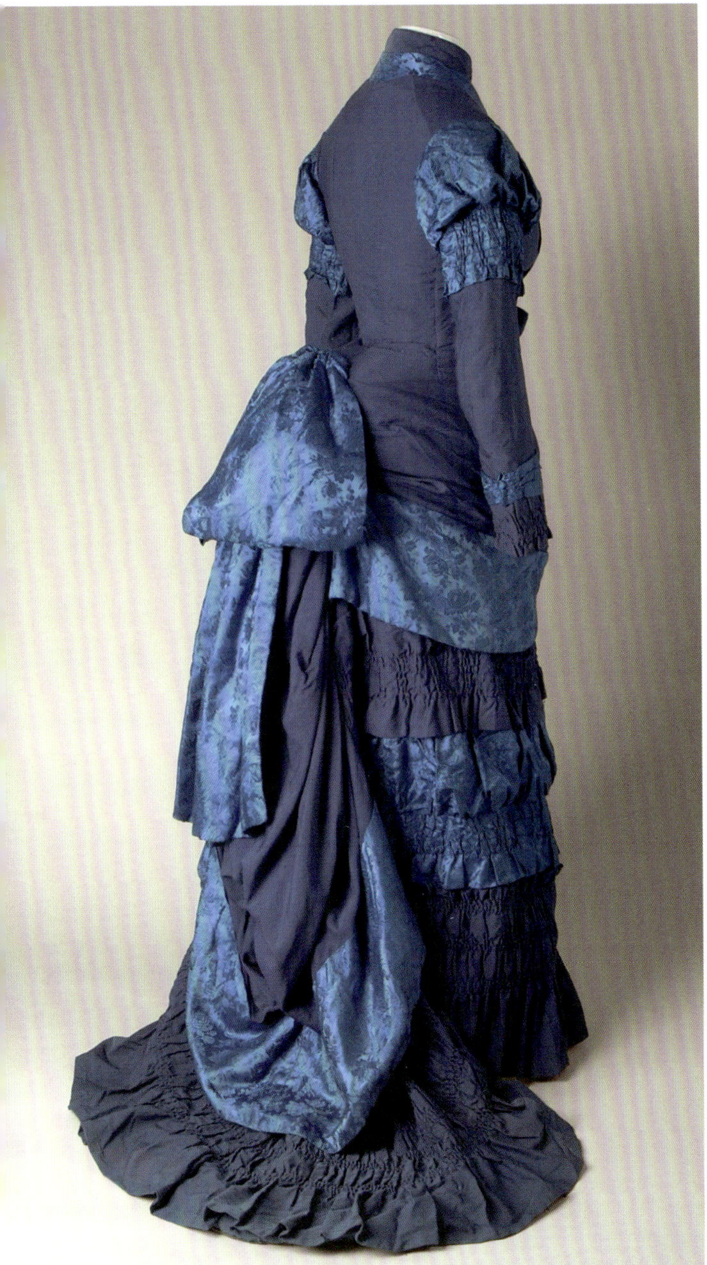

of the decade, persisting longer in evening wear. Some contemporary commentators had strong opinions on trains and mocked those who walked in the street with one trailing behind them. They suggest that only the wealthy who occupied a suitably clean environment should wear them. The writer Margaret Oliphant wrote in 1878:

> *Nothing can be a more certain indication that the wearer of a long train is not a lady, than the fact that she allows it to sweep the street behind her. As for the long skirt indoors… It is graceful and dignified in itself; it belongs to the fundamental idea of women's apparel, and possesses all the poetical and symbolical qualities which are necessary to a noble and fine ideal of dress. So long as it sweeps over carpets, or polished floors, clean and carefully kept… it has all the elements of beauty, and is not more inconvenient than a beautiful thing may be permitted to be.**

In order to protect the train from damage while walking this example has brush braid at the hem and coarse-woven brown linen/cotton mix fabric stitched under the train where it would have come into contact with the ground. This could be brushed to remove mud and dust.

OBJECT NUMBER – M.1994.14

*Oliphant, Mrs Margaret, *Dress*, Art at Home Series, (London 1878), quoted in Gernsheim, Alison, *Fashion and Reality* (London 1963), p.64.

Corset, 1885–1895

An attractive brown cotton sateen corset made by the firm Y&N, it features a steel spoon-shaped busk, steel supports at the sides and whalebone strips enclosed in lighter coloured boning channels (there are 30 separate supports in total). The white cotton lining includes the following label: 'The Y&N Corset Regd., The Y&N Diagonal Seam, trade mark, Awarded Three Gold Medals'. The 'Diagonal Seam' element of the corset is evident from an analysis of the construction. It is made up of 18 individually shaped pieces, most of which have at least one slanting or diagonal edge. These would have curved around the body, giving the figure an enhanced hourglass shape and adding strength to the corset. Most of the boning runs counter to this, extending in straight lines top to bottom, but on either side of the back opening at the top four bones have been stitched at a diagonal into channels between the layers of fabric; providing extra support to the upper back. Sixteen metal eyelets allow for the lacing of the corset, which was usually carried out by tightening from the top to the middle and from the bottom to the middle, gradually increasing the pressure, and tying off at natural waist level where the corset was narrowest. The spoon busk, which was first used in corsets during the 1880s, also provided extra support. In response to prevailing fashions for garments which were fitted to below hip level, corsets had started to extend lower over the stomach during the 1870s and continued to do so into the 1880s. The spoon busk curved in at the waist and slightly out over the abdomen, adding further strength and support to this area.

The Y&N corset manufacturer sold corsets through a wide variety of outlets. They marketed them in Europe as well as the United Kingdom, but there is also evidence of export abroad since one of the medals it received was at the New Zealand International Exhibition of 1882. Their adverts carry a quote from the newspaper *Ladies' Pictorial* stating that Y&N is 'the most comfortable corset ever made', and go on to claim that they 'will not split in the seams nor tear in the fabric. Made in white, black and all the fashionable colours and shades in Italian cloth, satin and coutil; also in the new sanitary Woollen Cloth. 4/11, 5/11, 6/11, 7/11 per pair upwards. Caution – every genuine Y&N Corset is stamped. Sold by all drapers and ladies' outfitters'.

Leigh Summers in her book *Bound to Please. A History of the Victorian Corset* notes that during the 1890s the Y&N brand were the only corset manufacturers to use women wearing glasses in their advertisements. She suggests that the company was responding to the greater emphasis on female education during this period, perhaps using a recognised symbol of intelligence – spectacles – as a way of associating cleverness with the purchase of a Y&N corset*. This was a period when concerns were being voiced about tight lacing within the dress reform movement and the medical establishment and corset manufacturers were attempting to respond by emphasising the comfort of their product; suggesting that it was the sensible choice for the intelligent woman.

OBJECT NUMBER – M.2009.03

*Summers, Leigh, *Bound to Please. A History of the Victorian Corset,* (Oxford 2001), pp.174–175.

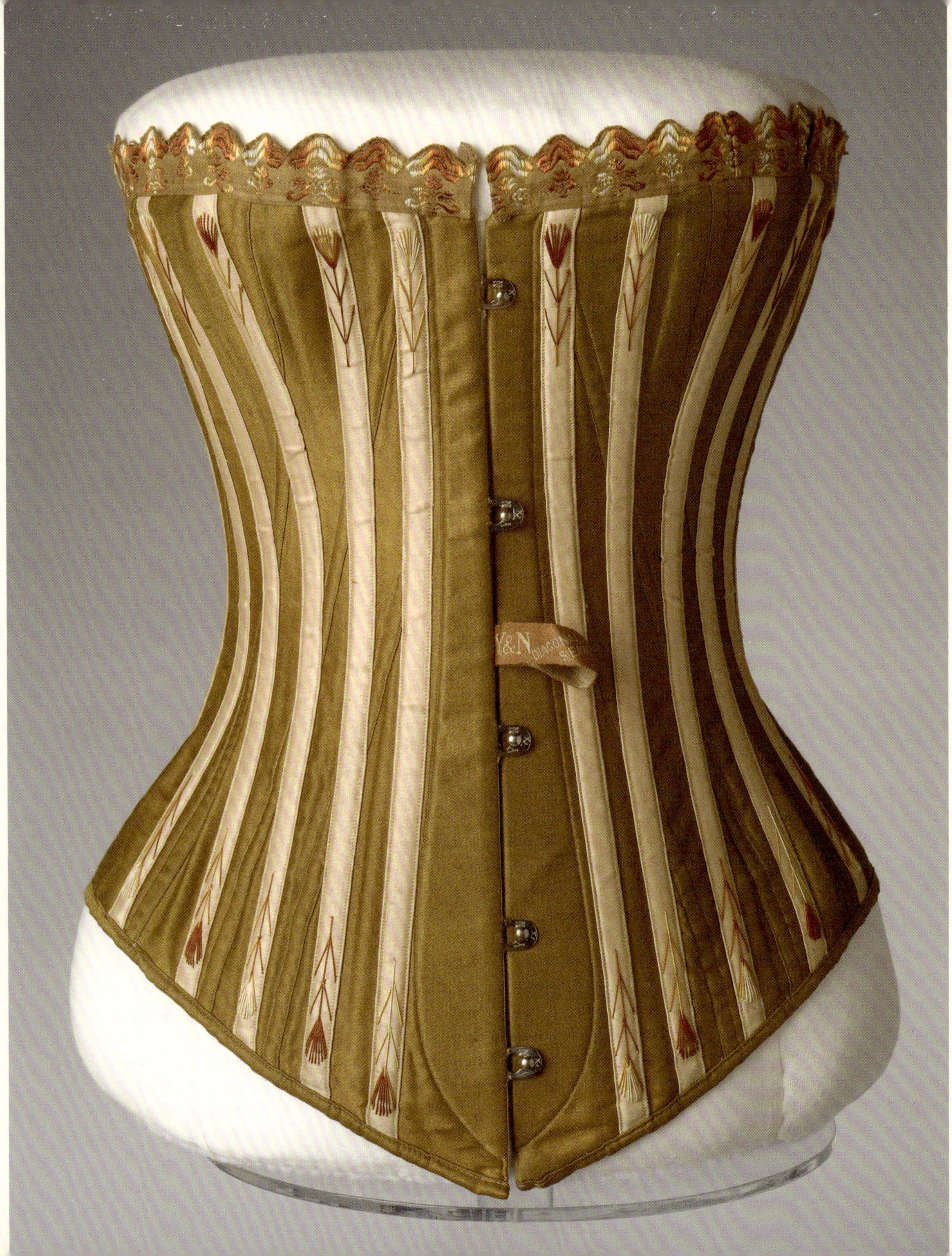
Y&N

Teagown, 1894–1897

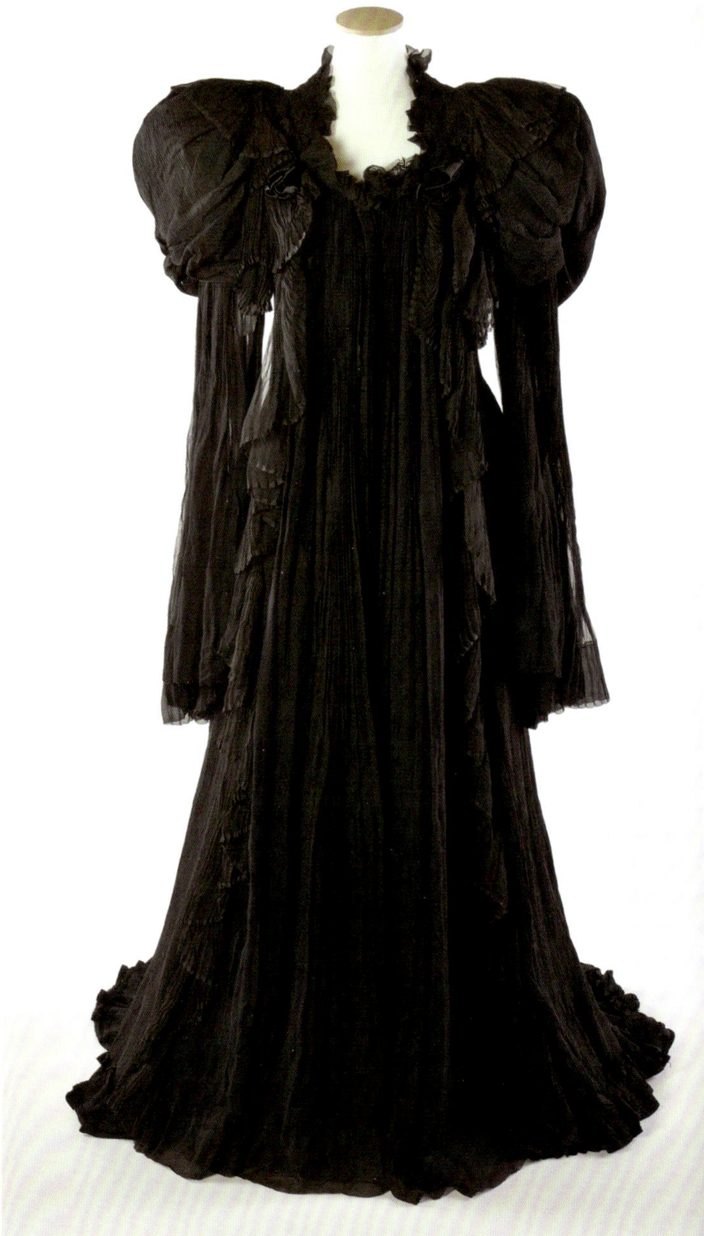

The overall impression given by this striking teagown is one of softness. The narrow pleats of the silk chiffon were achieved by a heat setting process, and the fabric falls in generous swathes from the neckline to the floor. Below the large puffs at the shoulder the chiffon fans out in bell shaped sleeves which are slit from the elbow for a draped and dramatic effect. A generous flounce of pleated chiffon has been added to the edge of a yoke of lace. This extends around the back of the dress and over the puffed sleeves before descending in ripples to the hem at the front. Though the gown is more fitted when seen from behind there is evidence to suggest that this is a later alteration relating to possible theatrical use. The back of the gown would once have continued to descend in an uninterrupted line to the wide train which is decorated with a soft ruffle at the hem. However, the softness and apparent comfort afforded by this gown is belied by the structure of the stiff silk taffeta beneath. The bodice is heavily boned with steels and fits tightly to the waistline, buttoning down the centre front and giving the garment a solid foundation which might have been glimpsed through the semi-transparent layers of chiffon. The underskirt is generously cut and finished with a pinked flounce at the hem, enabling the skirt to kick out at the bottom.

Said to have evolved as a respite from the extreme discomfort of heavy and tightly laced day and evening wear, teagowns became fashionable from around 1877. At first they were quite simple and more akin to dressing gowns, but they became increasingly elaborate during the 1880s. They were intended to be a relaxing garment, generally worn in the late afternoon – a restful period which incorporated tea at around 5 o'clock – but were also seen at informal dinners by the end of the '80s. Initially the fashion was only deemed appropriate for married women as the diaphanous nature of such garments might hold connotations of a loose character for young single women, but this soon changed as the fashion took hold. Though long and flowing and without a waist seam, teagowns did still incorporate features from mainstream

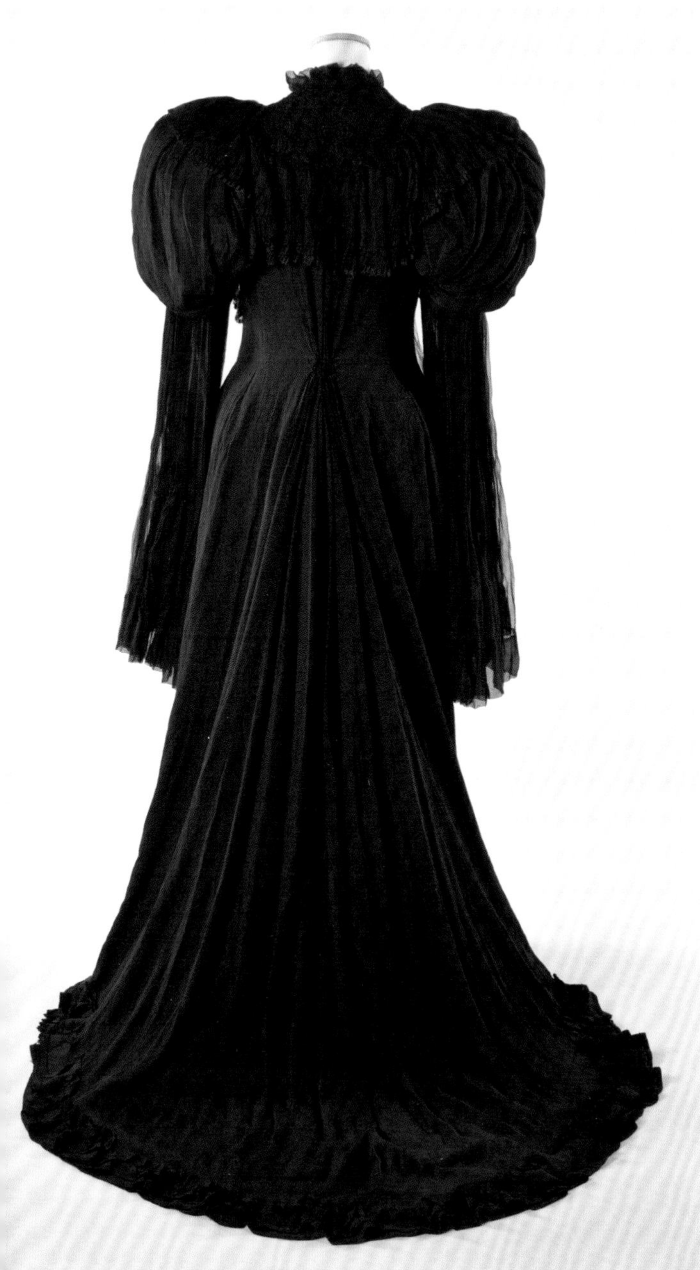

fashion. This example bears the hallmark balloon sleeves of the mid 1890s. The colour too is likely to have been selected for reasons of fashion rather than social etiquette. Despite the strong emphasis on mourning during the nineteenth century, by the 1890s black had also become an acceptable colour for fashionable clothing, especially for evening wear.

Teagowns were part of the endless round of changes of clothing that took place through the wealthy woman's day. Cynthia Asquith recounts how arduous and costly this could be when making visits to country houses during the early 1900s:

> *A large fraction of our time was spent in changing our clothes, particularly in winter when you came down to breakfast ready for church in your 'best dress' made probably of velvet if you could afford it, or velveteen if you couldn't. After church you went into tweeds. You always changed again before tea, into a 'tea-gown' if you possessed that special creation; the less affluent wore a summer day-frock. However small your dress allowance a different dinner dress for each night was considered necessary.**

OBJECT NUMBER – M.1998.49

*Asquith, Cynthia, *Remember and be Glad*, (James Barrie, London, 1952) p.165.

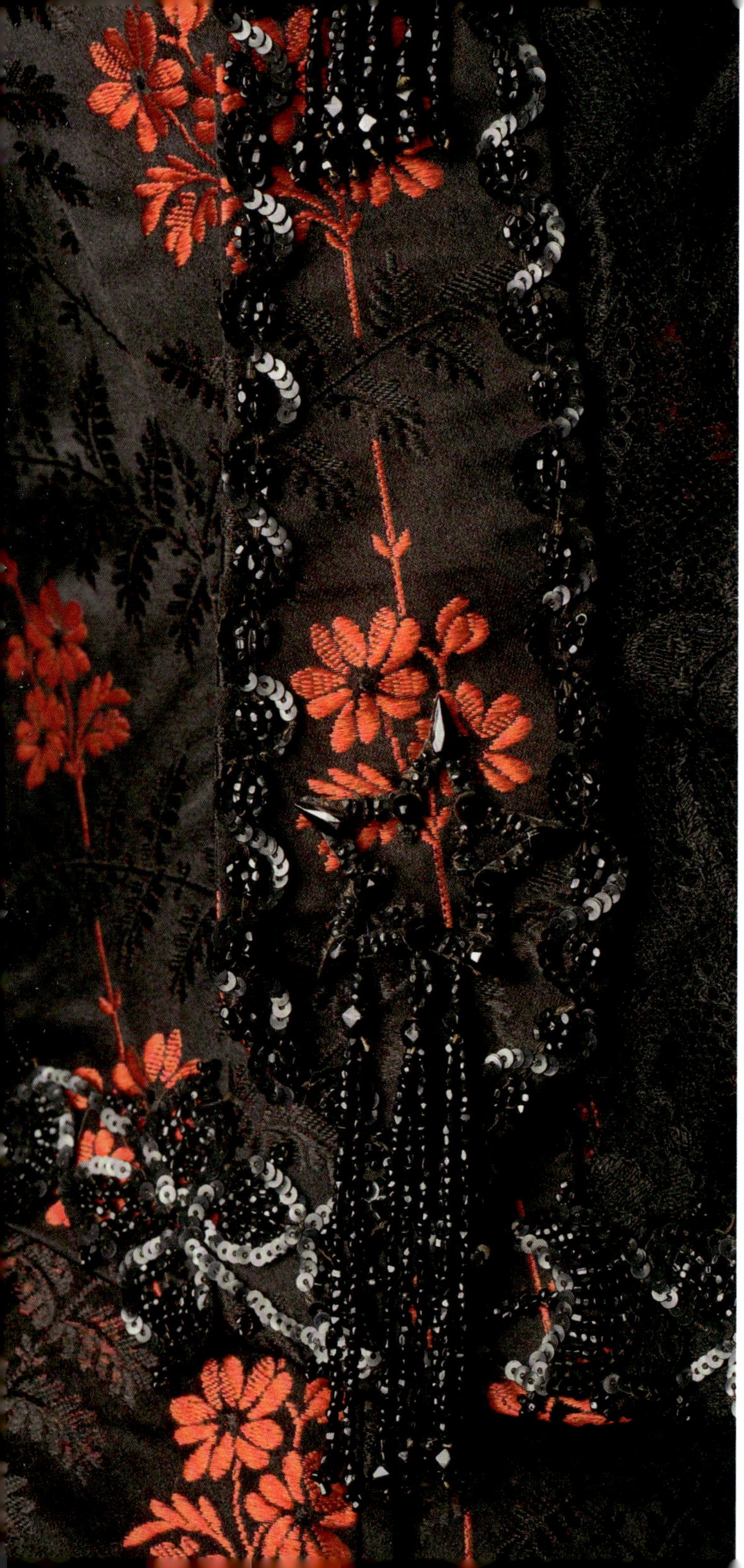

Day dress, 1897–1900

Consisting of a separate bodice and skirt and featuring a considerable variety of decorative devices, this lavish day dress epitomises late Victorian fashion at its elaborate and complex best. It is made from shot silk which has been brocaded in red and black with a flower and fern design. The high-collared bodice features an extra panel of fabric which extends like a small cape over the shoulders. This and much of the rest of the garment is generously trimmed with black glass beads and sequins. The 1890s saw a growing trend for such surface decoration – a fashion which would last well into the 1930s. At this date it was commonly used in evening wear, but was also liberally scattered over day wear. Further surface decoration is present in the shape of pleated black machine made lace, also with a fern motif, which runs down the centre of the bodice on either side of the front opening, giving the pouch effect which would become ubiquitous during the Edwardian era.

The dress is made of expensive materials and with meticulous attention to detail. Every part is finished to a very high standard, and an example of this is the way in which the bodice has been comprehensively boned with whalebone; each piece being carefully finished with shot silk. The boning gives the garment its fashionable shape, and was also designed to protect the fabric from strain; reinforcing the effect of the tightly laced corsets of the day. The gown also contains a maker's label which reads: 'Sheldrake & Tapp, Court Dressmakers, 55 Conduit St. W' – a business which appears in the Post Office Directories between 1895 and 1900. Intended to give an establishment an air of exclusivity, the term 'Court Dressmaker' was ostensibly used only by firms who had made garments for Court presentation. However, the sheer number of such establishments at the time – there are 345 Court Dressmakers listed in the 1895 Post Office Directory for London – suggests that this definition was quite loosely applied. The title also indicated that high quality and generally more expensive clothing was being produced.

OBJECT NUMBER – M.2005.03

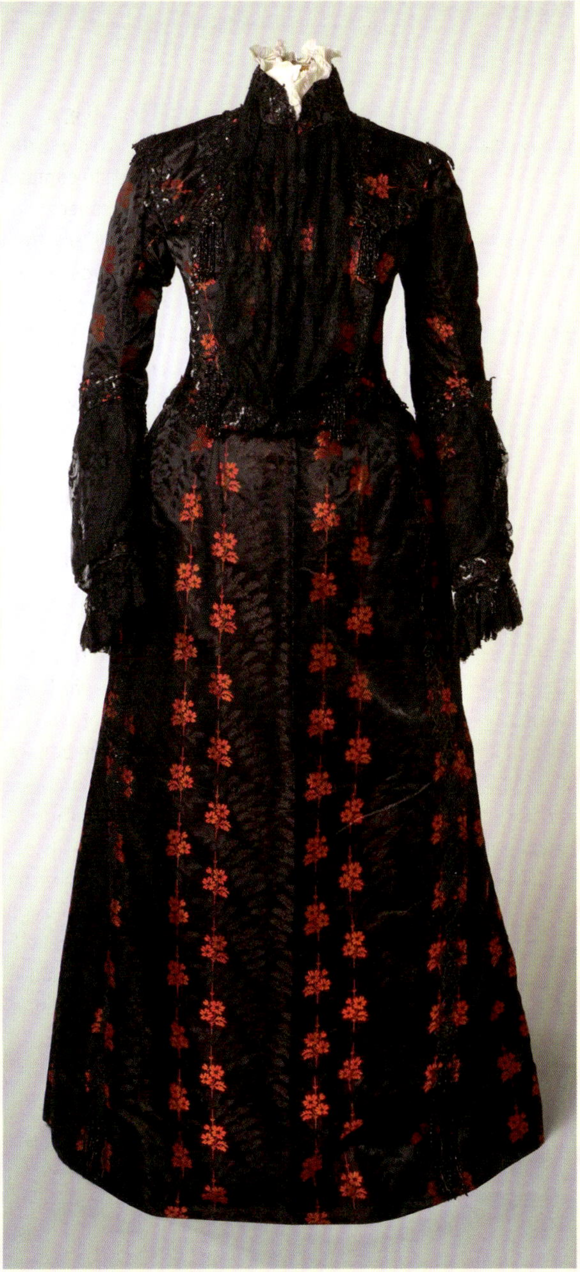
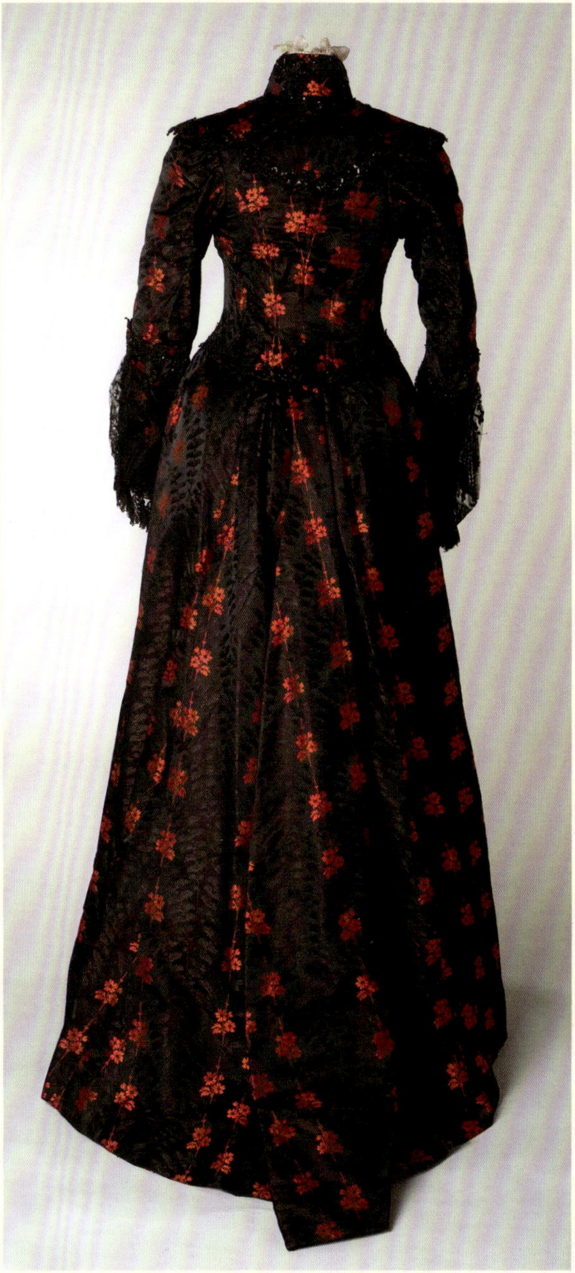

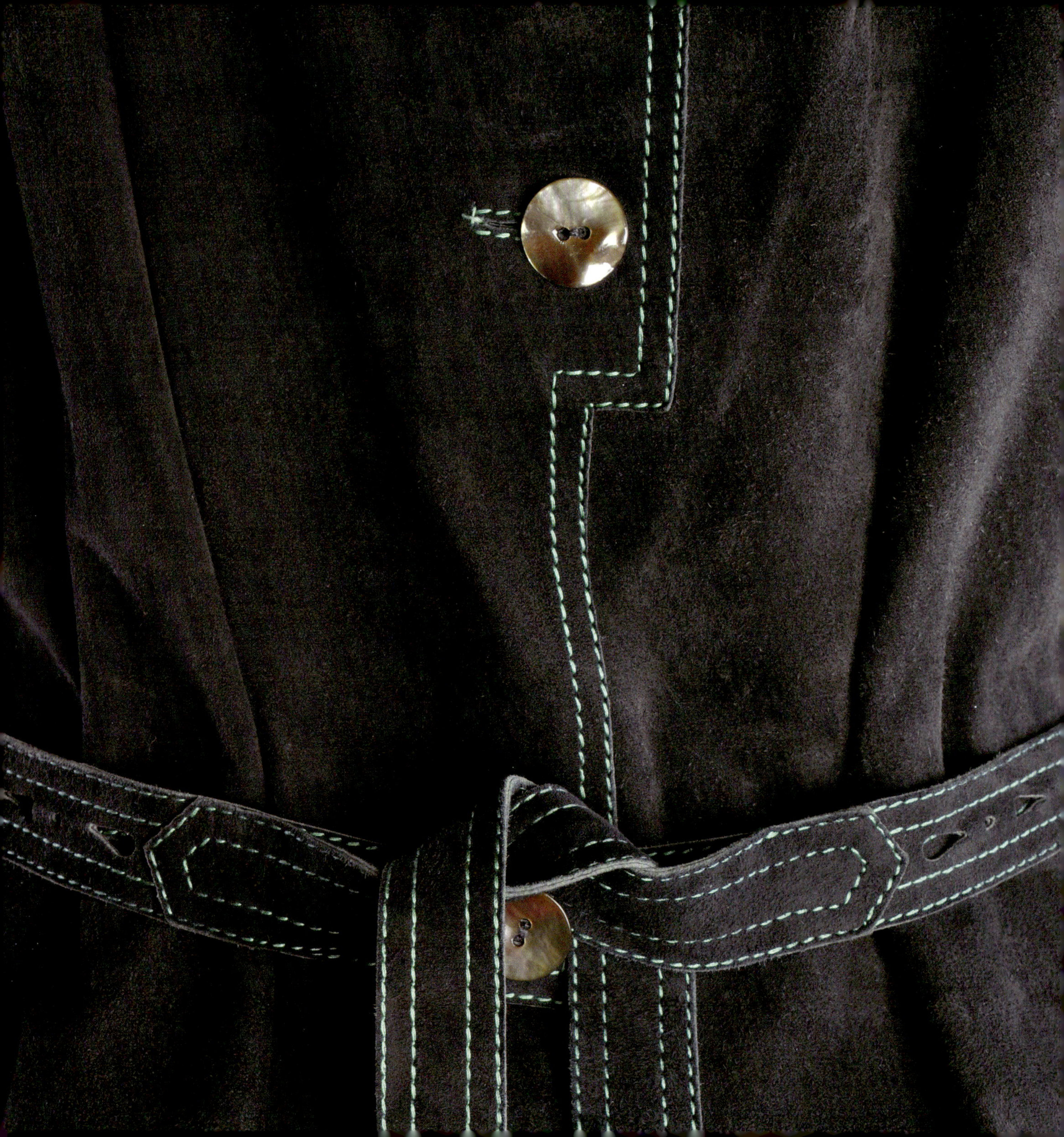

THE TWENTIETH CENTURY

*'I don't believe that fashion evolves on its own. There are more radical social changes behind it . . .it's about the lives we lead'**

People born in the early 1900s were to experience unprecedented changes during their lifetimes. A seemingly established western society was turned upside down by two World Wars and rapidly accelerated technological progress. There were huge implications for social, cultural and economic development, and fashion kept pace with change at every step of the way. There were developments which had particular implications for fashion. The first of these was the extension of women's rights. This had a significant effect on female clothing and, with some notable exceptions, encouraged a move towards more comfortable and practical women's garments – though there was still room for femininity and the occasional flight of fancy. Another important influence on fashion was the growth and efficiency of the manufacturing and retail industries. Breakthroughs in the production of man-made

*Helmut Lang in a 1998 interview, quoted in Steele, Valerie, *Fifty Years of Fashion: New Look to Now* (Yale University Press, New Haven and London, 2000), p.162.

LEFT Detail from a suede Jean Muir dress, 1973–1975 (see pages 136–137).

fibres and the advent of mass production meant that more people than ever before could afford to be fashionable. Style trends were no longer dictated by a privileged few. Instead they were progressively influenced by popular cultural forces such as music, film and celebrity.

The following chapter seeks to reflect the changes in style associated with this rapidly changing world. It incorporates key examples of high fashion from the period and, at a time when the importance of designers was growing, includes a number of labelled pieces, both well-known and less familiar. As mentioned previously, Olive Matthews was not an active collector of items dating later than the mid-nineteenth century. All of the garments discussed in this chapter have therefore entered the collection since her death. They consist either of donations or selective purchases made over the last thirty years. The twentieth century is a period of such dramatic contrasts and radical innovations in fashion that it could not be ignored by a collection which aims to educate and inspire fashion students and visitors alike. However, the tastes and passions of Miss Matthews have not been forgotten. Instead new additions remain in keeping with the collection as a whole. Successive curators have actively paid heed to Olive Matthews' love of intricate surface decoration and her preference for high quality examples of key fashion trends.

RIGHT Detail from a satin evening gown by Madame Clapham, 1901–1902 (see pages 112–113).

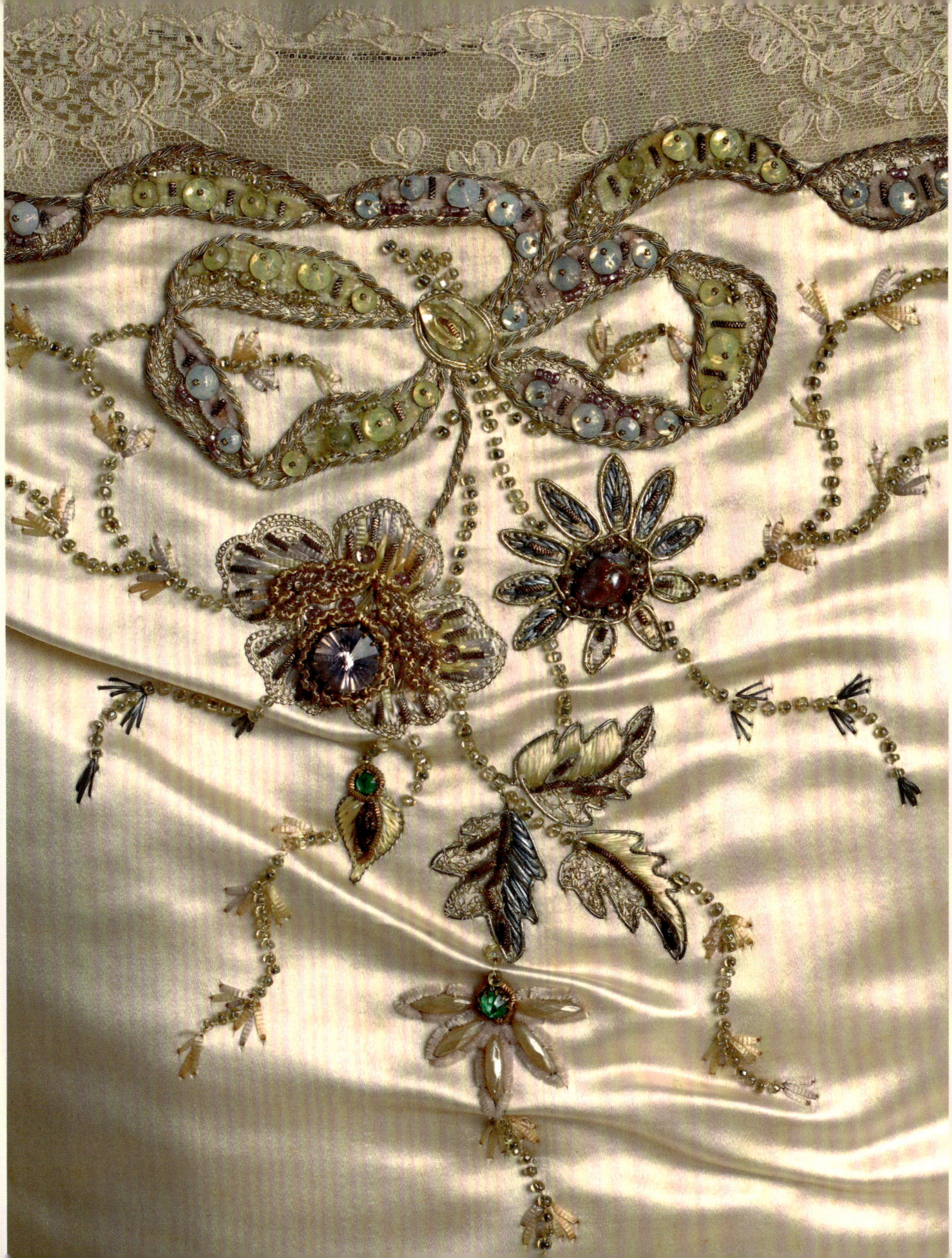

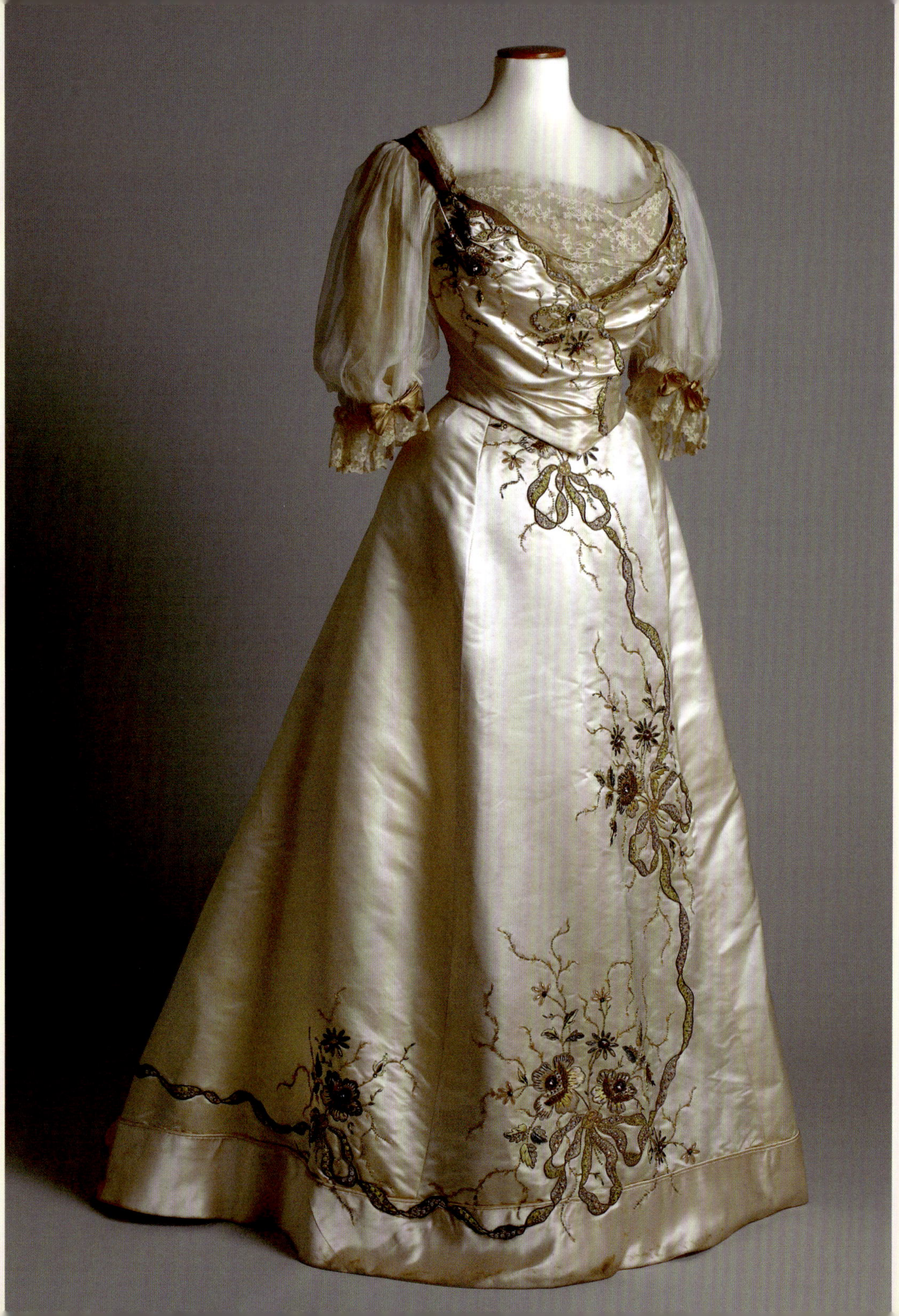

Evening gown, 1901–1902

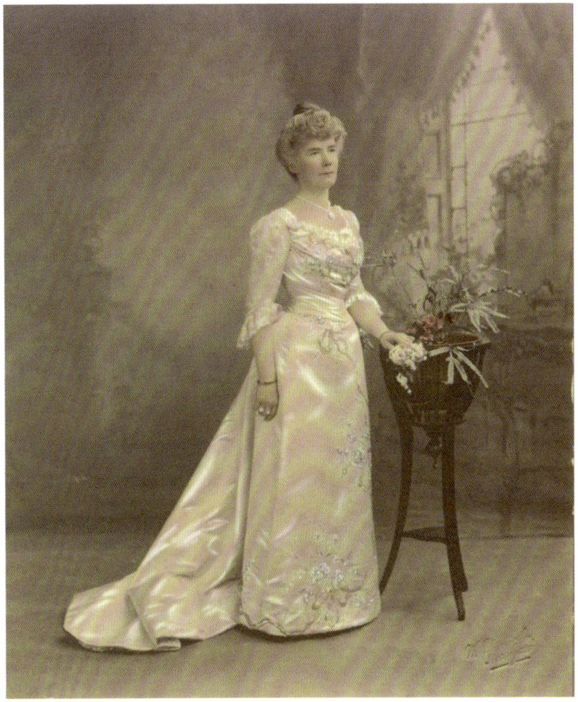

An evening dress of cream 'duchesse' silk satin trimmed with lace and chiffon. It is hand embroidered with silks, couched metallic thread, glass beads and paste stones. The thick pale coloured satin, elaborate hand embroidery and train are typical of the best quality dresses of the early Edwardian period, and a label indicates that the dress was made by Madame Clapham (1856–1952). This enterprising and fashionable Hull Court Dressmaker ran a very successful business making garments for wealthy clients, both in the North East of England and further afield. The fashion house opened in 1887, and by the 1890s she had built up a very good reputation. Madame Clapham was skilled at taking elements from the latest Paris fashions by haute couture houses such as Worth, Doucet or Paquin and merging them to create her own unique designs. She successfully courted a select clientele, and her creations were popular with society hostesses, even in fashionable London. She could boast that her client list included royalty since her most prestigious customer was Queen Maud of Norway. Madame Clapham's heyday lasted until the outbreak of the First World War in 1914 and it is not surprising that her house excelled at this time of unprecedented luxury in dress.

Garments of this sort are extremely labour intensive to make. At the height of her popularity, Madame Clapham employed approximately 150 skilled female seamstresses and cutters. The workforce was divided into separate workrooms, each being associated with a different element of the production process. The employees in each workroom were strictly supervised by a fitter who would maintain quality control and enforce swift production. Apprentices were taken from the local area, and trained in-house. They worked long hours for low pay with very few breaks and were also required to take on frequent periods of unpaid overtime. The sparse conditions of the workrooms contrasted significantly with the luxury of the salon where clients would come to view examples of gowns and attend the numerous fittings that would be required for each commission.

We are extremely lucky to have a photograph of this dress being worn by its original owner. Though the sleeves have since been altered and the skirt lengthened, the gown remains essentially the same. The photo is inscribed 'Alice Kettlewell, Beechwood, Driffield, East Riding', and research has uncovered that Alice was born in Leeds in 1854. Being a wealthy member of Yorkshire society, she fits perfectly into the mould of the typical Madame Clapham client. Alice married Alfred Kettlewell, a Corn Merchant, in 1882 when she was around 28 years old and they had two children, Sidney and Alice. The 1901 census states that Alfred was retired at the age of 47, suggesting that he was comfortable enough not to work, and Beechwood is indeed a large house which still stands today.

OBJECT NUMBER – M.1997.14

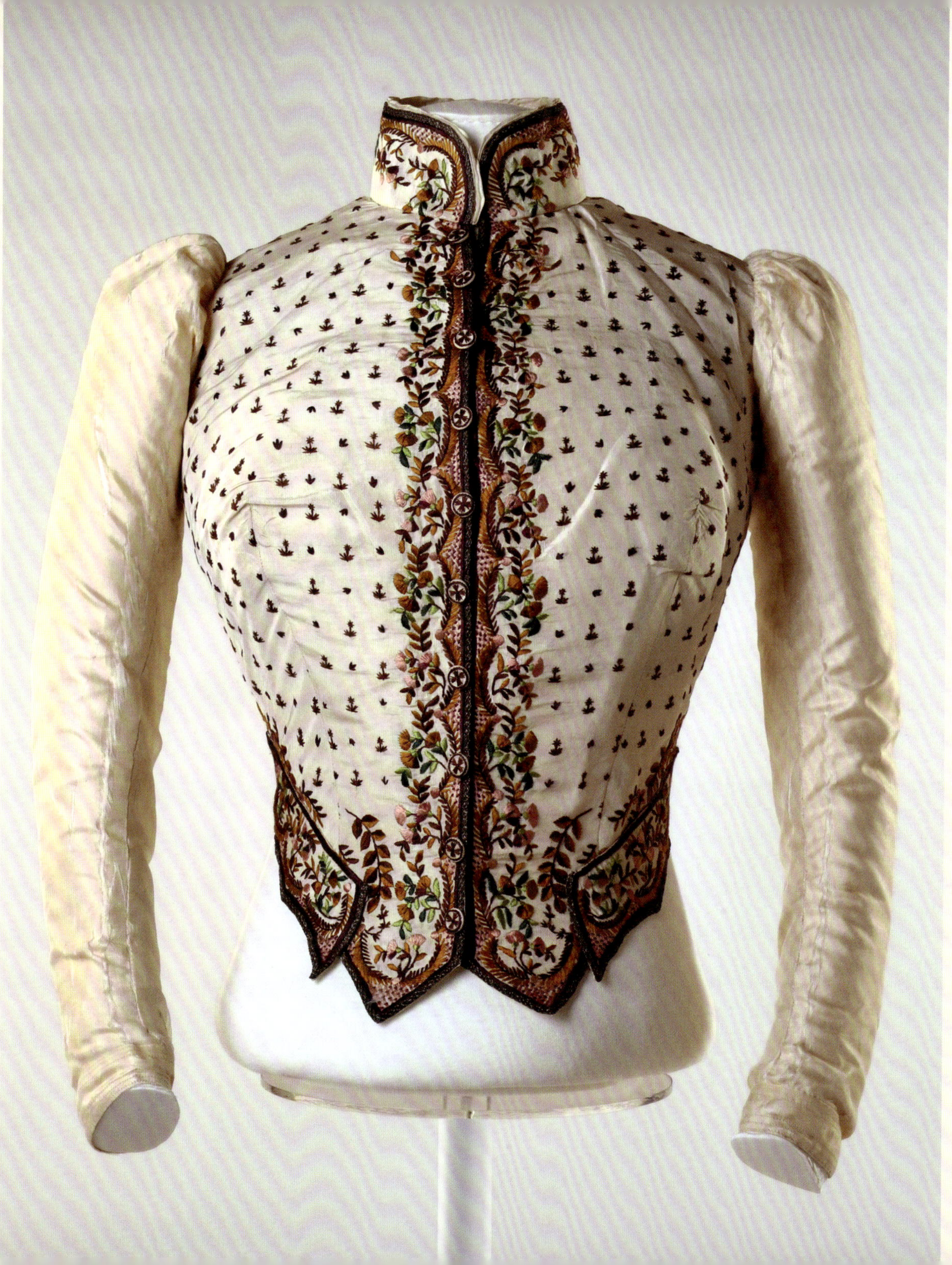

Woman's bodice, 1900–1910

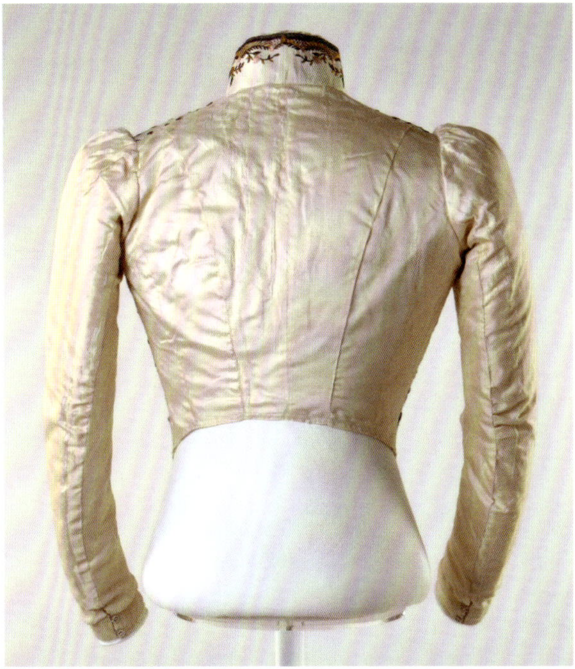

A man's evening court waistcoat from the 1840s has been re-used very creatively by the couturier Jacques Doucet (1853–1929) to make this attractive and flattering Edwardian woman's bodice. Boned shaping darts have been incorporated so that the bodice fits the curves of the female form, and parts of the bottom edges of the waistcoat have been removed and re-used to create the stand-up collar. The original silver braid edging and embroidered buttons remain, but the bodice fastens with hooks and eyes. Silk sleeves have been added and the pocket flaps moved to a slanting angle for added decoration. The back of the waistcoat has also been replaced with cream silk which matches that of the sleeves. The bodice is labelled 'Doucet Paris', and the style of the label helps date the garment as the design was only used from 1900.

The couturier Jacques Doucet's love of historic dress greatly influenced his work at Maison Doucet and he was an avid collector of eighteenth century artefacts until around 1912. As a founder of France's *Société de L'Histoire du Costume* (Society of Historical Costume), he donated a number of eighteenth century garments to the organisation. Although it dates from the nineteenth century, this waistcoat in its original form would have resembled an eighteenth century one and might have appealed to a wearer who enjoyed the quirky and historic. The recycling of antique textiles was quite common during the nineteenth and early twentieth century since the high quality of the fabrics and hand worked decoration was greatly valued during a time of increasing mechanisation. Indeed the quality of the older fabric of the waistcoat is in stark contrast to that of the more modern sleeves and back. These have deteriorated considerably due to the finishing process used on the silks of the time, whereas the silk of the waistcoat is almost pristine.

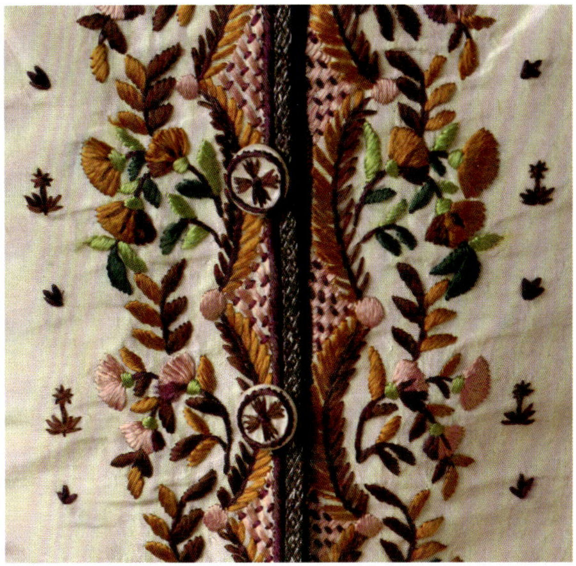

OBJECT NUMBER – MT.2115

Parasol, 1901–1910

Incorporating pale colours and soft, feminine fabrics, this parasol is typical of fashionable accessories from the Edwardian era and complemented clothing of a similar light style. It is trimmed with cream silk and a replacement cream silk satin ribbon, and lined with cotton lace. The wooden stick is surmounted by a ceramic handle, hand painted with flowers, and covered in an opalescent glaze.

The cover is warp printed with a delicate floral design, which is again in keeping with the soft, delicate fashions of the period. The blurred effect of warp printing was called chiné at the time. It was achieved by printing the pattern only on the warp or vertical threads of the fabric before weaving.

Parasols were regarded as important accessories from the late eighteenth century until the early twentieth, and fashion and technical innovation meant that they varied enormously over that period, both in size and materials. The large Edwardian examples are particularly attractive, but from this time onwards they would slowly disappear from mainstream fashion. Parasols went hand-in-hand with the preference for pale skin. In the 1920s the suntan took on a whole new significance as it began to be associated with wealth and the ability to afford a holiday abroad. Pale skin was no longer a status symbol, and before long parasols had all but disappeared from general usage.

OBJECT NUMBER – M.2000.11

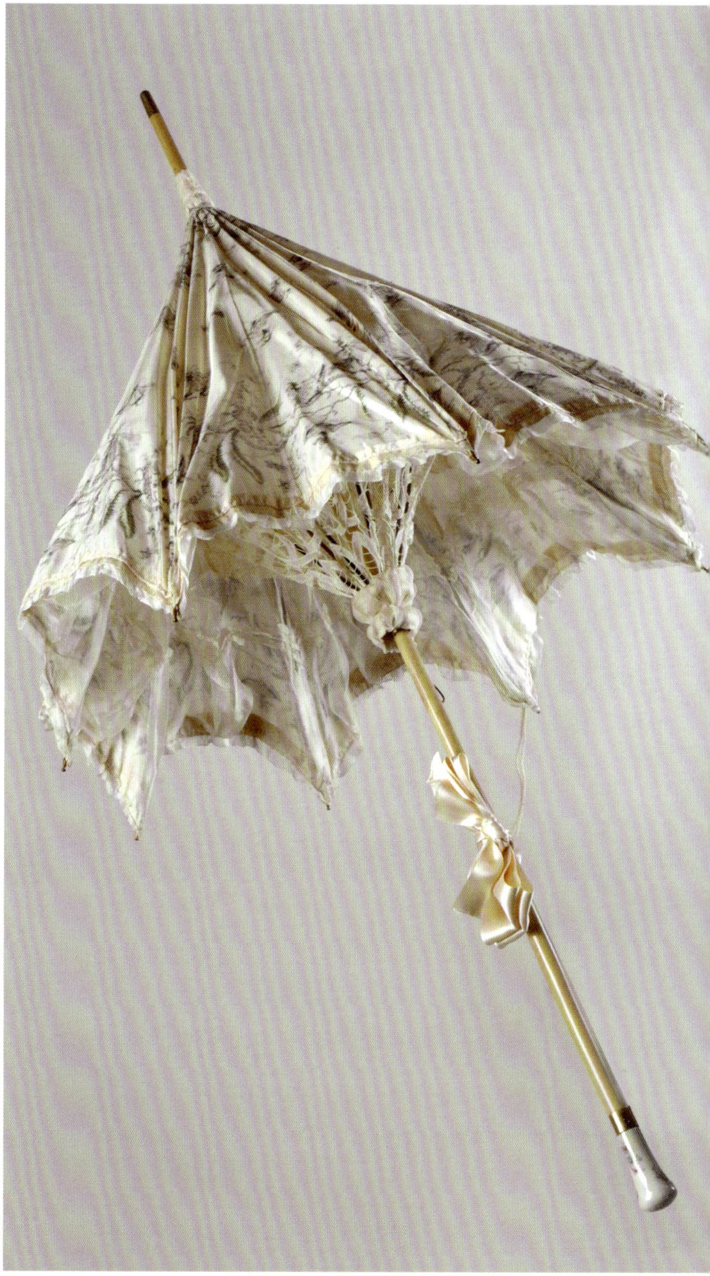

Woman's hat, 1909–1911

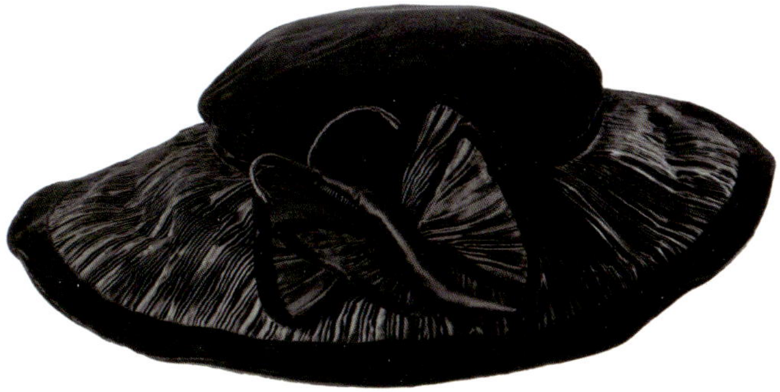

The exaggerated proportions of this elegant and wittily styled hat are typical of millinery fashions of the late Edwardian period. It is made from straw and the soft crown is covered with black silk velvet. The brim has been decorated with pleated black silk satin in a style which resembles the gills of a mushroom. The brim also features a bold wired butterfly, and the underside of the hat is trimmed with white lace. A label inside the crown identifies the hat as having been produced and sold by Harrods, the London department store.

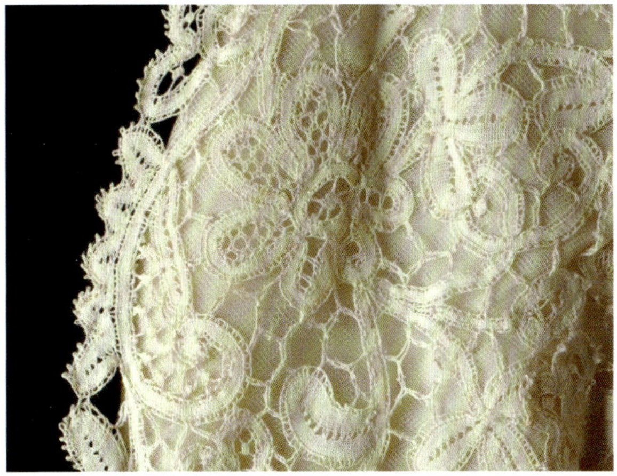

Though hats of fairly large proportions had been fashionable since the very early years of the twentieth century, the craze for extremely large and heavily trimmed hats is said to have begun around 1908. They were often called 'Merry Widow' hats, in reference to those worn by Lily Elsie in the first London production of Léhar's operetta of the same name. Hairstyles were designed to follow suit, and sections of false hair (sometimes called rats), dressed over large pads, gave width under the hat helping to secure it in place, and balanced the proportions in relation to the face. The burgeoning fashion for the hobble skirt from around 1910, which narrowed significantly towards the ankles, served to emphasise hat width even more.

OBJECT NUMBER – M.2006.06

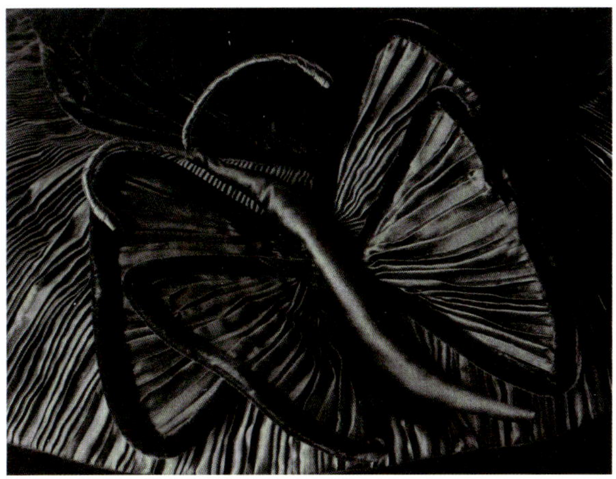

Opera coat, 1910–1912

Attributed to Paul Poiret (1879–1944), this opera coat is a striking example of the new and exciting garments that revolutionised fashion during the early twentieth century. It is made from black silk satin with a silk net insert at calf level. The generous shawl collar incorporates a large piece of chemical lace, and this and much of the rest of the garment is embellished with multi coloured silk embroidery stitched and woven into abstract patterns. The back of the collar is finished with a generous black silk tassel, while three large silk-covered wooden buttons are attached at hip level where the coat fastens. Two different styles of fastening are possible so that the coat can either be closed at the centre front or draped asymmetrically to fasten at the left hip.

Poiret is the designer credited with radically altering female fashion during the pre-First World War period. Having started his career designing for the exclusive couture houses of Doucet and Worth, Poiret opened his own Paris fashion house in 1903. Adept at gaining publicity and aligning himself with talented artists and illustrators, he drew upon a wide range of exotic and eclectic influences to create truly original, modern and challenging garments that chimed perfectly with the mood of the times. Looking back to the neo-classical French 'Directoire' period (c.1795–1799), he raised waistlines and dispensed with the need for cumbersome corsets and petticoats. He also drew from a myriad of other sources, making use of a bold colour palette and lavish decoration drawn from Middle and Far Eastern design as well as regional dress. Fashionable society became increasingly open to his approach, and this was partly due to the success of Serge Diaghilev's Ballets Russes. The lavish sets and costumes designed by Léon Bakst for productions such as *Schéhérazade* in 1910 captured the public imagination and caused a craze for all things oriental, which quickly crossed over into mainstream fashion. Poiret always paid a great deal of attention to marketing. He produced mouth-watering albums featuring the beautiful illustrations of Paul Iribe, Georges Lepape and Erté, while expansion into interior design and perfume production put him well ahead of his time.

The piece shown here incorporates many key aspects of Poiret's signature design style. He produced many elegant evening coats, and the wide sleeves and soft draping nature of this piece, as it wraps luxuriously around the body in the style of a Japanese kimono, are typical of his novel approach. The large tassel and lavish embroidery add to the exotic feel of the coat. The embroidery is inspired by the abstract patterns found in Middle Eastern architecture, and the oversized buttons lend further bold and quirky character to the piece. Another important element of the coat is its lining – a shot silk chiffon of green and blue which shines through the embroidered net. Poiret lined a number of his garments with green or turquoise silks, adding further richness and drama as the fabric is glimpsed when the wearer moves.

OBJECT NUMBER – M.2006.09

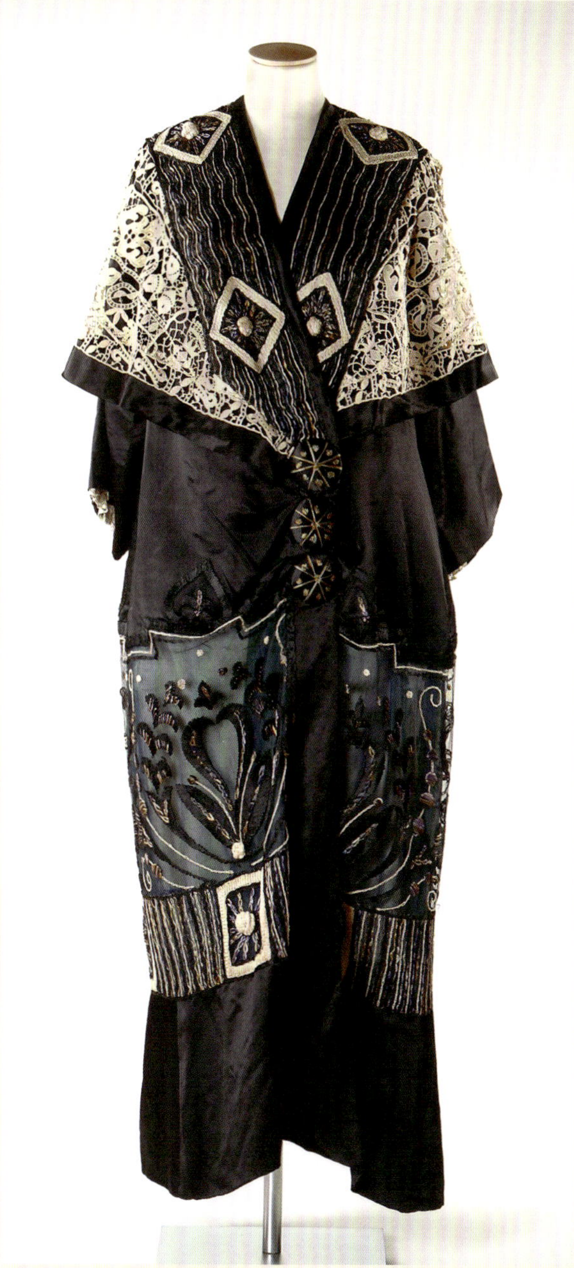

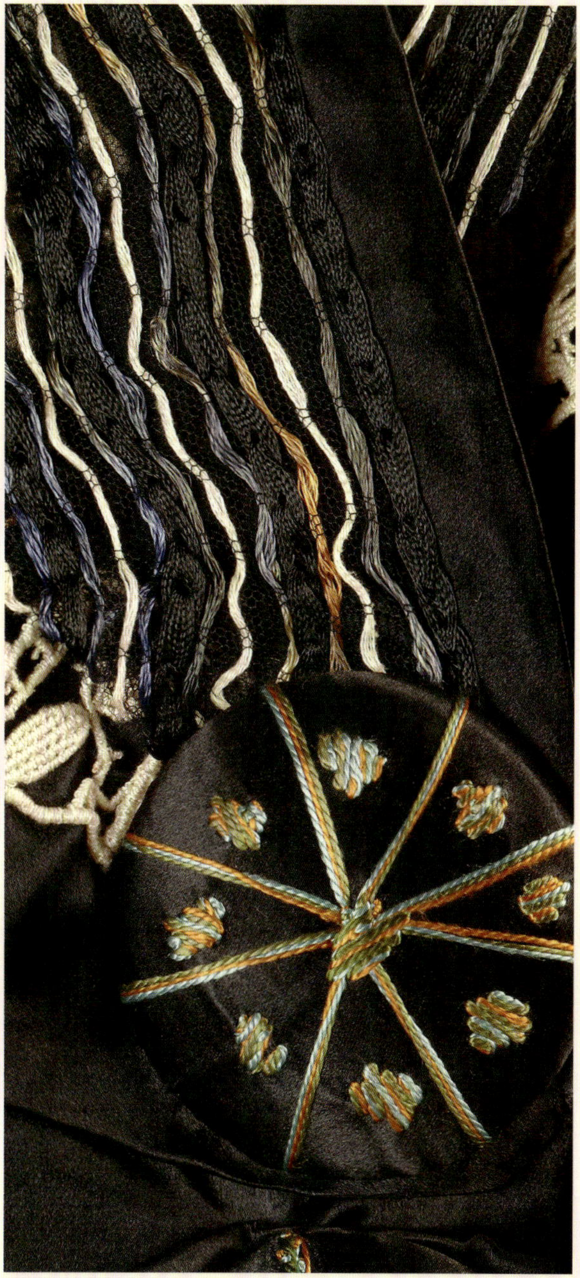

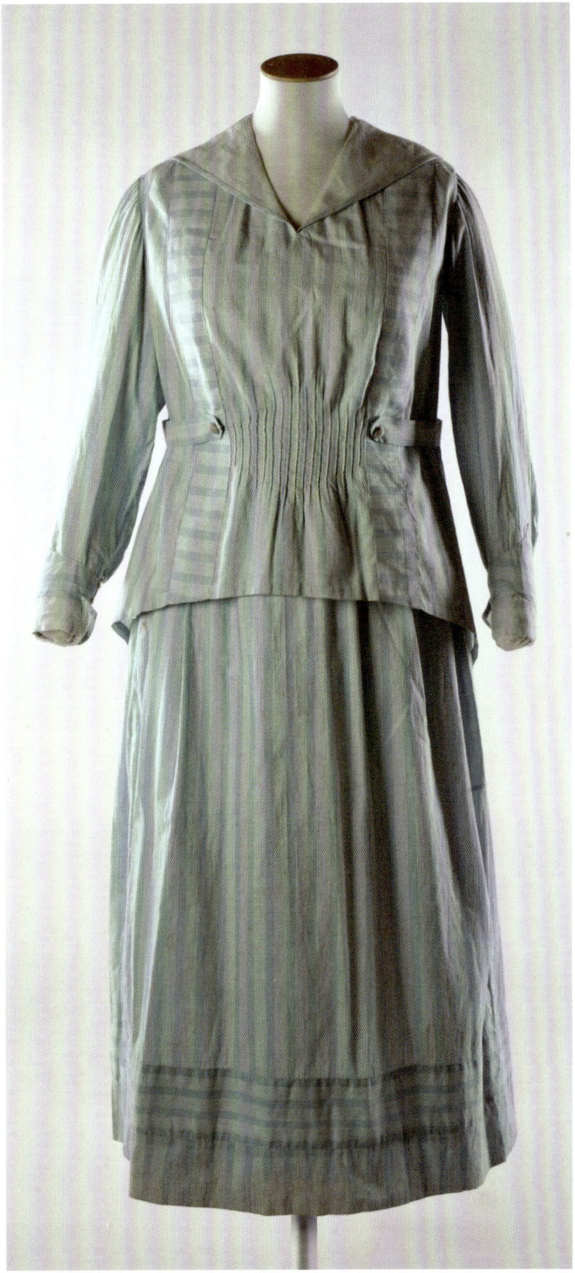

Seaside walking dress, 1916–1920

Made from a medium weight blue and white striped cotton with a white muslin sailor collar, this attractive nautical style summer dress is cleverly put together to make a comfortable yet stylish garment, ideal for a summer's day by the sea.

Despite its simple appearance the dress is carefully constructed along quite complicated lines. The fastening system is particularly complex – a common feature of garments dating from the first 20 years of the twentieth century. It is made up of two separate pieces; a dress with sleeves and a loose over-tunic. The bodice of the dress is close-fitting with hooks and eyes fastening down a centre panel of white cotton and along an overlap at waist level. Side panels of the striped cotton have been added, and the one-piece sleeves are generously cut, being gathered into the shoulders and the pointed turned-back cuffs. The V-necked tunic fastens down the left side and over the left shoulder with hooks and eyes. Vertical tucks provide simple decoration and shape, while further decorative features include bands of appliquéd cotton turned so that the stripes run horizontally. This device is also used to add interest to the skirt, which falls to mid-calf level in keeping with the new shorter hemlines which had begun to rise around 1915. Half belts with buttons give further structure and the hem of the tunic curves gently down to lead-weighted points at the sides, echoing the points at the cuffs. The fashion for layering clothing with over-tunics had begun around 1911. It softened the line and foreshadowed the loose drop-waisted styles which are associated with the 1920s.

A label on the inside waistband reads 'Madame Campbell, Court Dressmaker, Bournemouth', with the royal coat of arms. The label, attention to detail and high level of workmanship clearly indicate that this garment was produced by a maker of good quality, and her business establishment at 19 Old Christchurch Road, Bournemouth is listed as early as 1898 in Kelly's Directory. Madame Campbell's coastal town location may have meant that she specialised in holiday wear and was familiar with the practical issues associated with seaside fashions, such as the need to include lead weights to prevent the tunic from blowing about in the sea breezes.

Although clothing worn at the seaside during the nineteenth and early twentieth centuries can definitely be linked to mainstream trends, it is possible to identify this form of dress as a separate branch of fashion. Garments tended to be made from cotton for comfort and keeping cool as well as ease of care, and from the mid-nineteenth century simple, gaily coloured patterns were common; particularly stripes. Further modifications such as shorter skirts for ease of walking, or nautical elements, can also be found. The sailor suit, associated with children's wear since the 1840s, is clearly referenced in this piece. This links it to the sea, but also lends it a fun, light-hearted and carefree air which is very much in keeping with the holiday spirit.

OBJECT NUMBER – M.1995.22

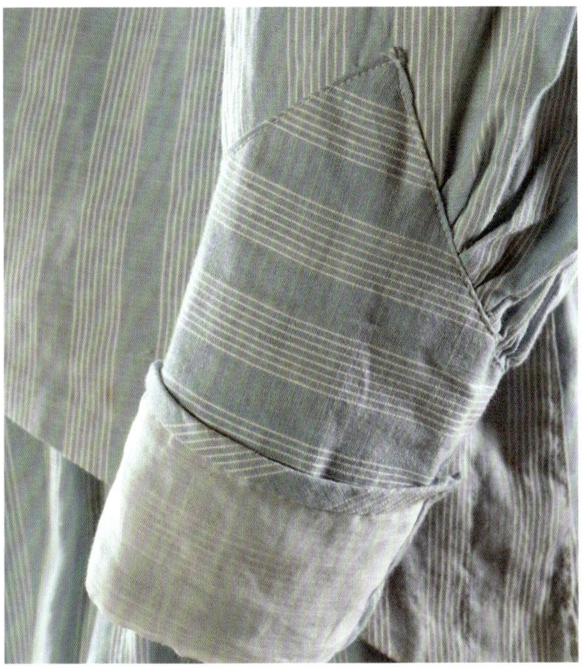

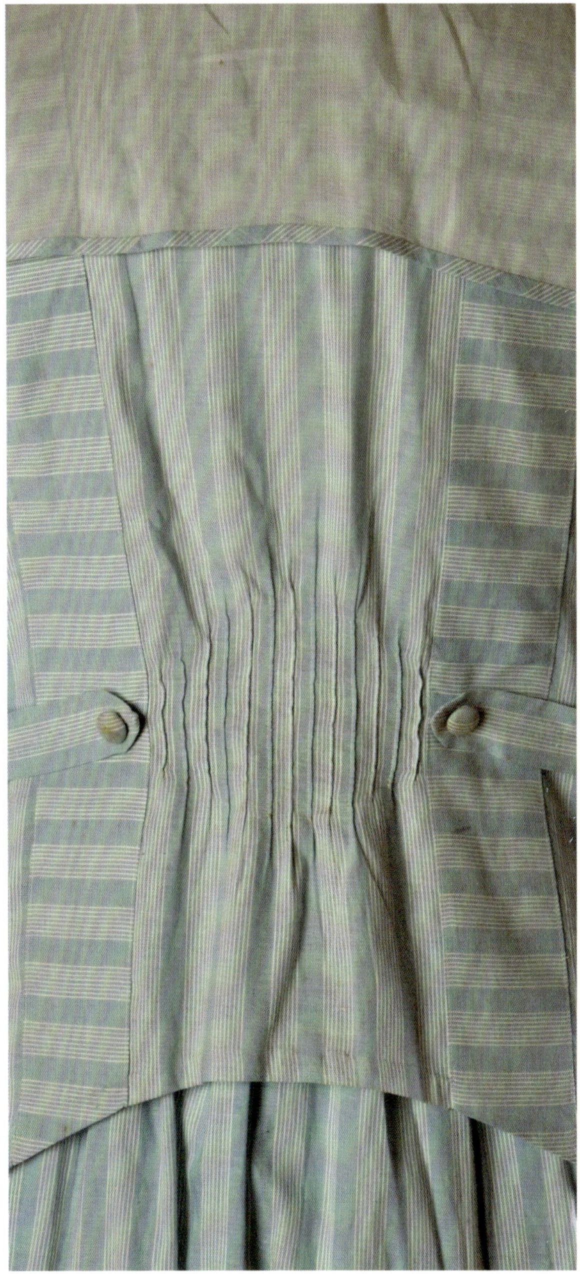

Evening dress, 1924–1926

Made from cream coloured silk georgette, this heavily beaded evening dress is cut in the straight, tubular line of the mid-1920s. The front of the skirt features three graduated flying panels, the shapes of which are emphasised by coloured strips of glass bead embroidery and white silk chain stitch. A cream georgette under-dress is worn beneath for modesty. This has a narrow border of white silk chain stitch and white beading at the hem. The dress bears the label of Premet, which was located at 8 Place Vendome, Paris. The fashion house existed from 1911 to 1931, and was where influential fashion designer Madame Grès (1903–1993) trained from 1930.

The straight, boyish lines prevalent during the mid 1920s owed much to the social and cultural attitudes of the time. The female silhouette celebrated the adolescent or even childlike body, and this was partly a response to the terrible loss of young life during the First World War. During the post-war period youth was celebrated above all things, and this is directly reflected in the style of clothing we see here. Other factors which influenced dress were changing attitudes towards women. During wartime many women had taken on traditionally male roles in the workplace, giving them the freedom of an independent wage and a different approach to the world outside the domestic sphere. Women's clothing became more suitable for this altered position in society, with a new emphasis on practicality, comfort and freedom of movement.

This dress has obviously been designed for dancing. The new dance crazes of the jazz age went hand in hand with garments designed to move seductively and glitter on the dance floor. The flying panels seen here would have undulated as the wearer shimmied; the beadwork catching the light with every move. The overall effect would have been stunning, and the weight of the beads meant that the dress hung well on the body; skimming the hips and bust.

The 1920s was very much part of the *Art Deco* period. The decade saw the flowering of new and innovative fashions in design of all kinds. Youthful exuberance and progress in transport and communications triggered an explosion of interest in the new, the exotic, and the glamorous. Designers greedily plundered ideas from ancient and modern art, as well as the cultures of the Far East and Africa. The result was an eclectic mix of decorative styles that evoked rather than replicated authentic originals. In clothing this manifested itself in strong design motifs, striking colour combinations and unusual mixtures of materials and textures. Emphasis was on surface decoration, and the flat, tubular line of fashionable dress was the perfect canvas for this new style. In keeping with the prevailing fashion for the exotic, the beadwork seen on this piece, which features peony flowers, storks, boxes and vases, is likely to have been inspired by Chinese decorative art.

OBJECT NUMBER – MT.1411

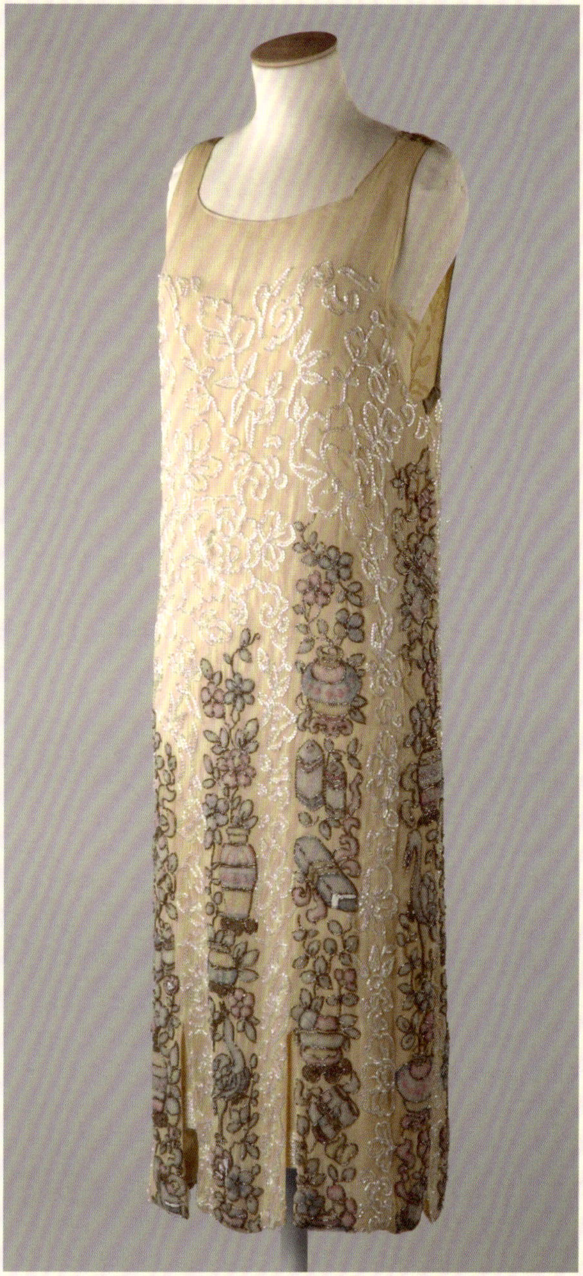

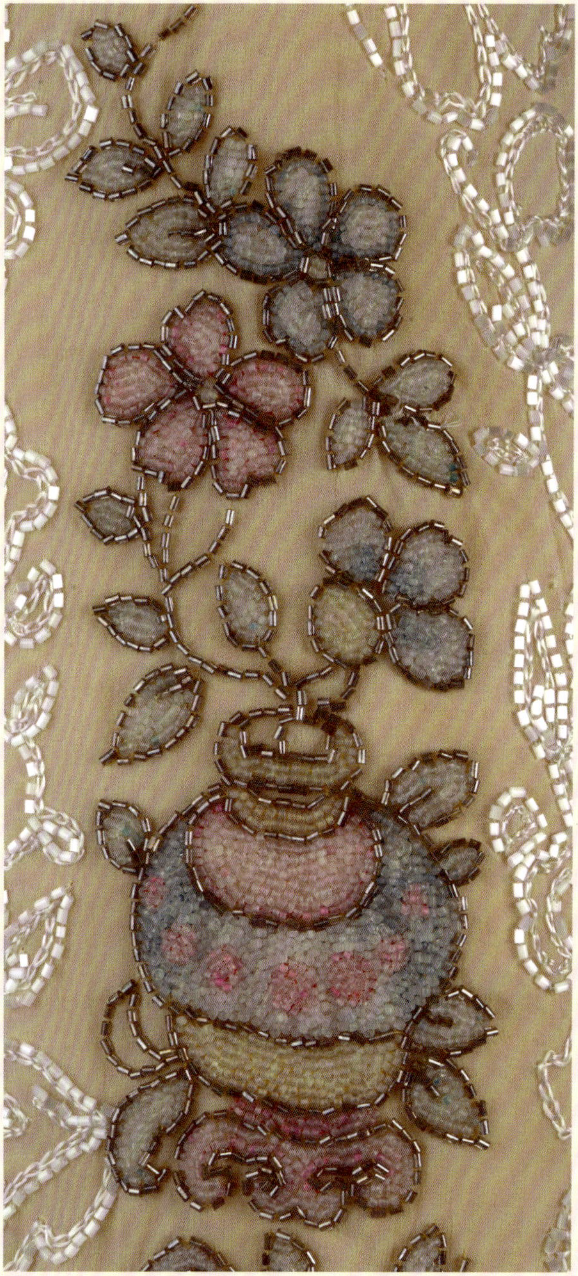

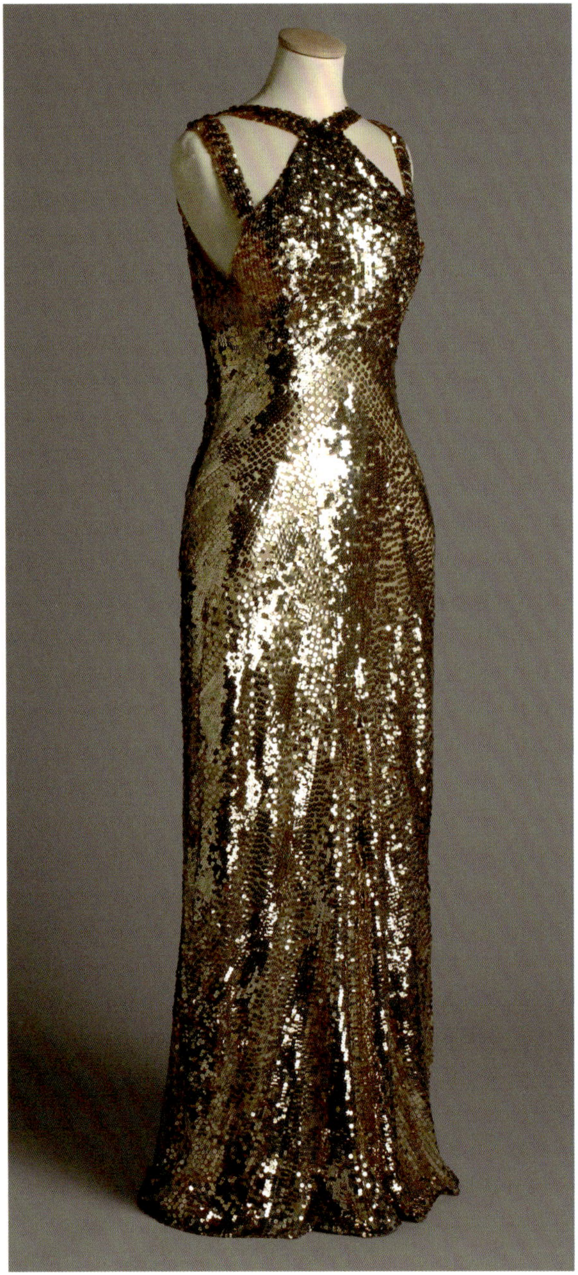

Evening dress, 1934–1935

Designed to dazzle onlookers, this glittering 1930s evening gown epitomises the glamour of the era. The effect is achieved by couching lengths of gold sequins on to a base of cream net. These change direction according to their position on the body, forming a subtle chevron pattern which flatters the figure and draws the eye upwards. Cut to emphasise fashion's new erogenous zones, this dress reveals much of the back and shoulders. It clings seductively to below hip level, and then falls in folds to the floor. A gold coloured silk under-dress is worn beneath.

The 1930s saw an emphatic reassertion of feminine curves in fashion. As early as 1928, the natural waistline had begun to return. Many fashion designers championed this trend, partly because such clothes were more difficult to construct than the simple, straight styles of the previous decade. They felt that more complicated construction might stem the rapid loss of exclusivity they had suffered through rampant copying and mass production. The need to set high-level fashion apart from the mainstream was particularly important following the catastrophic Wall Street Crash of 1929. The subsequent economic depression meant that many fashion houses were struggling and had to fight ever harder to carve out a niche in the marketplace.

This glittering evening gown with its sexy figure-skimming style was inspired by the costumes of glamorous film stars. Cinema was a very important factor in the creation and spread of fashion during the 1920s and '30s. This was the golden age of the film and cinemas sprang up in virtually every town and city. Young people, especially young women, were a key audience, particularly for glamorous Hollywood films, and many would attend several times a week. This phenomenon had several key influences on fashion. As a form of mass communication it had the capability to disseminate trends to the widest possible audience. Suddenly fashions were not shown as static images in magazines, but seen in motion and worn by the most glamorous people imaginable – film stars. No doubt the popularity of such fashions was also boosted by the luxury, wealth and style associated with Hollywood as it provided escapism from the everyday world.

During the 1920s Hollywood drew on the talents of European couturiers including Erté (1892–1990) and Chanel (1883–1971). Later the American film industry tended to use home-grown talent with designers such as Travis Banton (1894–1958) and Gilbert Adrian (1903–1959) creating pieces for stars such as Marlene Dietrich, Carole Lombard and Joan Crawford to wear both on and off screen. Their designs both popularised existing trends and initiated new ones. One of the most important innovations was the use of shiny or glittering fabrics. In a black and white film context these were the most effective visually but, as exemplified by this piece, they were quickly assimilated into mainstream fashion.

OBJECT NUMBER – M.2004.22

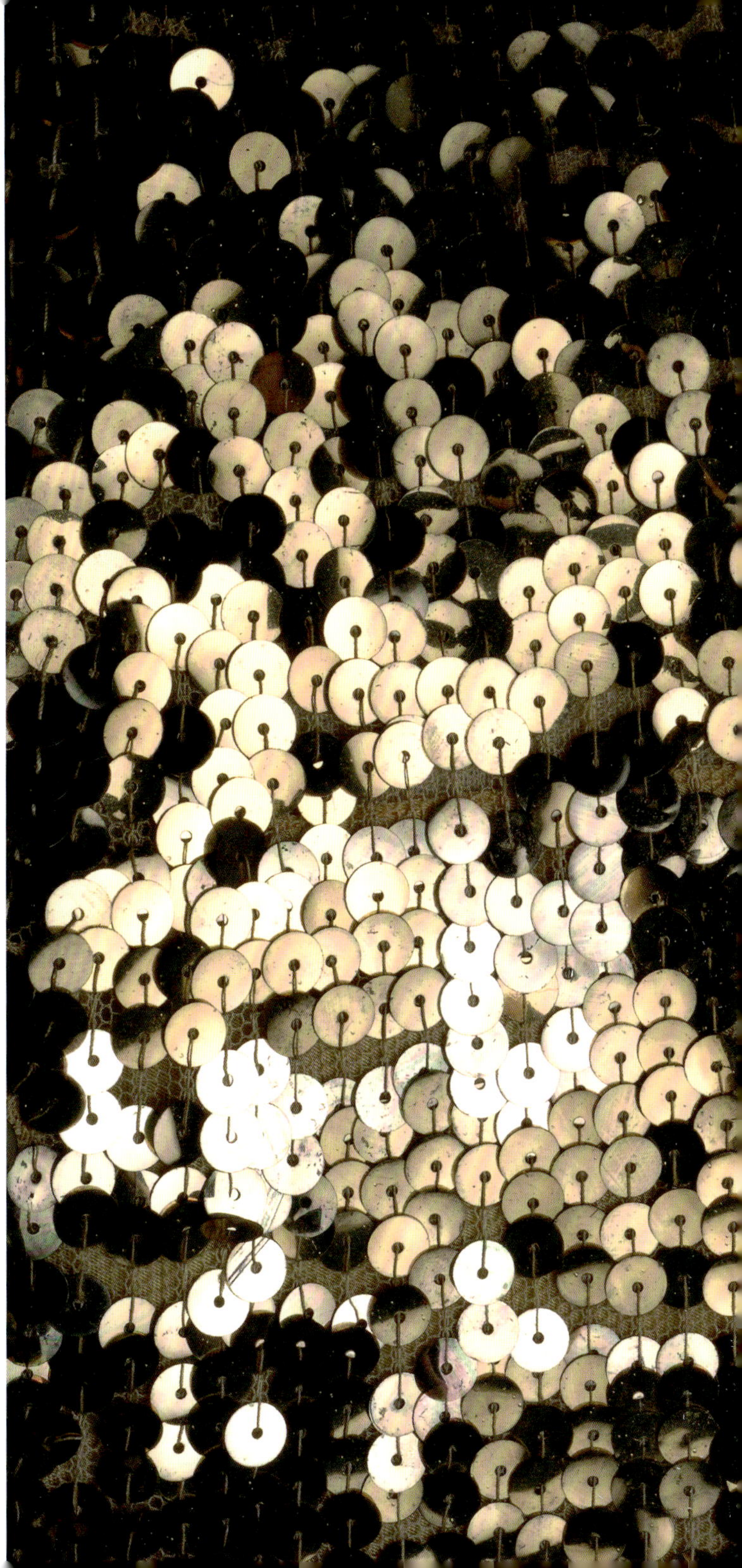

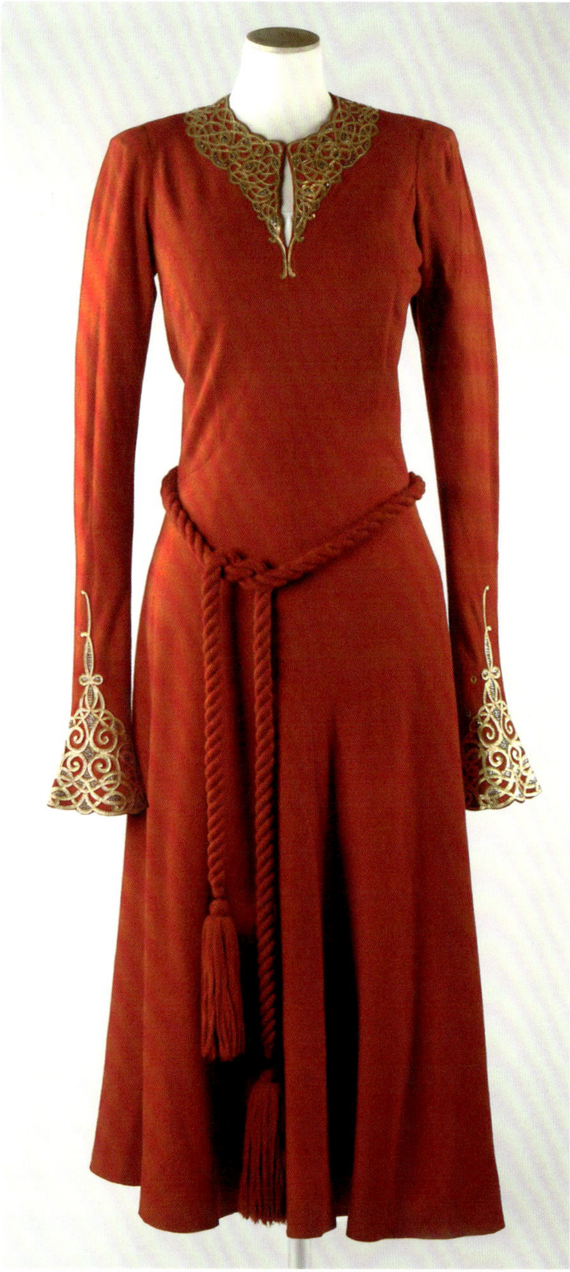

Evening dress, 1938

This dress is a stunning example of late 1930s style. Designed by influential Parisian couturier Jeanne Lanvin (1867–1946), it exemplifies many key aspects of the fashions of the period, as well as revealing the genius of a crucial player on the fashion stage. Sometimes referred to as a dinner dress this type of garment would have been worn during the evenings on less formal occasions. It is made from bias cut red wool, with a wide skirt that falls to calf level. Shoulder pads have been used to give the garment greater structure, and the long sleeves flare to a bell shape, covering the hands. The cuffs and neckline have been lavishly embroidered with appliquéd gold kid leather in a swirling design with sequins highlighting particular sections. A long rope-like belt is worn knotted loosely around the waist. Known during the 1920s for romantic picture dresses or *robes de style*, which were favourites for formal occasions such as weddings and garden parties, the 1930s saw Lanvin move towards a much more modern and sophisticated approach. Her work from this decade, with its subtle use of embroidery and rich colours, has come to epitomise the sophistication of the era.

During the 1930s the spotlight fell once more on shape as emphasis returned to the natural curves of the female body. The dual techniques of both cut and embellishment came together and resulted in glamorous and flattering garments that were inspired by an ever increasing range of subject matter. The design of this dress is a good indication of how eclectic high fashion had become, and here many influences combine to create a highly sophisticated and cohesive garment. The rich colour and applied leather decoration give a strong Middle Eastern feel. The long flared sleeves and the rope-style belt hark back to the medieval period, and the bias cut fabric is neo-classical in its inspiration.

The bias cut, perhaps one of the most recognisable aspects of 1930s fashion, is used to great effect in this piece. The originator and pioneer of this technique was the gifted designer Madeleine Vionnet (1876–1975). Cutting on the bias, or across the grain of the fabric, had been used for specific

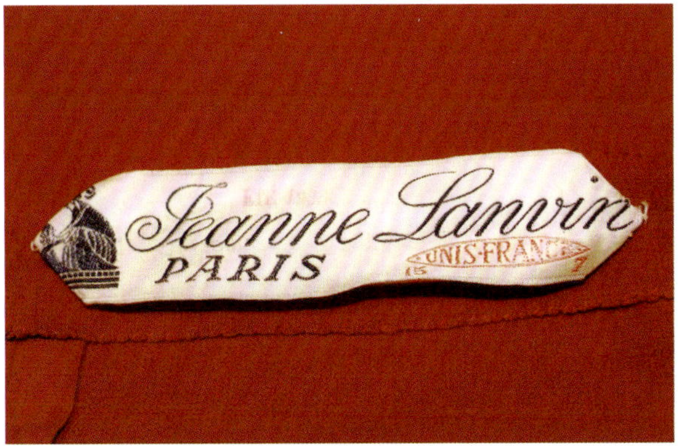

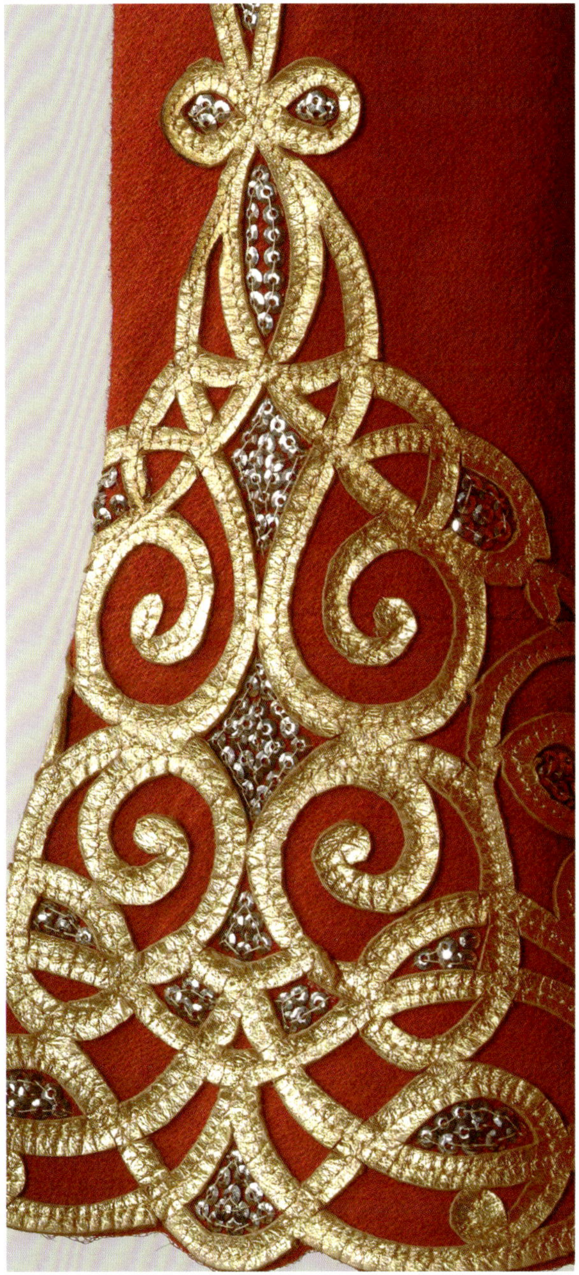

sections of dresses for many years, but Vionnet applied it to the whole garment using soft, sensual materials such as silk crêpes and satins. The result was beautifully streamlined clothing which clung to every curve in an elegant yet subtle way. The look caught on quickly and all the key designers of the era mastered the art. The Lanvin couture house was to become a leading practitioner of this sophisticated and complex technique, which required great skill and absolute accuracy in order to work successfully to flatter the body.

OBJECT NUMBER – M.2006.15

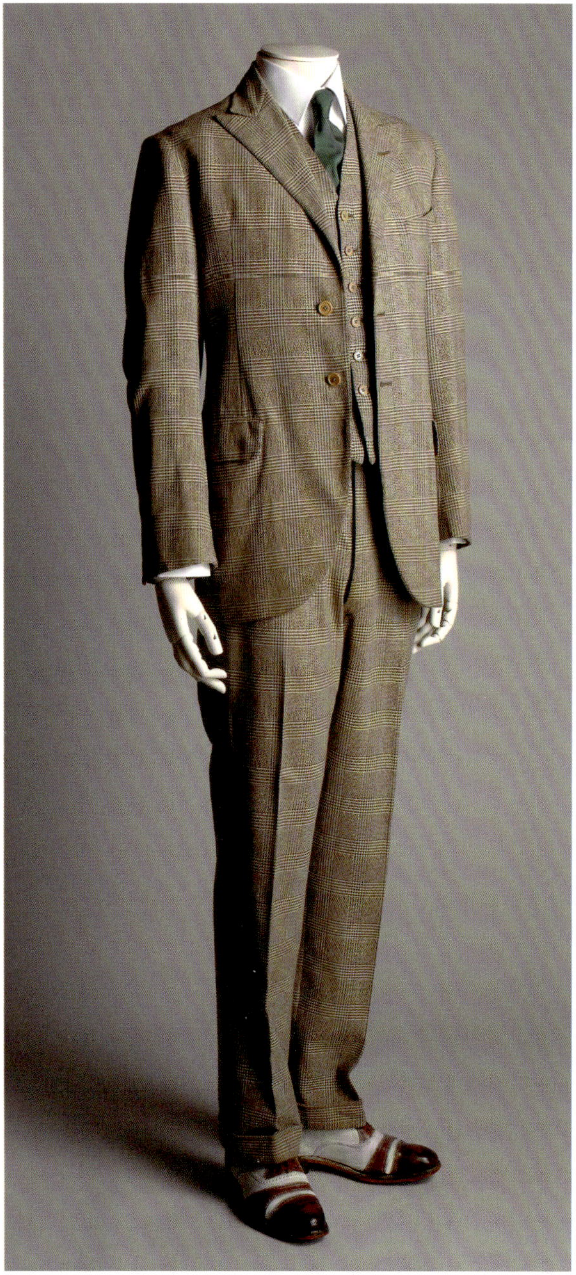

Man's three piece suit, 1935–1937

Consisting of beautifully tailored trousers, jacket and waistcoat, this comfortable man's suit was produced by Burberry, London. It is made from wool woven in the Glen Urquhart check design. The single breasted jacket fastens with two buttons. It has two breast pockets and two hip pockets. The long sleeves have wrist vents which are closed with four buttons, and a label inside the breast pocket reads '12/K model 3961'. The jacket is lined with brown rayon and cotton mix fabric, and the sleeves are lined with cream, purple and navy striped rayon. The single breasted waistcoat has a V-shaped neckline and two slanted breast pockets. There are a further two pockets at the waist. It fastens with six buttons at the front, and the back is made from the same material as the jacket lining. The trousers have a bound waistband and reversed pleats at the front waistband. They have a back strap for fit, a buttoned fly, side seam pockets and turn-ups. The buttons are engraved with 'Burberrys London'. The image shows it with a modern white cotton shirt, a narrow tie of sage green silk, which dates to around 1945, and a pair of brown and white co-respondent or brogue style leather shoes from around 1935.

Thomas Burberry started his clothing company in Basingstoke in 1856. By 1891 a store was opened in the Haymarket, London, and the company continues to go from strength to strength today. Burberry was famous for patenting a weatherproofed fabric called gabardine, a tightly twill-woven cotton cloth that was said to be both water resistant and breathable – gabardine was used, to great acclaim, by Shackleton's team of arctic explorers. During the Edwardian period Burberry was active in making tailored men's wear, but also made very stylish and practical motoring and sporting clothing for women. The familiar 'Burberry check' was introduced in the 1920s as a lining for trench coats – another garment for which they are famous. The owner of this suit bought it in a sale for £4 from the Burberry shop in London.

OBJECT NUMBER – M.1993.215

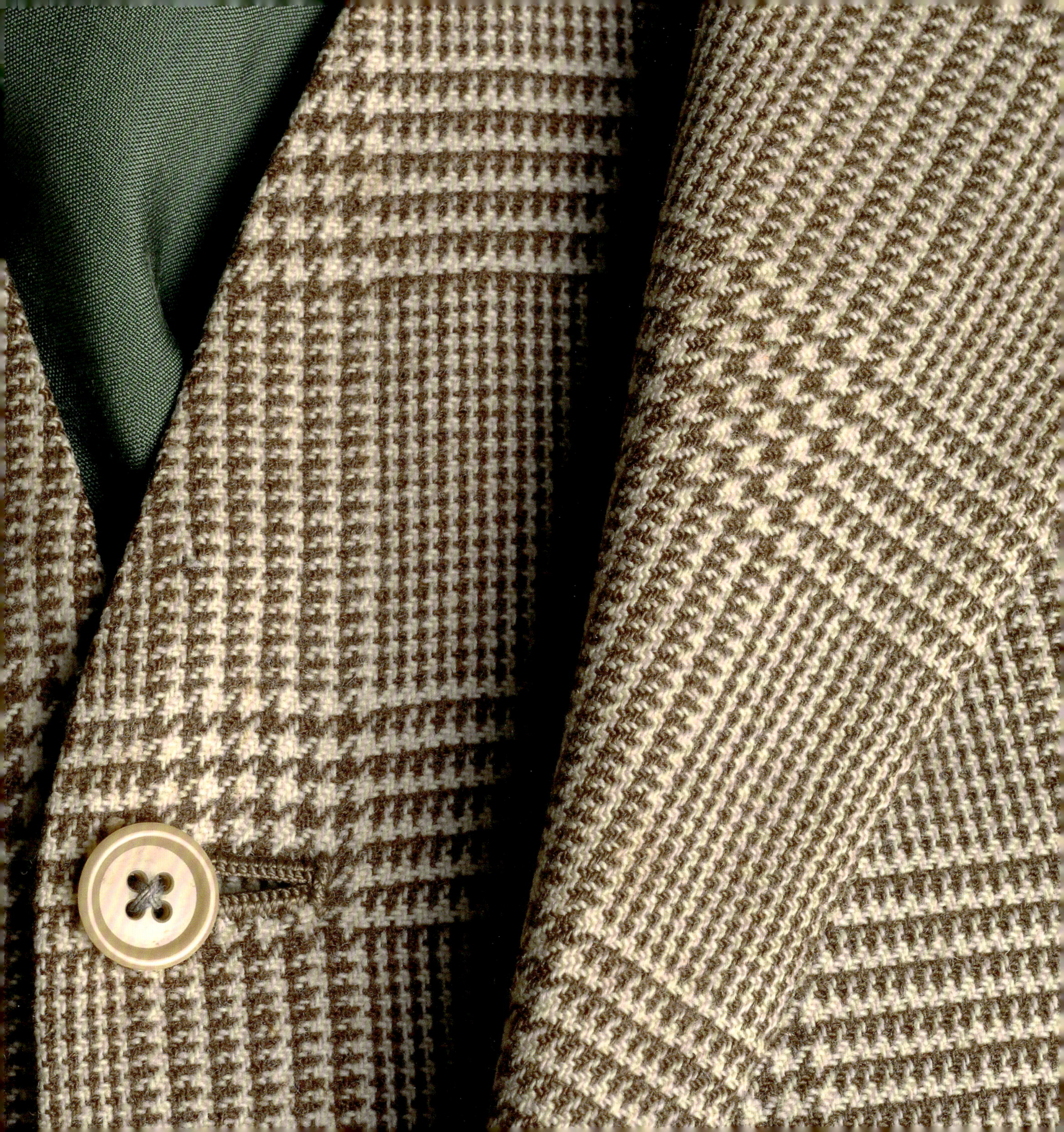

Woman's suit, 1943–1945

The neat military style of this two piece American suit of twill-woven wool by Hattie Carnegie (1889–1956) fits with its wartime date. It might have been worn with a high peaked cap or a small trilby hat with a feather trim. The jacket includes large shoulder pads, and has a generous double collar and turned-back cuffs. In an opulent flourish, it is fastened with four gilded brass buttons cast to look like gold nuggets. A pocket is positioned just below bust level on one side, and there are two further hip pockets. All have pocket flaps, and neat lines of top stitching have been used on these and the collar for added decoration. The lining is of navy rayon twill. The unlined skirt is knee length, slightly 'A-line' and fitted to the hips. It is constructed from five panels with a placket with zip fastening on the right hand side. It is not lined, and the sturdy waistband is of cream grosgrain ribbon. The military style of women's suits during this period amounted to a form of patriotic support for the forces. They were also extremely practical at a time when frivolity was virtually eliminated from clothing.

Clothing rationing and the Utility Scheme in Britain meant that all superfluous additions were removed from British made clothing of this date. The comparative prosperity of America during the same period meant that designers were able to make garments along similar lines, but with much more opulent and generous cutting and accessories. For example, the Utility Scheme limited the number of buttons on jackets to three where this suit has four. They also outlawed turned-back cuffs as seen here, and the double collar featured would definitely not have been seen on a British garment. As if to hammer home this feeling of wealth and bounty, the gold nugget buttons are the ultimate touch of luxury – quite out of step with British wartime austerity.

Hattie Carnegie, real name Henrietta Kanengeiser, was born in Vienna in 1889. Her family moved to America when she was six years old. By 1909, she had changed her name to that of the richest man in the U.S. and opened a small shop selling custom made clothes. This grew into a very successful fashion business, nurturing young designers and launching ready-to-wear and sports labels alongside her couture range. She was extremely good at marketing and networking, and wore her own designs to fashionable events. Her clothes, accessories, jewellery and perfumes soon became famous, and her clients included the Duchess of Windsor and Joan Crawford. She was known for her 'Little Carnegie Suits' (as shown here), but she also created very stylish evening wear. Interestingly, in the light of the military nature of this suit, Carnegie later went on to design new uniforms for the United States Women's Army Corps.

OBJECT NUMBER – M.2006.16

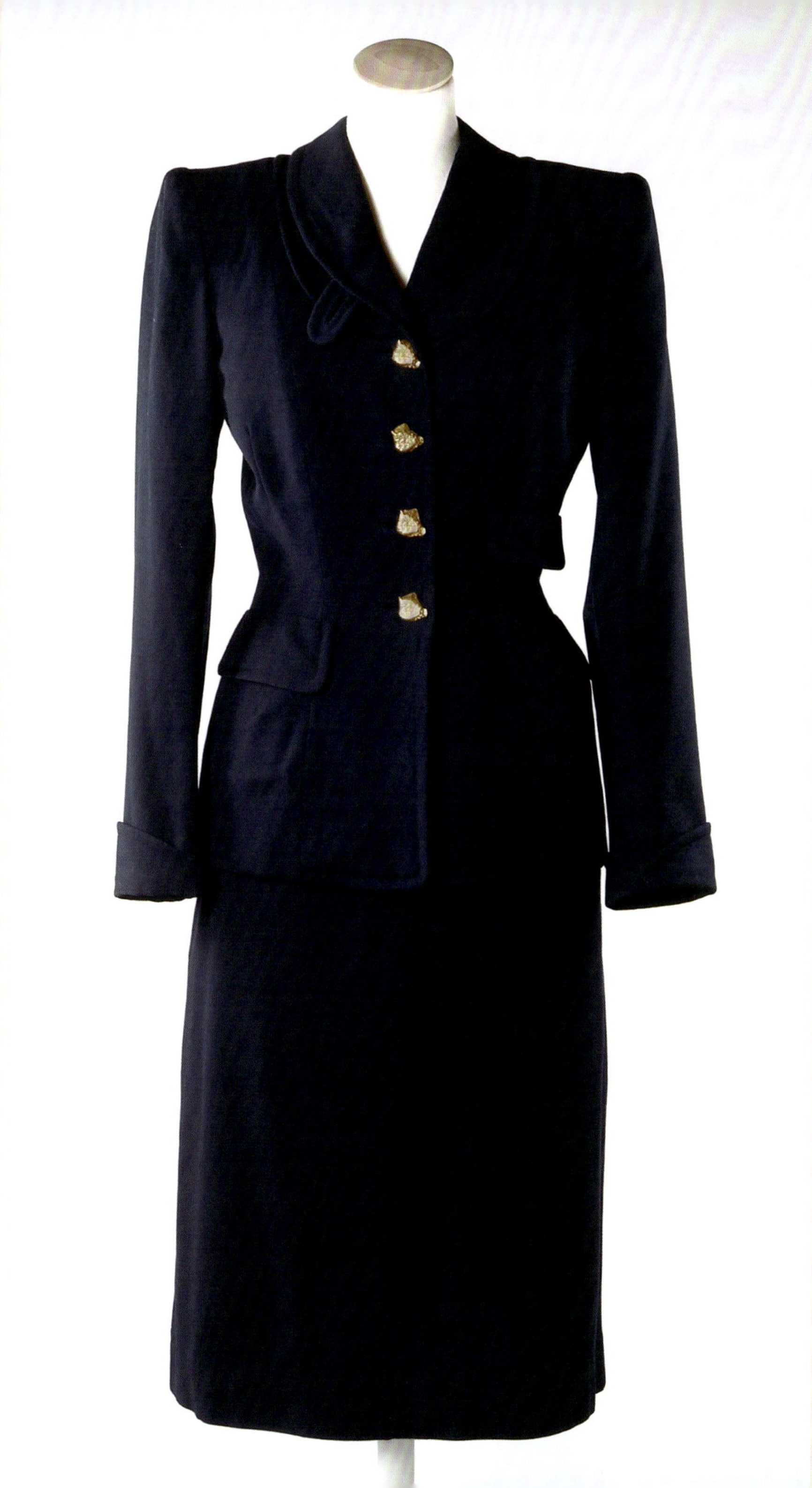

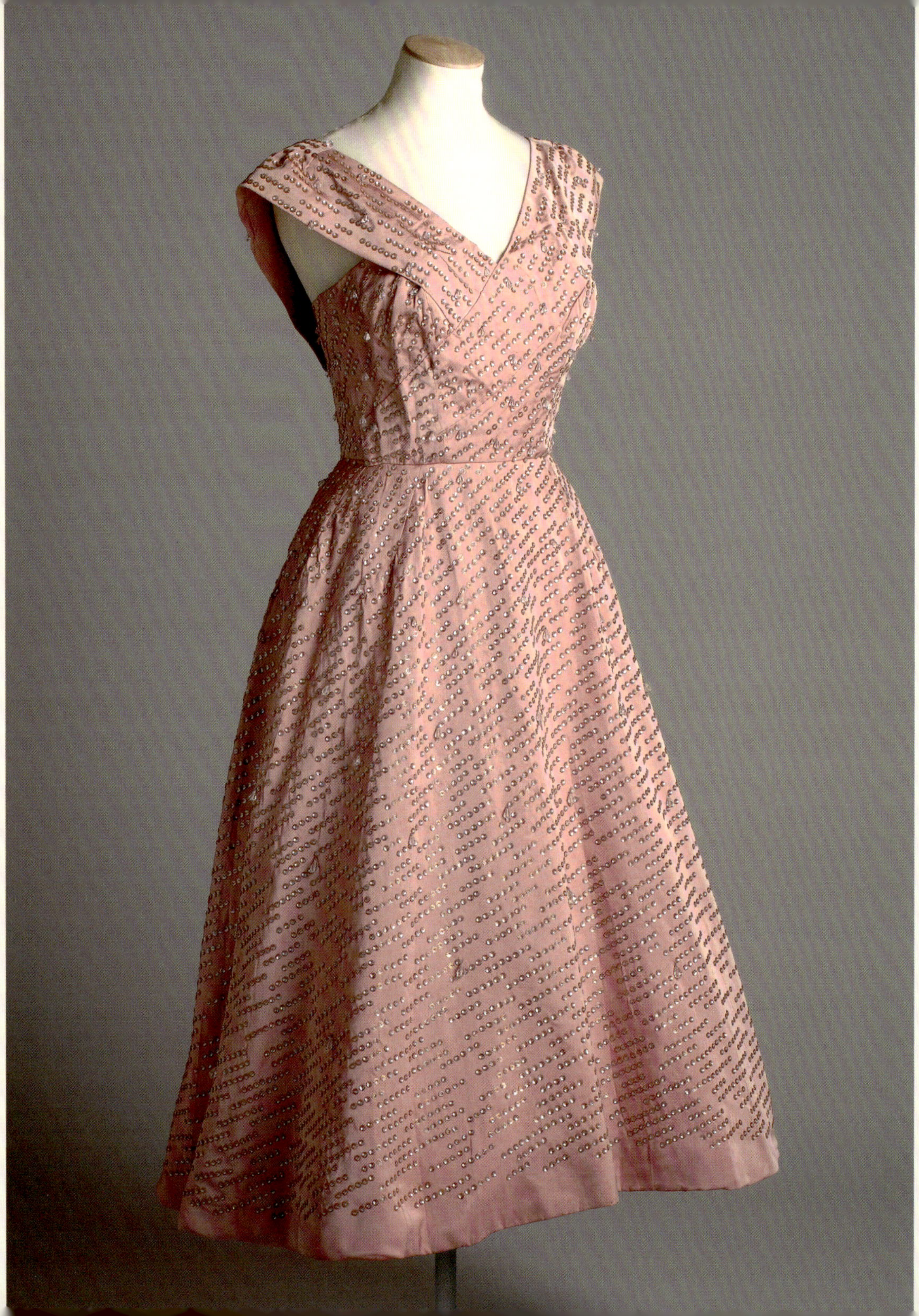

Evening dress, 1955–1957

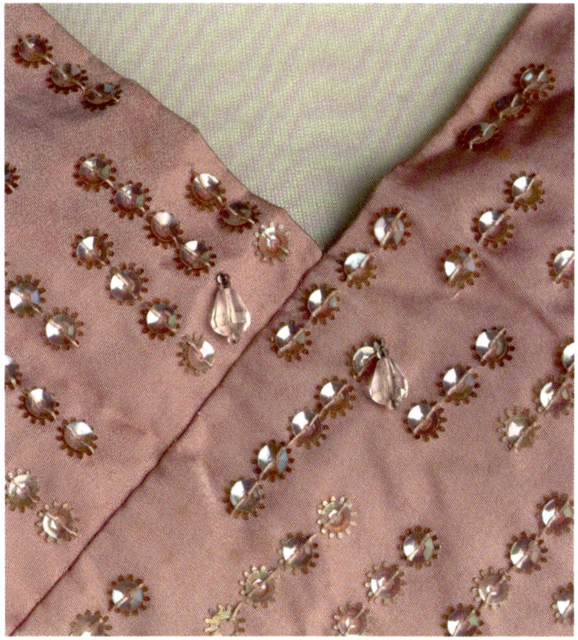

This attractive pink silk taffeta evening or cocktail dress is by Norman Hartnell (1901–1979). The glittering embellishment is particularly appealing, incorporating iridescent sequins and tear-drop shaped glass beads which move with the wearer. The bodice is heavily boned and has a deep 'V' shape both front and back. It is lined with pink rayon, and hidden elasticated straps extend over the shoulders to help the dress stay in place. The wide skirt is stiffened with net to make it stand away from the body, and further fullness would have been added with quantities of flounced petticoats. In addition to the boning in the bodice, a heavy foundation garment such as a corselette or girdle would have been worn in order to achieve a fashionably small waist. The soft, feminine colour, rich fabric and elaborate decoration are all typical of the period.

The gown is very much in the style of the New Look – a fashion which was all about fantasy and femininity. Despite the conclusion of the Second World War in 1945, the rationing of a wide range of commodities carried on for some years. Clothing coupons did not disappear until 1949, and the Utility Scheme continued until 1952. Into this world of post-war austerity burst a new and overwhelming fashion force. In 1947 Christian Dior (1905–1957) launched his now legendary New Look. Completely at odds with the plain and angular fashions of wartime, this new fashion celebrated femininity. Here Dior describes it in his own words: 'I designed clothes for flower-like women, with rounded shoulders, full, feminine busts and hand span waists above enormous spreading skirts'*. Women wholeheartedly embraced this celebration of femininity and extravagance, and they did so in the face of severe criticism from politicians and many branches of the press who believed the look to be wasteful.

The New Look reflected the mood of an era. Throughout the next decade society harked back to another age, as women conformed to traditional stereotypes. Norman Hartnell had first made his name in the pre-war period, but was the ideal designer to work in this mode. His clothes were romantic and feminine, often made of silk georgette or tulle and embroidered with beads and sequins, an approach which he clearly continued into the 1950s. Hartnell opened his own fashion house in 1923 after an initial period with the house of Lucile (1863–1935), and showed his collections successfully in both London and Paris. His couture house gained considerable success in the 1920s and '30s, and he was the designer of choice for garments associated with rites of passage such as weddings or presentation at court. Indeed he began to be commissioned by the royal family from 1935 when he designed the wedding dress and bridesmaids' dresses for the marriage of the Duke of Gloucester and Lady Alice Montagu Douglas Scott. Royal commissions continued to come in thick and fast, and perhaps his most famous creation was the Coronation dress of Queen Elizabeth II.

OBJECT NUMBER – M.1993.25

*Dior, Christian, *Christian Dior and I,* (New York, 1957) p.21.

Cream silk chiffon gown, 1969–1970

The flowing, feminine lines of this softly structured dress by Ossie Clark (1942–1996) for Quorum are a direct contrast to the angular, monochrome styles we associate with the mid 1960s. The mood of fashion was changing, and while Hippy flower-power was undeniably making its influence felt in the designer wardrobe, Ossie Clark was expertly incorporating many other design references in order to make ultra-flattering feminine garments. This full-length dress of white silk chiffon is printed all over with a stylised pineapple and leaf design by Clark's then wife, Celia Birtwell (b.1941). It has prominent shoulder pads and long sleeves with frills at the shoulder, elbow and cuff. The bodice is very low cut, and edged with printed silk satin. The waistband is also of silk satin, and the full skirt is gathered into it, opening right down the centre front, being fastened only at the waistband with hooks and eyes and silk chiffon ties.

Ossie Clark was one of the first designers to move towards a more flattering, feminine line in high fashion after the angular silhouette which had been fashionable for much of the 1960s. Often opting for the luxury and flowing movement of natural fibres rather than the novelty of the newer man-made fabrics, he was strongly influenced by the designers of the 1930s such as Madeleine Vionnet (1876–1975) and Charles James (1906–1978), whose work he studied at the Victoria and Albert Museum. Their garments were all about the precision of cut and a complete understanding of the properties of particular fabrics – techniques in which Ossie Clark became expert. Here he refers back to the late '30s and 1940s in his use of shoulder pads, and though this dress was designed to be worn in public, it is reminiscent of the negligees worn by Hollywood starlets. This gives the piece sex appeal; hinting at the seduction and femininity of the boudoir. The dress is also transparent – a style that Ossie Clark was to pioneer, though perhaps few clients outside the ultra-fashionable King's Road set that surrounded him were brave enough to wear such sheer fabrics without underwear.

The fabric prints that Ossie Clark used were a key element of his style. These were designed by Celia Birtwell, and they show an originality and a naive yet subtle character that complemented the exquisite cut of Ossie's clothes, whilst chiming perfectly with the feel of the times. In fact Celia's prints were hugely influential in the creation of Ossie Clark clothes. They were said to be the inspiration and starting point for many of his designs. This in tandem with his skills in draping and cutting on the stand meant that the style of the clothes worked perfectly with the textile patterns – an approach which was very fresh and hugely influential.

OBJECT NUMBER – M.2006.19

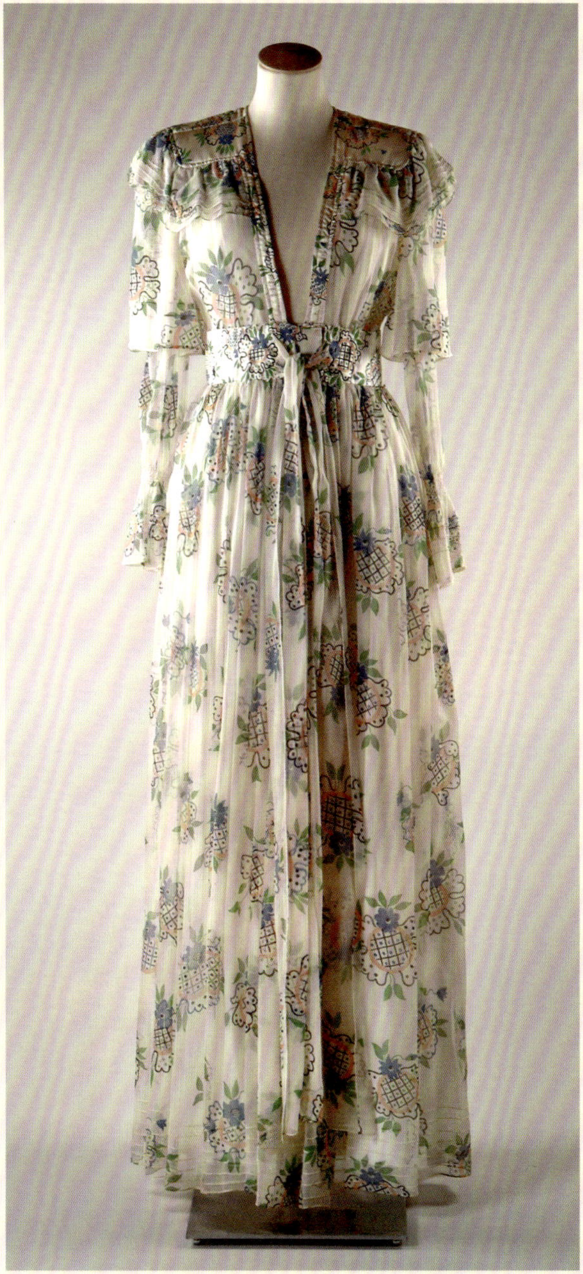

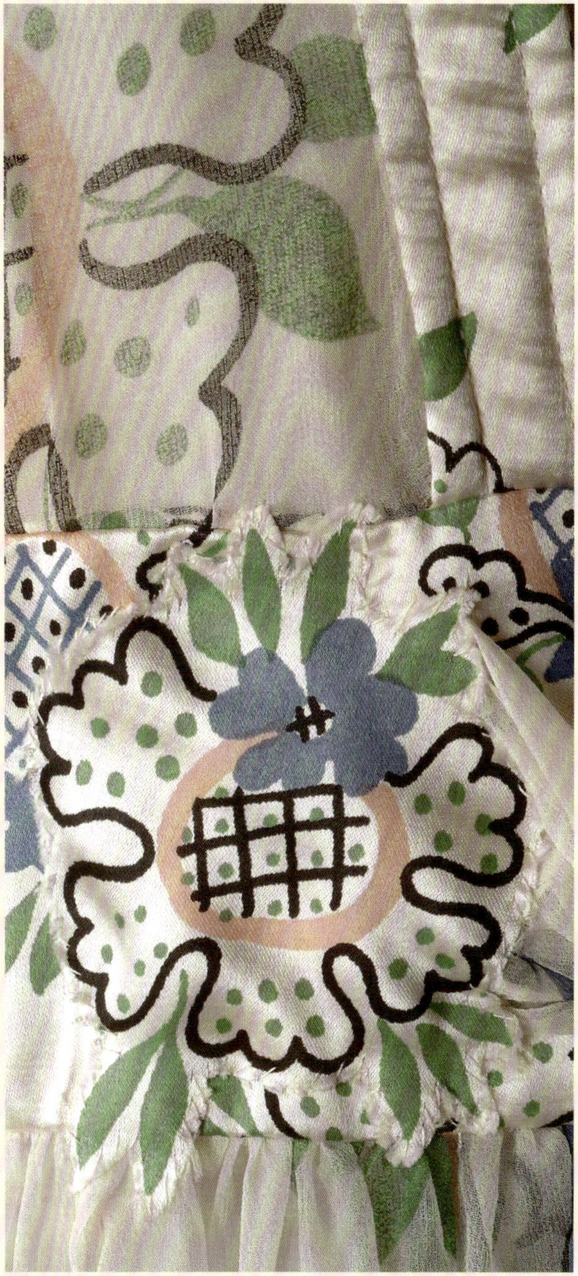

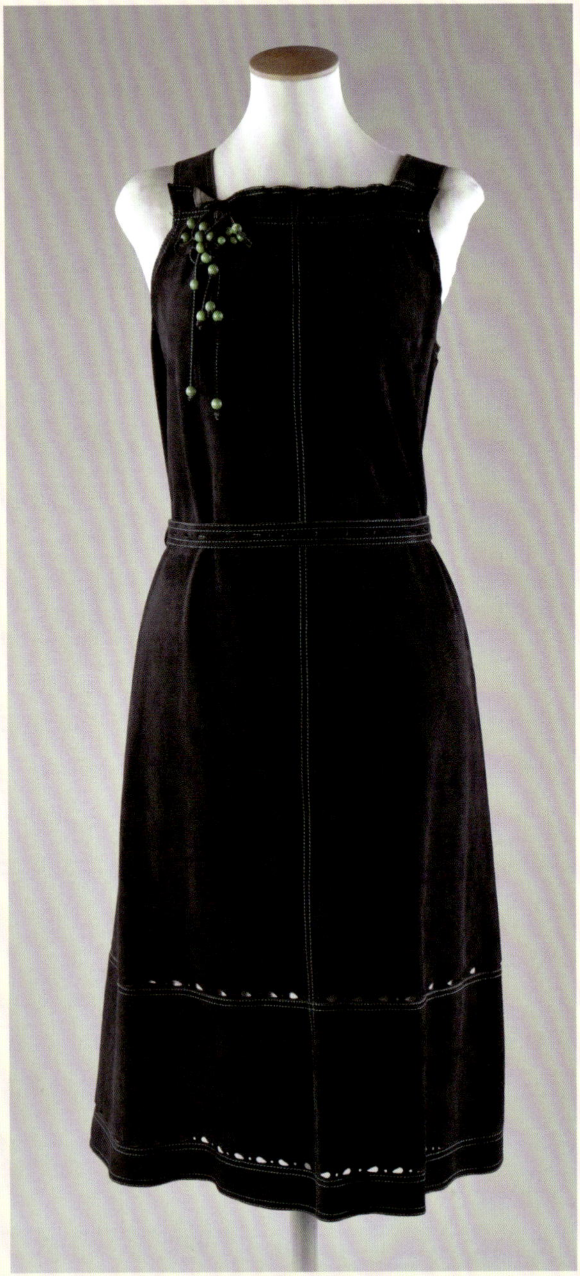

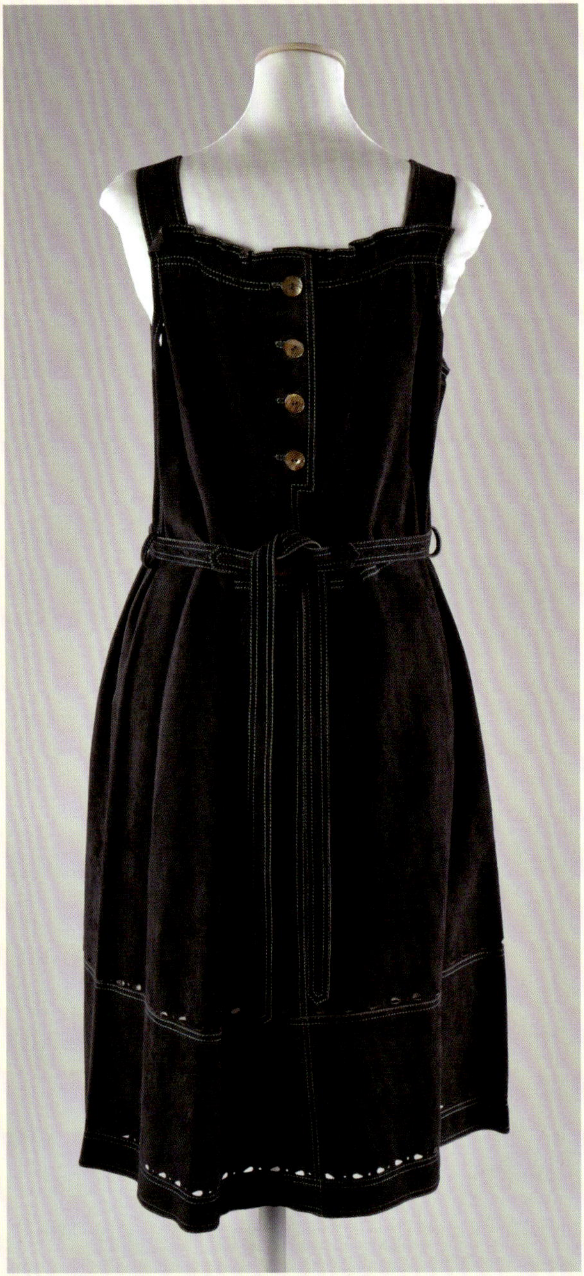

Day dress and matching cap, 1973–1975

Made from soft navy blue suede, the simple lines and subtle decoration of this day dress are the work of the gifted designer Jean Muir (1928–1995). The unlined dress is softly gathered at the top to create a frilled effect. A beaded tassel decoration is attached, and a suede belt buttons and ties together at the back or front to draw the dress in at waist level. The bodice fastens at the centre back with a four button placket. The knee length skirt is slightly flared, and features two lines of punched eyelets in a teardrop and dot pattern. This pattern is repeated at the edges of the armholes and along the belt. Green top stitching is the only other decorative element. The matching cap is also decorated with top stitched seams. It is made from six equal triangles and trimmed with a beaded tassel decoration which would have hung at the side of the face.

Jean Muir's attention to detail and timeless pieces have earned her a well deserved reputation for quality and style. Self-taught, she started her fashion career working for Liberty's department store, London. She then joined Jaeger where she excelled in working with jersey fabrics before leaving to set up her own label. In 1966 she showed for the first time under her own name with great success, gaining an international reputation by the early '70s which she maintained until her death in 1995. She is particularly known for her work in matte jersey, and for her 'little black dresses'. However, she also loved to work in leather and suede. She used the softest hides and skins to trim garments, but also to create complete pieces as seen here. By tailoring leather in the same way that one might work with woven or knitted fabrics, she pioneered a new approach which was all about luxury, sinuousness and the look and feel of this natural material on the body. The hand punched detailing seen on this garment was also a trademark Jean Muir technique which was described as 'brogueing' by the fashion press.

Miss Muir was also known for the quality of the accessories frequently added to her garments. She commissioned skilled craftspeople to work in a variety of media in order to create beautiful buttons, belt buckles and headwear. The addition of a matching hat for this dress is echoed in a number of her other ensembles. The simple construction used here suggests that this cap was probably produced in-house, but Muir frequently worked in partnership with talented milliners to create hats, caps and turbans to accompany her pieces. Never a slave to the dictates of fashion, she chose instead to create pieces that flattered the wearer with simple lines and understated elegance. This piece, though undeniably '70s in its style, transcends the often extreme fashions of the era by concentrating on cut, subtle decorative detailing and quality material.

OBJECT NUMBER – M.1994.26

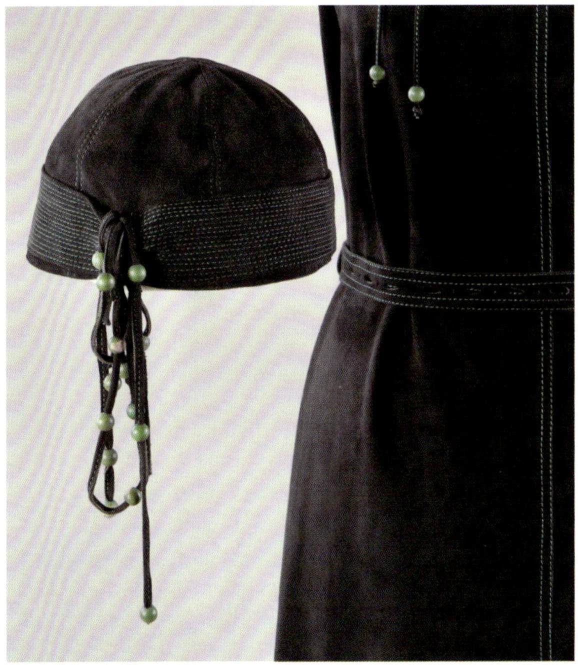

Printed silk chiffon gown, 1972–1974

Dubbed a *Field of Lilies dress* by Zandra Rhodes (b.1940), this piece is made from hand printed white silk chiffon, and drapes softly around the body. The dress is full length with wide 'bat wing' sleeves and has a low neckline with a lapel collar. Elastic has been used to create a ruched effect at the waist and the long skirt is lined with white silk chiffon. The dress is machine stitched but the cuffs are hand rolled – a time-consuming technique which helps the chiffon to hang correctly. A label inside the centre back reads 'Zandra Rhodes, London. Pure Silk. Made in England'. The fabric is printed with 'Lovely Lilies' text and Zandra Rhodes' signature as well as knitting stitch and lily motifs in green, pink and white.

Zandra Rhodes graduated from the Royal College of Art in 1964, and she began by selling her printed fabrics to the influential designers Marion Foale (b.1939) and Sally Tuffin (b.1938). However, she felt she lost control over the way the fabric was being used, so began to work in partnership with designer Sylvia Ayton (b.1937). They opened a shop called 'The Fulham Road Clothes Shop' but, partly due to financial difficulties, the shop and her partnership with Sylvia Ayton did not last. Eventually Zandra succeeded in securing backers and a market for her work, initially in America, and then in London. Her career took off as buyers and fashion journalists began to show a keen interest in her collections.

First and foremost Zandra Rhodes was trained as a textile designer, and this informed her garments from the very beginning. In this and many other pieces she has let the pattern dictate the way that the cloth should be cut and stitched, resulting in unusual, fluid lines. Here shape and pattern harmonise very effectively and the dress billows and flows when worn. The textile design also incorporates another favourite Zandra Rhodes print – lines of knitted or chain stitches which were influenced by knitting and embroidery patterns seen in childhood, as well as designs she found in the collections at the Victoria and Albert Museum. The 'Lovely Lilies' print was inspired by a gift of lilies which Zandra then began to draw. She was in Japan at the time, and there is an overall Japanese theme to the shape and style of the dress which resembles a kimono. This is further enhanced by the inclusion of a knotted silk satin sash, similar to an obi or kimono sash. The collection was launched in 1972 and was one of Zandra Rhodes' most important lines. It epitomises the pastoral, flowing modes that were fashionable at the time, and yet carries the distinct Zandra Rhodes signature style.

OBJECT NUMBER – M.2006.17

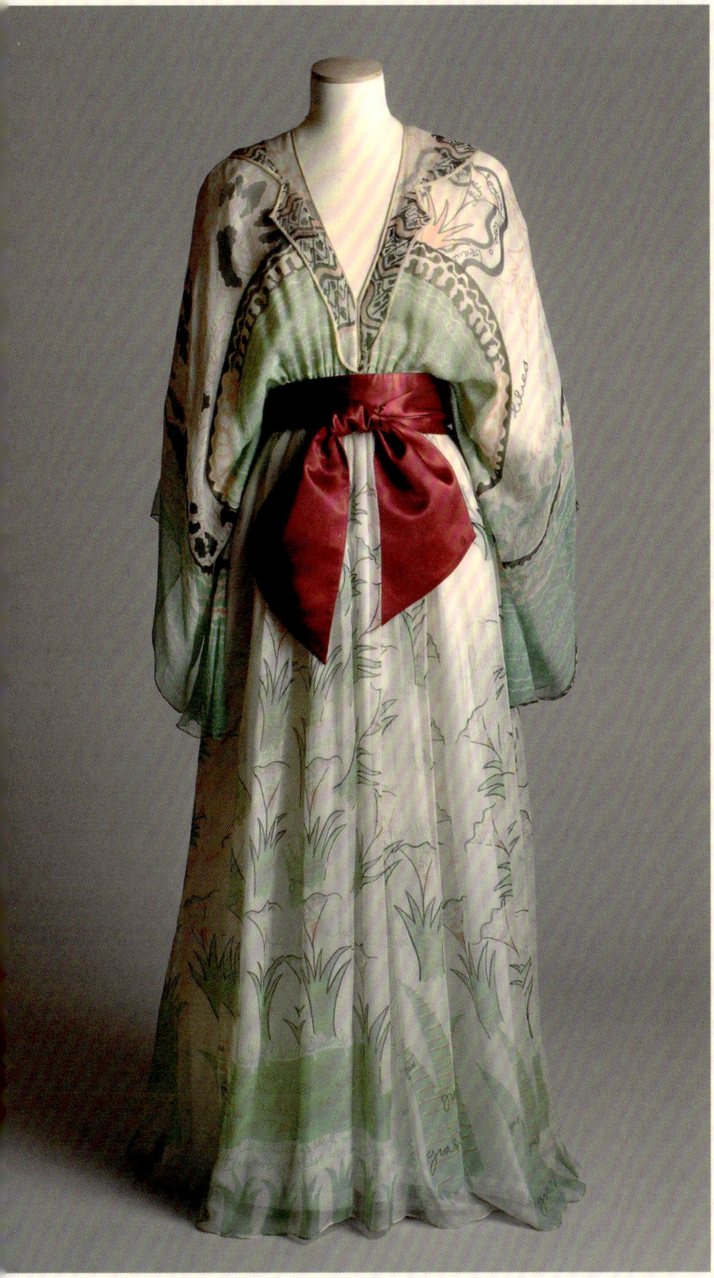

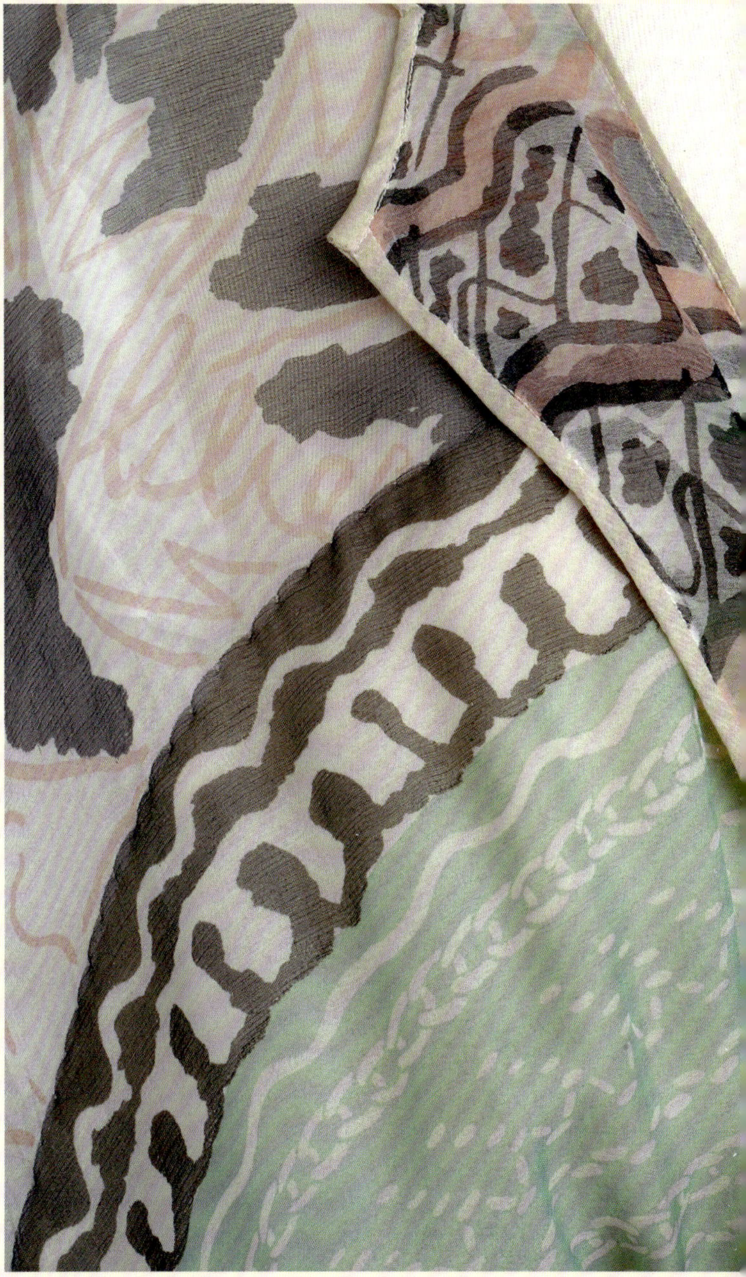

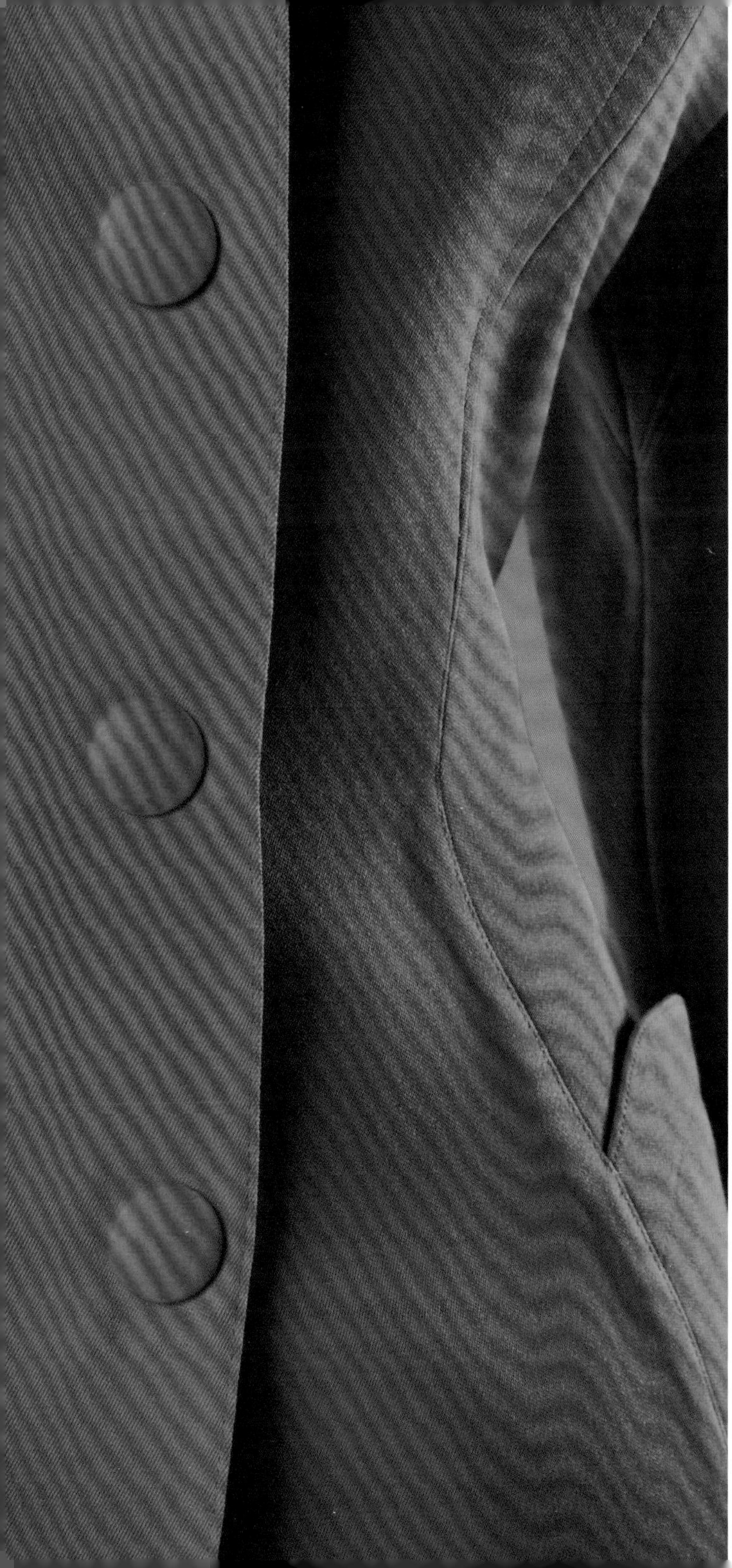

Woman's suit, 1985–1987

This particularly striking woman's suit is by influential French designer Thierry Mugler (b.1948). The oversized jacket is made from orange worsted wool and polyester mix and lined with orange polyester. It has wide padded shoulders, raglan sleeves and three press studs fasten the centre front. The use of topstitching or welt seams adds further decorative detail, and draws attention to the jacket's structure. The straight knee length pencil skirt is made from black wool. The use of such a simple line and a dark colour for the skirt serve to emphasise the bold hue and exaggerated proportions of the jacket.

Part of the 'power dressing' phenomenon, boxy suits with large shoulders became extremely fashionable during the mid-1980s with Thierry Mugler one of the key designers of this look; and one of the first. The 1940s Hattie Carnegie suit also shown in this chapter (pages 130–131) was an earlier exploration of this style, which evolved from the influence of uniforms on mainstream fashion and the role of women in wartime. Though initially likened to uniforms, and still linked to female occupation of a traditionally male space, the 1980s version became associated with career women and success in the male-dominated world of business.

The 1980s was a decade associated with conspicuous consumption. Men too wore 'power suits' with wide shoulders, but it is the women's suits that are the most memorable. There was a masculine element to these garments, but also an overt sexuality. The extension of the shoulders with padding and a boxy structure served to conceal some aspects of the female body, while other areas such as the legs were very much on show. Short, tight skirts were the norm, with legs often set off by a pair of high-heeled stiletto shoes. It was as if women were trying to use clothing to help them to succeed by any means necessary; playing with the ideas of power, androgyny and sexuality all at the same time and hoping to profit from all three.

OBJECT NUMBER – M.2010.02

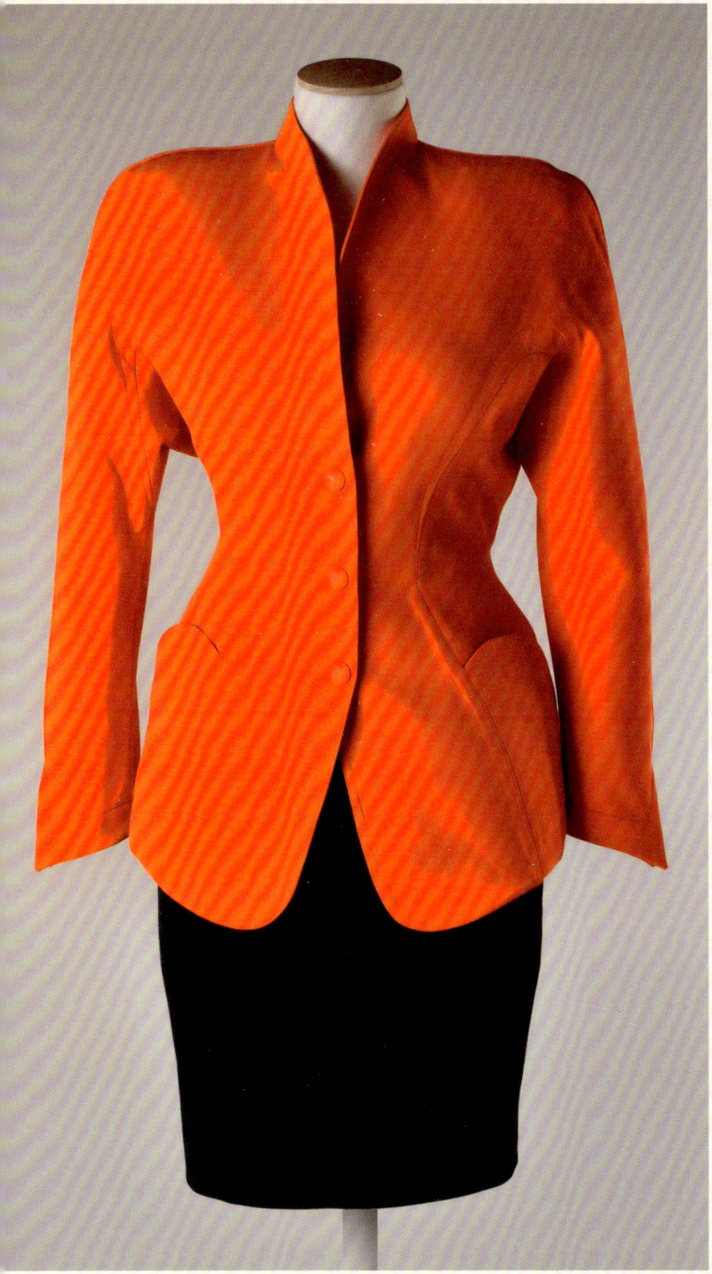
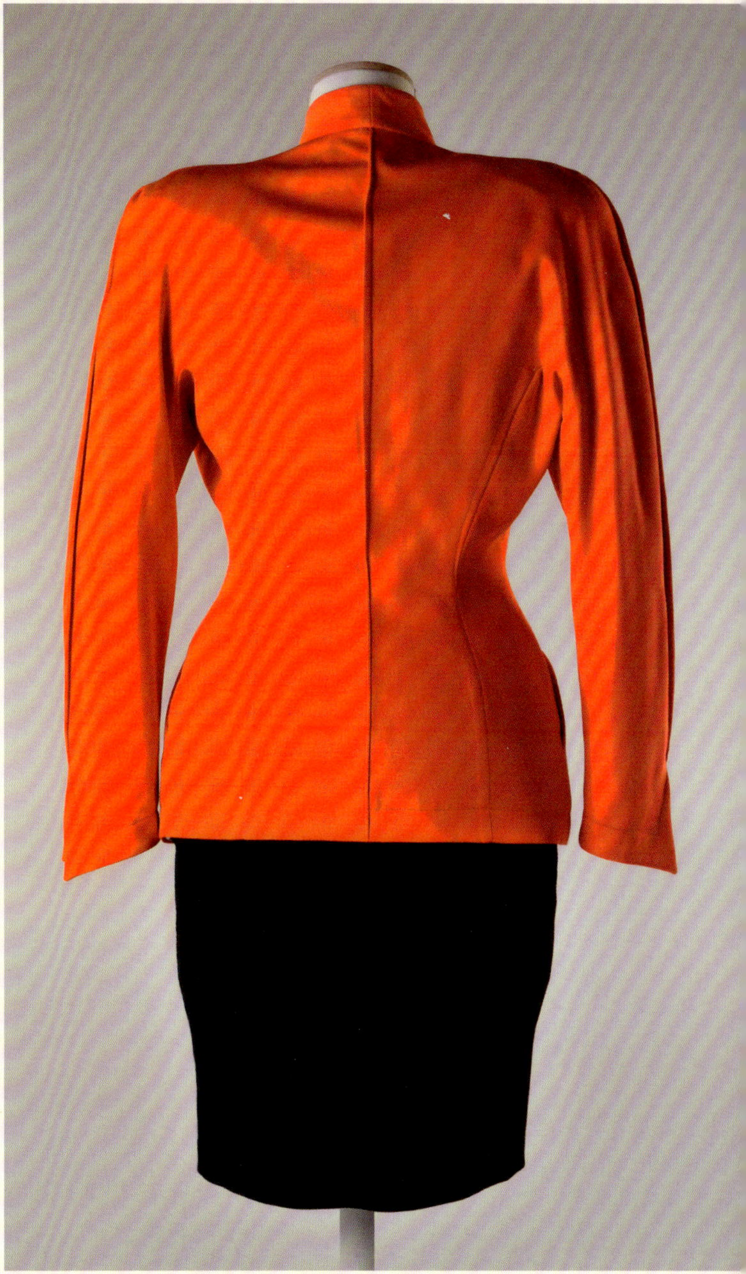

Epilogue

Collecting the twenty-first century

'Pleats Please' dress by Issey Miyake, 2009

The Olive Matthews Collection continues to expand through the acquisition of pieces which fill gaps and enhance existing themes. Though undoubtedly a challenging and controversial area, selective contemporary collecting is part of this process, and items are occasionally added in order to complete a temporary exhibition, bringing it up to date and helping to connect with today's audiences. This 'Pleats Please' dress was acquired for *An Image of Itself*; an exhibition which focused on the evolution of fashion and the constant inspiration provided by styles of the past. It was shown alongside a borrowed 1910 'Delphos' gown by Mariano Fortuny in order to highlight the links between Fortuny's revolutionary pleating technique and that employed by Miyake. A classic garment, the 'Pleats Please' dress has had a lasting impact on recent fashion, whilst also serving to highlight important connections with other pieces both old and new.

The dress is made from grey polyester. Before pleating it has been cut and stitched in a size three times larger than the eventual finished article. It has then been passed through a heated press in order to produce permanent pleats. The pleats have transformed the garment into a narrow, figure-hugging dress of a simple, classic style which, in common with Fortuny's designs, echoes the clinging draperies seen in ancient Greek sculpture as well as the body-skimming lines of 1930s bias cut dresses. The piece also evokes the fluidity of organic form and the simple styles of traditional Japanese clothing. The columnar, sheath-like cut and the body-lengthening effects of the vertical pleats add texture and elegance, as well as creating a very modern, minimalist look which alters according to the individual body shape of the wearer. With no fastenings or waist seam, the dress can be pulled on over the head with little effort, and the man-made fabric and pleated style make it simple to launder, store and wear.

Issey Miyake (b.1938) held his first fashion shows during the early 1970s. In 1976 he presented the collection 'A Piece of Cloth' which marked the emergence of his characteristic approach to fabric and design. He explored the concept of using flat fabrics on the three-dimensional body, drawing on techniques found in traditional Japanese clothing and updating them, using man-made fabrics and innovative cutting. Miyake began to work with pleats in 1988, and his 'Pleats Please' range, which was launched in 1993, has become one of his most classic and enduring lines. Miyake's work can also be seen within the broader context of modern Japanese fashion design. Since the early 1980s Miyake and his contemporaries, such as Rei Kawakubo (b.1942) and Yohji Yamamoto (b.1943), have had a significant and lasting impact on the world fashion stage. Each has demonstrated distinctive approaches whilst also acknowledging Japanese cultural and sartorial values and traditions. With techniques such as the use of monochromatic fabrics, deconstructed tailoring and cutting and an open-minded approach to technology, they have challenged and subverted preconceived ideas about dress in uniquely innovative ways.

OBJECT NUMBER – M.2010.26

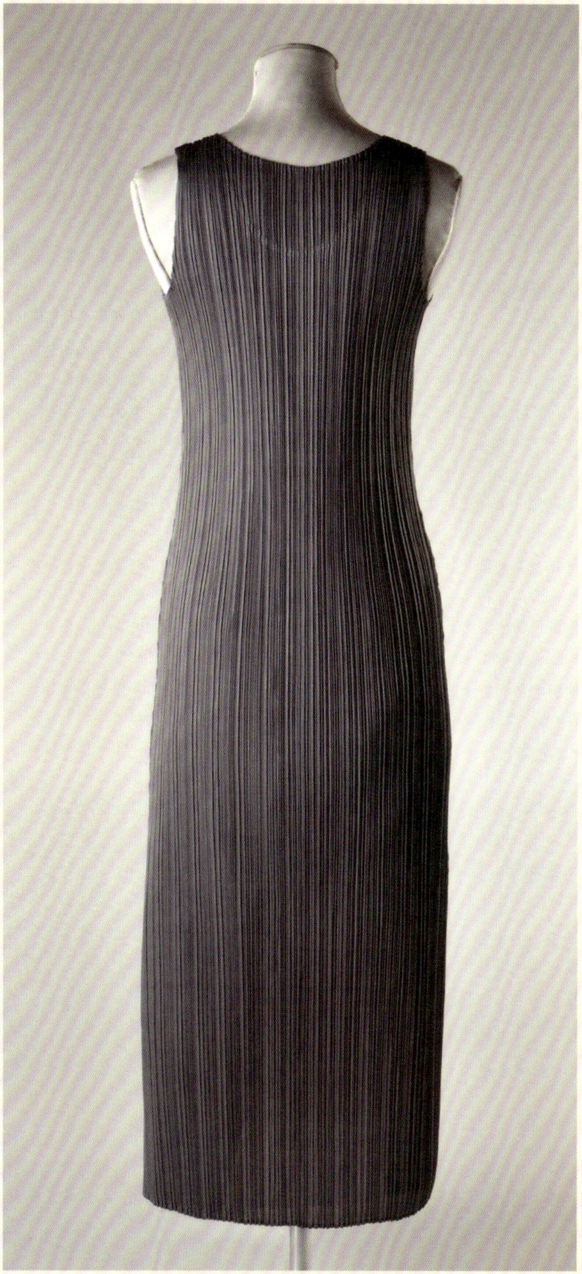

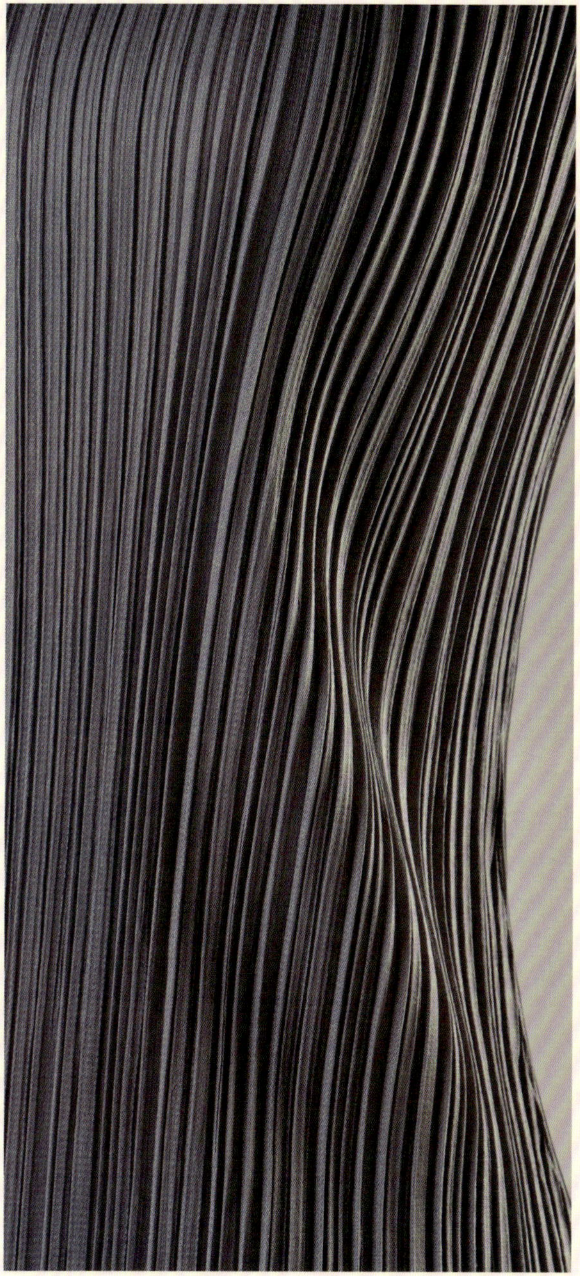

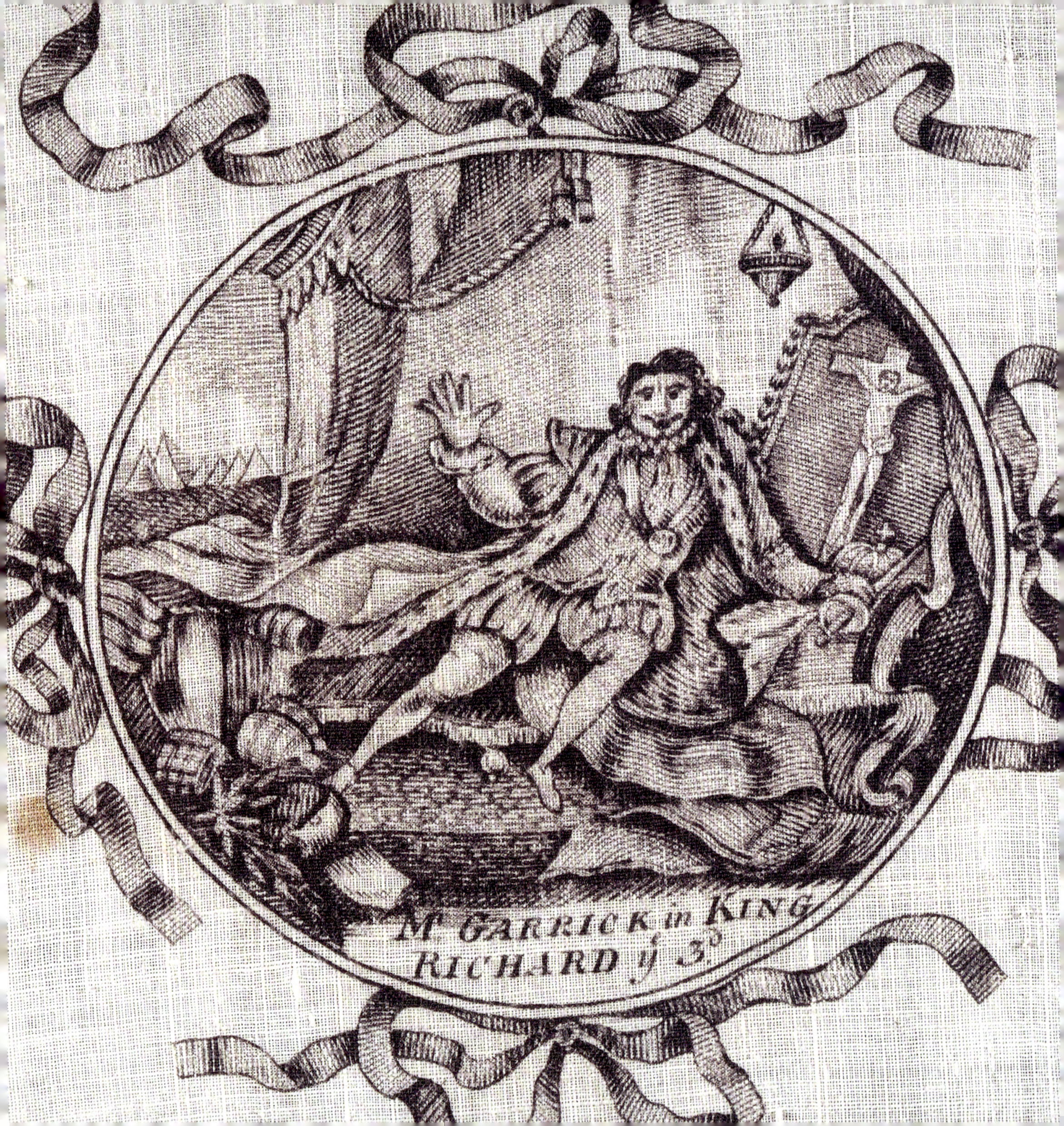
Mr. GARRICK in KING
RICHARD ye 3d

The Garrick Handkerchief

List of actors, characters and playwrights depicted on the Garrick handkerchief (see pages 64–65).

Mr Beard in the character of Hawthorn in *Love in a Village*
Mr Dibden in the character of Mongo in *The Padlock*
Mr Dunstall in the character of Hodge in *Love in a Village*
Mr Foot in the character of Mother Cole in *The Minor*
Mr Foot in the character of The Devil in *The Devil on Two Sticks*
Mr Foot in the character of the Doctor in *The Devil on Two Sticks*
Mr Foot in the character of Major Sturgeon in *The Mayor of Garrat*
Mr Garrick in the character of Abel Drugger in *The Alchymist*
Mr Garrick in the character of Fribble in *Miss in Her Teens*
Mr Garrick in the character of Hamlet
Mr Garrick in the character of King Lear
Mr Garrick in King Richard the Third
Mr Garrick in the character of Sir John Brute
Mr Garrick in the character of Tancred
Mr Jacobs in the character of Doctor Jallop in *The Mayor of Garrat*
Mr King in the character of Ancient Pistoll in *Henry the Fourth*
Mr Macklin in the character of Shylock in *The Merchant of Venice*
Mr Macklin in the character of Sir Archie in *Love à la Mode*
Mr Mattocks in the character of Squire in *Thomas and Sally*
Mr Moody in the character of Foiguard in the *Beaux Stratagem*
Mrs Pitt in the character of Mrs Quickly in *Henry the Fourth*
Mr Powell in the character of Lovewell in the *Clandestine Marriage*
Mr Shuter (sic) in the character of Master Stephen in *Every Man in his Humour*
Mr Shutter in the character of Sir John Falstaff
Mr Shutter in the character of Justice Woodcock in *Love in a Village*
Mr Smith in the character of Edgar in *King Lear*
Mr Weston in the character of Dr Last in *The Devil on Two Sticks*
Mr Woodward in the character of Captain Bobadil in *Every Man in His Humour*
Mr Woodward in the character of Captain Flash in *Miss in her Teens*
Mr Woodward in the character of Dutchman in the *Bold Stroke for a Wife*
Mr Yates in the character of Sir Callighan in *Love à la Mode*
Mrs Yates in the character of Mandane in *Cyrus*

Plus playwrights in the four corners:
Ben Jonson (top left)
William Shakespeare (top right)
John Fletcher (bottom left)
John Dryden (bottom right)

LEFT Detail from the centre of the Garrick handkerchief, showing Mr David Garrick as Richard III in Shakespeare's play of the same name. The image is taken from William Hogarth's 1745 portrait of Garrick.

Select Bibliography

Adburgham, Alison, *Shops and Shopping 1800–1914,* (George Allen and Unwin Ltd., London, 1964)

Arnold, Janet, *Patterns of Fashion Vol 1, Englishwomen's Dresses and their Construction c.1660–1860,* (Macmillan Ltd., London, 1972)

Arnold, Janet, *Patterns of Fashion Vol 2, Englishwomen's Dresses and their Construction, c.1860–1940,* (Macmillan Ltd., London, 1972)

Ashelford, Jane, *The Art of Dress Clothes and Society 1500–1914,* (National Trust Enterprises Ltd., London, 2000), (first published 1996)

Asquith, Cynthia, *Remember and be Glad*, (James Barrie, London, 1952)

Benn, Elizabeth, *Treasures from the Embroiderers' Guild Collection*, (David and Charles plc., Newton Abbot, 1995), (first published 1991)

Bradfield, Nancy, *Costume in Detail, 1730–1930,* (Harrap, London, 1989)

Breward, Christopher, Ehrman, Edwina and Evans, Caroline, *The London Look, Fashion from Street to Catwalk*, (Yale University Press, New Haven and London, 2004)

Browne, Clare, *Lace from the Victoria and Albert Museum*, (V&A Publications, London, 2004)

Buck, Anne M., *Victorian Costume and Costume Accessories,* (Herbert Jenkins, London, 1961)

Buck, Anne M., *Dress in Eighteenth Century England,* (B.T. Batsford Ltd., London, 1991)

Byrde, Penelope, *The Twentieth Century, A Visual History of Costume,* (B.T. Batsford Ltd., London, 1986)

Carter, Alison, *Underwear, the Fashion History,* (B.T. Batsford Ltd., London, 1992)

Christie, Archibald, *Samplers and Stitches. A Handbook of the Embroiderer's Art,* (B. T. Batsford Ltd., London, 1950), (first published 1920)

Clabburn, Pamela, *Beadwork,* (Shire Publications, Princess Risborough, Bucks, 2001), (first published 1980)

Clabburn, Pamela, *The Norwich Shawl, its History,* (Stationery Office Books, Norwich, 1996)

Clark, Fiona, *The Costume Accessories Series; Hats,* (B. T. Batsford Ltd., London, 1985), (first published 1982)

Colby, Averil, *Samplers,* (B.T. Batsford Ltd., London, 1984), (first published 1964)

Coleman , Elizabeth Ann, *The Opulent Era, Fashion of Worth, Doucet and Pingat,* (Thames and Hudson and the Brooklyn Museum, London, 1989)

Cumming, Valerie and Ribeiro, Aileen, *The Visual History of Costume,* (B.T. Batsford Ltd., London, 2000), (first published 1989)

Cumming, Valerie, Cunnington C.W. and Cunnington, P.E., *The Dictionary of Fashion History*, (Berg, Oxford, New York, 2010)

Cumming, Valerie, *The Costume Accessories Series; Gloves* (B.T. Batsford Ltd., London 1982)

Cumming, Valerie, *The Visual History of Costume Accessories,* (B. T. Batsford Ltd., London, 1998)

Cumming, Valerie, *Understanding Fashion History,* (B.T. Batsford Ltd., London, 2004)

Cunnington, C. Willett and Phillis, *Handbook of English Costume in the 17th Century*, (Faber and Faber Ltd., 1963), (first published 1955)

Cunnington, Willett C. and Phillis, *Handbook of English Costume in the 18th Century,* (Faber and Faber, London,1972), (first published 1957)

Cunnington, C. Willett and Phillis, *Handbook of English Costume in the 19th Century,* (Faber and Faber, London, 1970), (first published 1959)

Cunnington, C. Willett, *English Women's Clothing in the Nineteenth Century,* (Faber and Faber Ltd., London, 1937)

Cunnington, C. Willett, *English Women's Clothing in the Present Century,* (Faber and Faber Ltd., London, 1952)

Dior, Christian, *Christian Dior and I*, (Dutton, New York, 1957)

Earnshaw, Pat, *Lace in Fashion from the Sixteenth to the Twentieth Centuries,* (B. T. Batsford Ltd., London, 1985)

Earnshaw, Pat, *The Identification of Lace,* (Shire Publications, Princess Risborough, Bucks, 1980)

Evans, Grace, 'Marriage à la Mode, An Eighteenth-Century Wedding Dress, Hat and Shoes Set from the Olive Matthews Collection, Chertsey Museum', *Costume,* (Vol. 42, 2008), pp.50–65

Evans, Grace, 'Shapshot: The Corset', *Berg Encyclopedia of World Dress and Fashion, Vol 8, West Europe,* (Berg, Oxford, New York, 2010), pp.393–395

Evans, Grace, 'Underwear', *Berg Encyclopedia of World Dress and Fashion, Vol 8, West Europe,* (Berg, Oxford, New York, 2010), pp.389–393

Ewing, Elizabeth, *Dress and Undress, A History of Women's Underwear,* (B.T. Batsford Ltd., London, 1986)

Ewing, Elizabeth, *History of Twentieth Century Fashion,* (B.T. Batsford Ltd., London, 1975)

Farrell, Jeremy, *The Costume Accessories Series; Umbrellas and Parasols,* (B. T. Batsford Ltd., London, 1985)

Foster, Vanda, *A Visual History of Costume, The Nineteenth Century,* (B. T. Batsford Ltd., London 1986), (first published 1984)

Foster, Vanda, *Costume Accessories Series; Bags and Purses,* (B T. Batsford Ltd., London, 1985), (first published 1982)

Fukai, Akiko, *Fashion*, *The Collection of the Kyoto Costume Institute, a History from 18th to 20th Century,* (Taschen, London, 2002)

Gernsheim, Alison, *Fashion and Reality, 1840–1914*, (Faber and Faber, London, 1963)

Ginsberg, Madeleine, *The Hat, Trends and Traditions,* (Studio Editions Ltd., London, 1990)

Ginsburg, Madeleine, Hart, Avril and Mendes, Valerie D, *Four Hundred Years of Fashion* (V&A Publications in association with William Collins Sons and Co Ltd., London, 1984)

Goodhart, Douglas, *One Man's Samplers. The Goodhart Collection.* (The Embroiderer's Guild, London, 1983)

Hart, Avril and North, Susan, *Historical Fashion in Detail, the Seventeenth and Eighteenth Centuries*, (V&A Publications, London, 2000), (first published 1998)

Hart, Avril and Taylor, Emma, *Fans*, (V&A Publications, London, 1998)

Hashagen, Joanna and Levey, Santina. M. *Fine and Fashionable Lace from the Blackborne Collection,* (Bowes Museum Publications, London 2006)

Hefford, Wendy, *The V&A Museum's Textile Collection: Design for Printed Textiles in England from 1750 to 1850*, (V&A Publications, London 2002)

Hill, June, 'Chertsey Museum, The Olive Matthews Collection', *Embroidery,* (July / August 2010), pp.42–47

Hughes, Therle, *English Domestic Needlework 1660–1860,* (Lutterworth Press, London 1961)

Huish, Marcus B., *Samplers and Tapestry Embroideries*, (Longmans, Green and Co., London 1913)

Irwin, John, *The Kashmir Shawl*, (V&A Publications, London, 1973)

Johnson, Lucy, *Nineteenth Century Fashion in Detail*, (V&A Publications, London, 2006), (first published 2005)

Koda, Harold and Bolton, Andrew, *Poiret*, (Metropolitan Museum of Art, New York, 2007)

Lambert, Miles, *Fashion in Photographs 1860–1880*, (B. T. Batsford Ltd., London, 1991)

Lansdell, Avril, *Seaside Fashions, History in Camera 1860–1939*, (Shire Publications Ltd., Princess Risborough, Bucks, 1990)

Levey, Santina. M., *Lace, A History*, (V&A Publications, London, 1983)

Levi-Strauss, Monique, *The Cashmere Shawl*, (Dryad Press Ltd., London, 1987)

Levitt, Sarah, *Fashion in Photographs 1880-1900*, (B. T. Batsford Ltd., London, 1991)

Levitt, Sarah, *Victorians Unbuttoned*, (Harper Collins Publishers Ltd., New York, 1986)

Lewis, M.D.S. *Antique Paste Jewellery*, (Faber and Faber, London, 1970)

Lussier, Suzanne, *Art Deco Fashion*, (V&A Publications, London, 2006), (first published 2003)

Mackrell, Alice, *Paul Poiret*, (Holmes and Meier, New York, 1990), (first published 1992)

Mackrell, Alice, *Shawls, Stoles and Scarves*, (B. T. Batsford Ltd., London, 1986)

McDowell, Colin, *McDowell's Directory of Twentieth Century Fashion*, (Frederick Muller Ltd., London, 1987)

Mendes, Valerie and de la Haye, Amy, *Fashion since 1900*, (Thames and Hudson, London, 2010)

Mulvagh, Jane, *The Vogue History of Twentieth Century Fashion*, (Viking adult, New York, 1989)

Nicoll, Allardyce, *The Garrick Stage, Theatres and Audiences in the Eighteenth Century*, (Manchester University Press, Manchester, 1980)

O'Connor, Deryn and Granger-Taylor, Hero, *Colour–the Calico Printer, an Exhibition of Printed and Died Textiles 1750–1850*, (P. J. Henderson and Co., Guildford, 1982)

Owen, Elizabeth, *Fashion in Photographs 1920–1940*, (B. T. Batsford Ltd., London, 1993)

Persson, Helen, 'Straw – The Blond Goddess: The Adaptation of a Folk Tradition to Fashion', *Costume*, (Vol. 38, 2004), pp.50–62

Reilly, Valerie, *The Paisley Pattern: The Official Illustrated History*, (Gibbs Smith, Utah, 1989)

Rhodes, Zandra and Knight, Anne, *The Art of Zandra Rhodes*, (Zandra Rhodes Publications Ltd., Michael O'Mara Books Ltd., London, 1994), (first published 1984)

Ribeiro, Aileen, *A Visual History of Costume in the Eighteenth Century*, (B. T. Batsford, London, 1986), (first published 1983)

Ribeiro, Aileen, *Dress in Eighteenth Century Europe 1715–1789*, (Yale University Press, New Haven and London, 2002), (first published 1984)

Ribeiro, Aileen, *Fashion and Fiction. Dress in Art and Literature in Stuart England*, (Yale University Press, New Haven and London, 2005)

Rothstein, Natalie, (ed.), *Barbara Johnson's Album of Fashions and Fabrics*, (Thames and Hudson, London, 1987)

Rothstein, Natalie, (ed.), *Four Hundred Years of Fashion*, (William Collins and Sons and Co. Ltd., London, 1984)

Rothstein, Natalie, *Silk Designs of the Eighteenth Century in the Collection of the V&A Museum London*, (Thames and Hudson, London, 1990)

Rowley, Christina, *Costume in Chertsey Museum, 1700–1800,* (Runnymede District Council, Addlestone, 1976)

Schoeser, Mary, *Printed Handkerchiefs,* (Museum of London Publications, London, 1988)

Steele, Valerie, *Fifty Years of Fashion, New Look to Now*, (Yale University Press, New Haven and London, 2000), (first published 1997)

Steele, Valerie, *The Corset, A Cultural History,* (Yale University Press, New Haven, London, 2001)

Stemp, Sinty, *Jean Muir: Beyond Fashion,* (Antique Collectors Club, Woodbridge, Suffolk, 2007)

Summers, Leigh, *Bound to Please. A History of the Victorian Corset*, (Berg, Oxford, New York, 2001)

Swann, June, *The Costume Accessories Series; Shoes* (B.T. Batsford Ltd., London, 1982)

Sykas, Philip, 'Calico Catalogues: Nineteenth-Century Printed Dress fabrics from Pattern Books', *Costume,* (Vol. 33, 1999), pp.57–67

Thornton, Peter, *Baroque and Rococo Silks*, (Faber and Faber, London, 1965)

Tozer, Jane and Levitt, Sarah, *The Fabric of Society, a Century of People and their Clothes 1770–1870,* (Laura Ashley Publications Ltd., Powys, Wales, 1983)

Vickery, Amanda, *The Gentleman's Daughter, Women's Lives in Georgian England,* (Yale University Press, New Haven and London, 2003), (first published 1998)

Wardle, Patricia, *75 X Lace,* (Rijksmuseum, Amsterdam, 2000)

Wardle, Patricia, *Guide to English Embroidery*, (V&A Publications, London 1970)

Warren, Philip, *Foundations of Fashion, The Symington Corsetry Collection 1860–1990,* (Leicestershire County Council, Leicester, 2001)

Watt, Judith, *Ossie Clark 1965–1974*, (V&A Publications, London, 2003)

Waugh, Norah, *Corsets and Crinolines,* (B. T. Batsford Ltd., London, 1987), (first published 1954)

Waugh, Norah, *The Cut of Men's Clothes, 1600–1900*, (Faber and Faber Ltd., London, 1972), (first published 1964)

Waugh, Norah, *The Cut of Women's Clothes, 1600–1930*, (Faber and Faber Ltd., London, 1968)

Wilcox, Claire and Mendes, Valerie, *Modern Fashion in Detail*, (V&A Publications, London, 2007)

Wilcox, Claire, (ed.),*The Golden Age of Couture; Paris and London 1947-1957*, (V&A Publications, London, 2007)

Wilcox, Claire, *Bags*, (V&A Publications, London, 2008), (first published 1999)

Glossary

Algerian eye stitch – An embroidery stitch which takes the form of a square star shape, often with a hole in the centre. The stars are often repeated to create a geometric pattern.

Basque – An extension of the bodice below the waistline.

Black work – A type of embroidery carried out in black silk, usually on linen. Popular from the early sixteenth century.

Brides – A lace term denoting narrow linking threads which run between lace motifs.

Brides picotées – A lace term for brides which are decorated with small loops.

Brocade – A slightly raised pattern of coloured or metal threads woven into silk. The pattern is produced by using extra weft or horizontal threads which, rather than running across the entire width of the fabric, are located only in the patterned areas.

Busk – A stiffened section or insert located at the front of a bodice or corset to make it rigid and inflexible. By the mid nineteenth century this was usually made of steel, but earlier versions could be of wood, horn or whalebone.

Cordonnet – A lace term referring to the clear outlines around patterned sections.

Couched – An embroidery technique, where threads of any thickness are stitched onto a ground material using a different finer thread which is usually seen as a pattern.

OPPOSITE **Detail from a drawstring bag, 1640–1670 (see page 22).**

Coutil – A type of cotton cloth with a twill weave.

Cuirasse bodice – A type of bodice which was fashionable during the 1870s and early 1880s. It was long and tight; usually boned and extending down over the hips.

Damask – A patterned or figured fabric of one colour in linen, wool or most frequently silk. The pattern is reversible.

Diaper pattern – A pattern of repeated geometric shapes, usually diamonds or lozenges, often used in embroidery, but also found in patterned fabrics of linen or cotton as well as other forms of decorative art.

Gauging – A method of fixing gathered or pleated fabric in place by a series of running stitches made in parallel lines.

Georgette – A type of light silk crêpe or crimped silk gauze.

Gobelin stitch – A stitch used in canvas work embroidery. It is often used for shaded work or backgrounds. A slanting stitch; the thread is worked over two horizontal and one perpendicular thread of the ground. Each row slants in the opposite direction. A variation of this is **plaited gobelin stitch**, where the stitches slightly overlap each other.

Gored skirt – A technique in which fabric panels are cut and stitched in triangular shapes in order to avoid pleating and bulk at the waist, whilst creating a widening circumference towards the bottom of the skirt.

Kerchief – A shortened version of 'neckerchief', or covering for the neck and top of the chest. From the sixteenth to the eighteenth-century this term usually referred to a scarf of fine linen, cotton or lace which was tied, tucked or otherwise fastened around the top of the bodice on women's dresses.

They were worn for modesty and in order to create a fashionable look. The term 'kerchief' can also mean a draped head covering, and may be used as a shortened version of 'handkerchief'.

Paste – A hard, transparent and shiny compound, of similar make-up to glass. It was used for making imitation jewels.

Picots – Lace term meaning short loops used to embellish the brides (see above) or the pattern itself. Also used to decorate the heading or top edge of a piece of lace.

Placket – An opening or slit extending from the waistband of a skirt or at the waist level of a dress, usually at the back or side. It allows the skirt to be slipped on over the hips before fastening.

Resist dyeing – A method of covering certain areas of cloth in order to preserve the colour beneath before dyeing. The covering material or 'resist', used was primarily pure wax up until the 1830s, and the dye used in conjunction with the process was indigo. Later other compounds were used to produce more varied effects.

Robings – Trimmings, often of the same fabric as the dress, which are quite wide and flat in style. Common during the eighteenth century, they were usually stitched down the edges of the bodice front and could extend down the edges of the dress where it falls open to reveal the petticoat. They can be gathered or feature padded sections, and some are stitched in curving lines (serpentine robings).

Spangles – An early form of sequin: they consist of small, flat, circular discs made from shiny metal. Usually pierced with a hole; this allowed them to be stitched to garments for decoration, but they could also be attached using adhesive. They were particularly common as a form of decoration in seventeenth and eighteenth century clothing and accessories.

Tulle – A form of very fine silk net.

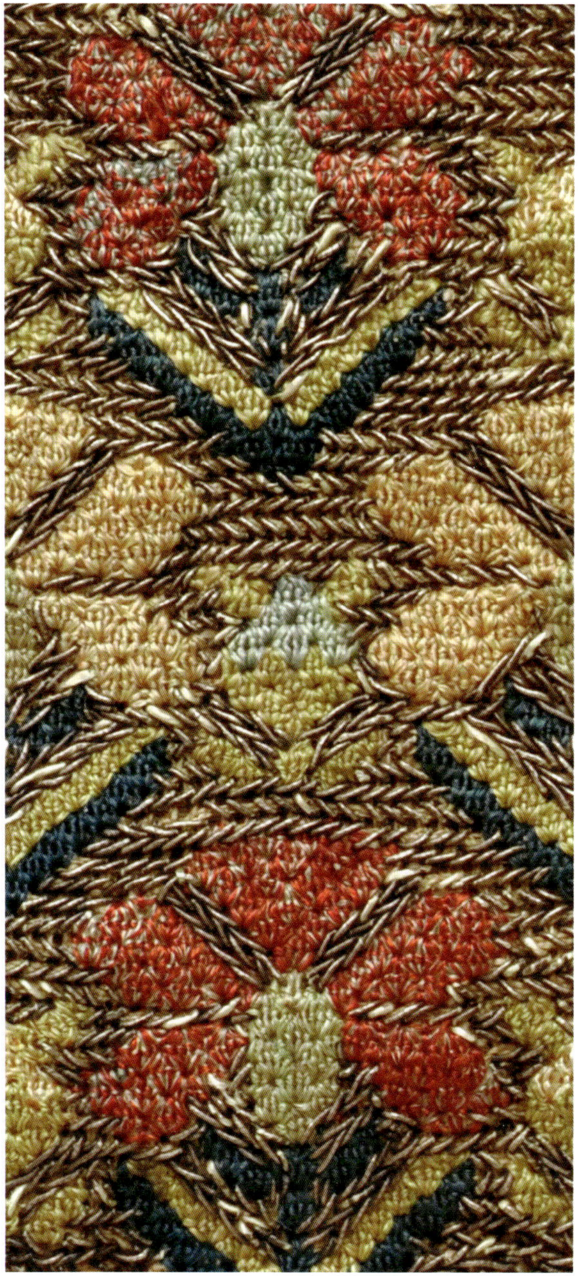

Acknowledgements

I have received a great deal of help and advice during the creation of this publication, and would like to thank the following people for their support: the Leche Trust for their funding of the design and photographic elements of the book; the Trustees of the Olive Matthews Collection for their ongoing support, with particular thanks to Valerie Cumming, dress and social historian and Chairman of the Olive Matthews Collection Trustees, who has given a great deal of her time, advice and expertise; Clare Browne, Curator of European Textiles in the Department of Furniture, Textiles and Fashion at the V&A; Emma Warren, Curator of Chertsey Museum; Judith Norman and Barbara Prowle, Chertsey Museum volunteers and Alex Evans for his patience and proofing skills.

The stunning photographs were taken by John Chase, and the book has been beautifully designed by Anne Wilson.

BELOW **Detail from a printed cotton seaside walking dress, 1916–1920 (see pages 120–121).**

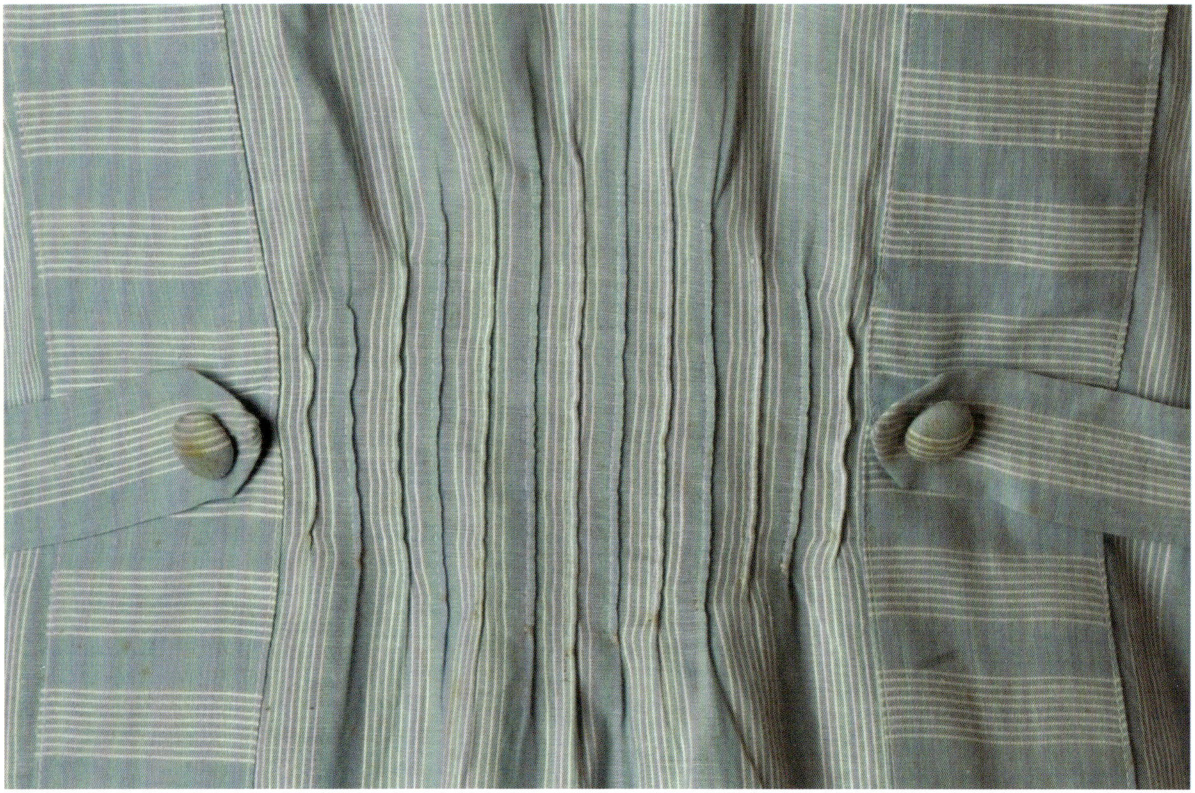